NYSTCE

Multi-Subject:
Teachers of Early Childhood
(211/212/245 Birth-Grade 2)
Part 2 of 2

SECRETS

Study Guide
Your Key to Exam Success

NYSTCE Test Review for the
New York State Teacher Certification
Examinations

Dear Future Exam Success Story:

Congratulations on your purchase of our study guide. Our goal in writing our study guide was to cover the content on the test, as well as provide insight into typical test taking mistakes and how to overcome them.

Standardized tests are a key component of being successful, which only increases the importance of doing well in the high-pressure high-stakes environment of test day. How well you do on this test will have a significant impact on your future, and we have the research and practical advice to help you execute on test day.

The product you're reading now is designed to exploit weaknesses in the test itself, and help you avoid the most common errors test takers frequently make.

How to use this study guide

We don't want to waste your time. Our study guide is fast-paced and fluff-free. We suggest going through it a number of times, as repetition is an important part of learning new information and concepts.

First, read through the study guide completely to get a feel for the content and organization. Read the general success strategies first, and then proceed to the content sections. Each tip has been carefully selected for its effectiveness.

Second, read through the study guide again, and take notes in the margins and highlight those sections where you may have a particular weakness.

Finally, bring the manual with you on test day and study it before the exam begins.

Your success is our success

We would be delighted to hear about your success. Send us an email and tell us your story. Thanks for your business and we wish you continued success.

Sincerely,

Mometrix Test Preparation Team

Need more help? Check out our flashcards at: http://MometrixFlashcards.com/NYSTCE

Copyright © 2018 by Mometrix Media LLC. All rights reserved.
Written and edited by the Mometrix Exam Secrets Test Prep Team
Printed in the United States of America

TABLE OF CONTENTS

Social Studies - Continued 1
   Economics and Politics 1
   Roles, Rights, and Responsibilities of Citizenship 11
   Maps and Data in Social Studies 22
Fine Arts 26
   Visual Arts 26
   Music 32
   Theatre and Dance 46
Health and Fitness 54
Family and Consumer Science and Career Development 68
Practice Test 114
   Literacy and English Language Arts 114
   Mathematics 122
   Arts and Sciences 132
Answers and Explanations 138
   Literacy and English Language Arts 138
   Mathematics 143
   Arts and Sciences 148
Secret Key #1 - Time is Your Greatest Enemy 153
   Pace Yourself 153
Secret Key #2 - Guessing is not Guesswork 154
   Monkeys Take the Test 154
   $5 Challenge 155
Secret Key #3 - Practice Smarter, Not Harder 156
   Success Strategy 156
Secret Key #4 - Prepare, Don't Procrastinate 157
Secret Key #5 - Test Yourself 158
General Strategies 159
Special Report: How to Overcome Test Anxiety 164
   Lack of Preparation 164
   Physical Signals 165
   Nervousness 165
   Study Steps 167
   Helpful Techniques 168
Additional Bonus Material 172

Social Studies - Continued

Economics and Politics

Economics

Economics is the study of the ways specific societies allocate resources to individuals and groups within that society. Also important are the choices society makes regarding what efforts or initiatives are funded and which are not. Since resources in any society are finite, allocation becomes a vivid reflection of that society's values. In general, the economic system that drives an individual society is based on:
- What goods are produced
- How those goods are produced
- Who acquires the goods or benefits from them

Economics consists of two main categories: macroeconomics, which studies larger systems, and microeconomics, which studies smaller systems.

Market economy

A market economy is based on supply and demand. Demand has to do with what customers want and need, as well as what quantity those consumers are able to purchase based on other economic factors. Supply refers to how much can be produced to meet demand, or how much suppliers are willing and able to sell. Where the needs of consumers meet the needs of suppliers is referred to as a market equilibrium price. This price varies depending on many factors, including the overall health of a society's economy, overall beliefs and considerations of individuals in society. The following is a list of terms defined in the context of a market economy:
- Elasticity—this is based on how the quantity of a particular product responds to the price demanded for that product. If quantity responds quickly to changes in price, the supply/demand for that product is said to be elastic. If it does not respond quickly, then the supply/demand is inelastic.
- Market efficiency—this occurs when a market is capable of producing output high enough to meet consumer demand, that market is efficient.
- Comparative advantage—in the field of international trade, this refers to a country focusing on a specific product that it can produce it more efficiently and more cheaply, or at a lower opportunity cost, than another country, thus giving it a comparative advantage in production.

> ➤ **Review Video:** Market Economy
> Visit *mometrix.com/academy* and enter **Code: 460547**

Comparison to planned economy
In a market economy, supply and demand are determined by consumers. In a planned economy, a public entity or planning authority makes the decisions about what resources will be produced, how they will be produced, and who will be able to benefit from them. The means of production, such as factories, are also owned by a public entity rather than by private interests. In market socialism, the economic structure falls somewhere between the market economy and the planned

economy. Planning authorities determine allocation of resources at higher economic levels, while consumer goods are driven by a market economy.

Microeconomics

While economics generally studies how resources are allocated, microeconomics focuses on economic factors such as the way consumers behave, how income is distributed, and output and input markets. Studies are limited to the industry or firm level, rather than an entire country or society. Among the elements studied in microeconomics are factors of production, costs of production, and factor income. These factors determine production decisions of individual firms, based on resources and costs.

> **Review Video:** Microeconomics
> Visit **mometrix.com/academy** and enter **Code: 779207**

Classification of markets

The conditions prevailing in a given market are used to classify markets. Conditions considered include:
- Existence of competition
- Number and size of suppliers
- Influence of suppliers over price
- Variety of available products
- Ease of entering the market

Once these questions are answered, an economist can classify a certain market according to its structure and the nature of competition within the market.

Market failure

When any of the elements for a successfully competitive market are missing, this can lead to a market failure. Certain elements are necessary to create what economists call "perfect competition." If one of these factors is weak or lacking, the market is classified as having "imperfect competition." Worse than imperfect competition, though, is a market failure. There are five major types of market failure:
- Inadequate competition
- Inadequate information
- Immobile resources
- Negative externalities, or side effects
- Failure to provide public goods

Externalities are side effects of a market that affect third parties. These effects can be either negative or positive.

> **Review Video:** Market Failure
> Visit **mometrix.com/academy** and enter **Code: 198450**

Factors of production and costs of production

Every good and service requires certain resources, or inputs. These inputs are referred to as factors of production. Every good and service requires four factors of production:
- Labor
- Capital
- Land
- Entrepreneurship

These factors can be fixed or variable, and can produce fixed or variable costs. Examples of fixed costs include land and equipment. Variable costs include labor. The total of fixed and variable costs makes up the cost of production.

Factor income

Factors of production each have an associated factor income. Factors that earn income include:
- Labor—earns wages
- Capital—earns interest
- Land—earns rent
- Entrepreneurship—earns profit

Each factor's income is determined by its contribution. In a market economy, this income is not guaranteed to be equal. How scarce the factor is and the weight of its contribution to the overall production process determines the final factor income.

Output market

The four kinds of market structures in an output market are:
- Perfect competition—all existing firms sell an identical product. The firms are not able to control the final price. In addition, there is nothing that makes it difficult to become involved in or leave the industry. Anything that would prevent entering or leaving an industry is called a barrier to entry. An example of this market structure is agriculture.
- Monopoly—a single seller controls the product and its price. Barriers to entry, such as prohibitively high fixed cost structures, prevent other sellers from entering the market.
- Monopolistic competition—a number of firms sell similar products, but they are not identical, such as different brands of clothes or food. Barriers to entry are low.
- Oligopoly—only a few firms control the production and distribution of products, such as automobiles. Barriers to entry are high, preventing large numbers of firms from entering the market.

Monopolies

Four types of monopolies are:
- Natural monopoly—a single supplier has a distinct advantage over the others.
- Geographic monopoly—only one business offers the product in a certain area.
- Technological monopoly—a single company controls the technology necessary to supply the product.
- Government monopoly—a government agency is the only provider of a specific good or service.

Control by the US government
The US government has passed several acts to regulate businesses, including:
- Sherman Antitrust Act (1890)—this prohibited trusts, monopolies, and any other situations that eliminated competition.
- Clayton Antitrust Act (1914)—this prohibited price discrimination.
- Robinson-Patman Act (1936)—this strengthened provisions of the Clayton Antitrust Act, requiring businesses to offer the same pricing on products to any customer.

The government has also taken other actions to ensure competition, including requirements for public disclosure. The Securities and Exchange Commission (SEC) requires companies that provide public stock to provide financial reports on a regular basis. Because of the nature of their business, banks are further regulated and required to provide various information to the government.

Marketing and utility

Marketing consists of all of the activity necessary to convince consumers to acquire goods. One major way to move products into the hands of consumers is to convince them that any single product will satisfy a need. The ability of a product or service to satisfy the need of a consumer is called utility. There are four types of utility:
- Form utility—a product's desirability lies in its physical characteristics.
- Place utility—a product's desirability is connected to its location and convenience.
- Time utility—a product's desirability is determined by its availability at a certain time.
- Ownership utility—a product's desirability is increased because ownership of the product passes to the consumer.

Marketing behavior will stress any or all of these types of utility when marketing to the consumer.

Determining a product's market

Successful marketing depends not only on convincing customers they need the product, but also on focusing the marketing towards those who already have a need or desire for the product. Before releasing a product into the general marketplace, many producers will test markets to determine which will be the most receptive to the product.

There are three steps usually taken to evaluate a product's market:
- Market research—this involves researching a market to determine if it will be receptive to the product.
- Market surveys—a part of market research, market surveys ask consumers specific questions to help determine the marketability of a product to a specific group.
- Test marketing—this includes releasing the product into a small geographical area to see how it sells. Often test marketing is followed by wider marketing if the product does well.

Marketing plan

Once these elements have all been determined, the producer can proceed with production and distribution of his product.
- Product—this includes any elements pertaining directly to the product, such as packaging, presentation, or services to include along with it.
- Price—this calculates cost of production, distribution, advertising, etc., as well as the desired profit to determine the final price.

- Place—this determines which outlets will be used to sell the product, whether traditional outlets or through direct mail or Internet marketing.
- Promotion—this involves ways to let consumers know the product is available, through advertising and other means.

> ➢ **Review Video:** Marketing Plan
> Visit *mometrix.com/academy* and enter **Code**: **983409**

Distribution channels

Distribution channels determine the route a product takes on its journey from producer to consumer, and can also influence the final price and availability of the product. There are two major forms of distributions: wholesale and retail. A wholesale distributor buys in large quantities and then resells smaller amounts to other businesses. Retailers sell directly to the consumers rather than to businesses. In the modern marketplace, additional distribution channels have grown up with the rise of markets such as club warehouse stores as well as purchasing through catalogs or over the Internet. Most of these newer distribution channels bring products more directly to the consumer, eliminating the need for middlemen.

Distribution of income and poverty

Distribution of income in any society ranges from poorest to richest. In most societies, income is not distributed evenly. To determine income distribution, family incomes are ranked from lowest to highest. These rankings are divided into five sections called quintiles, which are compared to each other. The uneven distribution of income is often linked to higher levels of education and ability in the upper classes, but can also be due to other factors such as discrimination and existing monopolies. The income gap in America continues to grow, largely due to growth in the service industry, changes in the American family unit and reduced influence of labor unions. Poverty is defined by comparing incomes to poverty guidelines. Poverty guidelines determine the level of income necessary for a family to function. Those below the poverty line are often eligible for assistance from government agencies.

Consumer behavior

The two major types of consumer behavior as defined in macroeconomics are:
- Marginal propensity to consume defines the tendency of consumers to increase spending in conjunction with increases in income. In general, individuals with greater income will buy more. As individuals increase their income through job changes or growth of experience, they will also increase spending.
- Utility is a term that describes the satisfaction experienced by a consumer in relation to acquiring and using a good or service. Providers of goods and services will stress utility to convince consumers they want the products being presented.

Macroeconomics

Macroeconomics examines economies on a much larger level than microeconomics. While microeconomics studies economics on a firm or industry level, macroeconomics looks at economic trends and structures on a national level. Variables studied in macroeconomics include:
- Output
- Consumption

- Investment
- Government spending
- Net exports

The overall economic condition of a nation is defined as the Gross Domestic Product, or GDP. GDP measures a nation's economic output over a limited time period, such as a year.

> ➤ **Review Video:** Microeconomics and Macroeconomics
> *Visit **mometrix.com/academy** and enter **Code**: 538837*

GDP

The two major ways to measure the Gross Domestic Product of a country are:
- The expenditures approach calculates the GDP based on how much money is spent in each individual sector.
- The income approach calculates the GDP based on how much money is earned in each sector.

Both methods yield the same results and both of these calculation methods are based on four economic sectors that make up a country's macro-economy:
- Consumers
- Business
- Government
- Foreign sector

Several factors must be considered in order to accurately calculate the GDP using the incomes approach. Income factors are:
- Wages paid to laborers, or Compensation of Employees
- Rental income derived from land
- Interest income derived from invested capital
- Entrepreneurial income

Entrepreneurial income consists of two forms. Proprietor's income is income that comes back to the entrepreneur himself. Corporate profit is income that goes back into the corporation as a whole. Corporate profit is divided by the corporation into corporate profits taxes, dividends, and retained earnings. Two other figures must be subtracted in the incomes approach. These are indirect business taxes, including property and sales taxes, and depreciation.

Effects of the population
Changes in population can affect the calculation of a nation's GDP, particularly since GDP and GNP (Gross National Product) are generally measured per capita. If a country's economic production is low, but the population is high, the income per individual will be lower than if the income is high and the population is lower. Also, if the population grows quickly and the income grows slowly, individual income will remain low or even drop drastically. Population growth can also affect overall economic growth. Economic growth requires both that consumers purchase goods and workers produce them. A population that does not grow quickly enough will not supply enough workers to support rapid economic growth.

Ideal balance in an economy and phases in national economies

Ideally, an economy functions efficiently, with the aggregate supply, or the amount of national output, equal to the aggregate demand, or the amount of the output that is purchased. In these cases, the economy is stable and prosperous. However, economies more typically go through phases. These phases are:
- Boom—GDP is high and the economy prospers
- Recession—GDP falls, unemployment rises
- Trough—the recession reaches its lowest point
- Recovery—unemployment lessens, prices rise, and the economy begins to stabilize again

These phases tend to repeat in cycles that are not necessarily predictable or regular.

Unemployment and inflation

When demand outstrips supply, prices are driven artificially high, or inflated. This occurs when too much spending causes an imbalance in the economy. In general, inflation occurs because an economy is growing too quickly. When there is too little spending and supply has moved far beyond demand, a surplus of product results. Companies cut back on production, reduce the number of employees, and unemployment rises as people lose their jobs. This imbalance occurs when an economy becomes sluggish. In general, both these economic instability situations are caused by an imbalance between supply and demand. Government intervention may be necessary to stabilize an economy when either inflation or unemployment becomes too serious.

Forms of unemployment
- Frictional—when workers change jobs and are unemployed while waiting for new jobs
- Structural—when economic shifts reduce the need for workers
- Cyclical—when natural business cycles bring about loss of jobs
- Seasonal—when seasonal cycles reduce the need for certain jobs
- Technological—when advances in technology result in elimination of certain jobs

Any of these factors can increase unemployment in certain sectors. Inflation is classified by the overall rate at which it occurs:
- Creeping inflation—this is an inflation rate of about 1-3% annually.
- Walking inflation—this is an inflation rate of 3-10% annually.
- Galloping inflation—this is a high inflation rate of more than 10% but less than 1000% annually.
- Hyperinflation—this is an inflation rate over 1000% per year. Hyperinflation usually leads to complete monetary collapse in a society, as individuals become unable to generate sufficient income to purchase necessary goods.

Government intervention policies

When an economy becomes too imbalanced, either due to excessive spending or not enough spending, government intervention often becomes necessary to put the economy back on track. Government Fiscal Policy can take several forms, including:
- Contractionary policy
- Expansionary policy
- Monetary policy

Contractionary policies help counteract inflation. These include increasing taxes and decreasing government spending to slow spending in the overall economy. Expansionary policies increase government spending and lower taxes in order to reduce unemployment and increase the level of spending in the economy overall. Monetary policy can take several forms, and affects the amount of funds available to banks for making loans.

Populations and population growth

Populations are studied by size, rates of growth due to immigration, the overall fertility rate, and life expectancy. For example, though the population of the United States is considerably larger than it was two hundred years ago, the rate of population growth has decreased greatly, from about three percent per year to less than one percent per year. In the US, the fertility rate is fairly low, with most choosing not to have large families, and life expectancy is high, creating a projected imbalance between older and younger people in the near future. In addition, immigration and the mixing of racially diverse cultures are projected to increase the percentages of Asians, Hispanics and African-Americans.

Money

Money is used in three major ways:
- As an accounting unit
- As a store of value
- As an exchange medium

In general, money must be acceptable throughout a society in exchange for debts or to purchase goods and services. Money should be relatively scarce, its value should remain stable, and it should be easily carried, durable, and easy to divide up. There are three basic types of money: commodity, representative and fiat. Commodity money includes gems or precious metals. Representative money can be exchanged for items such as gold or silver which have inherent value. Fiat money, or legal tender, has no inherent value but has been declared to function as money by the government. It is often backed by gold or silver, but not necessarily on a one-to-one ratio.

<u>US money</u>
Money in the US is not just currency. When economists calculate the amount of money available, they must take into account other factors such as deposits that have been placed in checking accounts, debit cards and "near moneys" such as savings accounts, that can be quickly converted into cash. Currency, checkable deposits and traveler's checks, referred to as M1, are added up, and then M2 is calculated by adding savings deposits, CDs and various other monetary deposits. The final result is the total quantity of available money.

Monetary policy and the Federal Reserve System

The Federal Reserve System, also known as the Fed, implements all monetary policy in the US. Monetary policy regulates the amount of money available in the American banking system. The Fed can decrease or increase the amount of available money for loans, thus helping regulate the national economy.

Monetary policies implemented by the Fed are part of expansionary or contractionary monetary policies that help counteract inflation or unemployment. The discount rate is an interest rate charged by the Fed when banks borrow money from them. A lower discount rate leads banks to borrow more money, leading to increased spending. A higher discount rate has the opposite effect.

> **Review Video:** Monetary Policy
> *Visit **mometrix.com/academy** and enter **Code**: 662298*

Banks

Banks earn their income by loaning out money and charging interest on those loans. If less money is available, fewer loans can be made, which affects the amount of spending in the overall economy. While banks function by making loans, they are not allowed to loan out all the money they hold in deposit. The amount of money they must maintain in reserve is known as the reserve ratio. If the reserve ratio is raised, less money is available for loans and spending decreases. A lower reserve ratio increases available funds and increases spending. This ratio is determined by the Federal Reserve System.

Open Market Operations

The Federal Reserve System can also expand or contract the overall money supply through open market operations. In this case, the Fed can buy or sell bonds it has purchased from banks or individuals. When the Fed buys bonds, more money is put into circulation, creating an expansionary situation to stimulate the economy. When the Fed sells bonds, money is withdrawn from the system, creating a contractionary situation to slow an economy suffering from inflation. Because of international financial markets, however, American banks often borrow and lend money in markets outside the US. By shifting their attention to international markets, domestic banks and other businesses can circumvent whatever contractionary policies the Fed may have put into place.

International trade

International trade can take advantage of broader markets, bringing a wider variety of products within easy reach. By contrast, it can also allow individual countries to specialize in particular products that they can produce easily, such as those for which they have easy access to raw materials. Other products, more difficult to make domestically, can be acquired through trade with other nations. International trade requires efficient use of native resources as well as sufficient disposable income to purchase native and imported products. Many countries in the world engage extensively in international trade, but others still face major economic challenges.

Developing nations

The five major characteristics of a developing nation are:
- Low GDP
- Rapid growth of population
- Economy that depends on subsistence agriculture
- Poor conditions, including high infant mortality rates, high disease rates, poor sanitation, and insufficient housing
- Low literacy rate

Developing nations often function under oppressive governments that do not provide private property rights and withhold education and other rights from women. They also often feature an extreme disparity between upper and lower classes, with little opportunity for the lower classes to improve their position.

Stages of economic development
Economic development occurs in three stages that are defined by the activities that drive the economy:
- Agricultural stage
- Manufacturing stage
- Service sector stage

In developing countries, it is often difficult to acquire the necessary funding to provide equipment and training to move into the advanced stages of economic development. Some can receive help from developed countries via foreign aid and investment or international organizations such as the International Monetary Fund or the World Bank. Having developed countries provide monetary, technical, or military assistance can help developing countries move forward to the next stage in their development.

Obstacles to economic growth
Developing nations typically struggle to overcome obstacles that prevent or slow economic development. Major obstacles can include:
- Rapid, uncontrolled population growth
- Trade restrictions
- Misused resources, often perpetrated by the government
- Traditional beliefs that can slow or reject change

Corrupt, oppressive governments often hamper the economic growth of developing nations, creating huge economic disparities and making it impossible for individuals to advance, in turn preventing overall growth. Governments sometimes export currency, called capital flight, which is detrimental to a country's economic development. In general, countries are more likely to experience economic growth if their governments encourage entrepreneurship and provide private property rights.

Problems with rapid industrialization

Rapid growth throughout the world leaves some nations behind, and sometimes spurs their governments to move forward too quickly into industrialization and artificially rapid economic growth. While slow or nonexistent economic growth causes problems in a country, overly rapid industrialization carries its own issues. Problems encountered due to rapid industrialization are:
- Use of technology not suited to the products or services being supplied
- Poor investment of capital
- Lack of time for the population to adapt to new paradigms
- Lack of time to experience all stages of development and adjust to each stage

Economic failures in Indonesia were largely due to rapid growth that was poorly handled.

Roles, Rights, and Responsibilities of Citizenship

Political science

Political science focuses on studying different governments and how they compare to each other, general political theory, ways political theory is put into action, how nations and governments interact with each other, and a general study of governmental structure and function. Other elements of political science include the study of elections, governmental administration at various levels, development and action of political parties, and how values such as freedom, power, justice and equality are expressed in different political cultures. Political science also encompasses elements of other disciplines, including:
- History—how historical events have shaped political thought and process
- Sociology—the effects of various stages of social development on the growth and development of government and politics
- Anthropology—the effects of governmental process on the culture of an individual group and its relationships with other groups
- Economics—how government policies regulate distribution of products and how they can control and/or influence the economy in general

Government

Based on general political theory, the four major purposes of any given government are:
- Ensuring national security—the government protects against international, domestic and terrorist attacks and also ensures ongoing security through negotiating and establishing relationships with other governments.
- Providing public services—the government should "promote the general welfare," as stated in the Preamble to the US Constitution, by providing whatever is needed to its citizens.
- Ensuring social order—the government supplies means of settling conflicts among citizens as well as making laws to govern the nation, state, or city.
- Making decisions regarding the economy—laws help form the economic policy of the country, regarding both domestic and international trade and related issues. The government also has the ability to distribute goods and wealth to some extent among its citizens.

Origin of the state

There are four main theories regarding the origin of the state:
- Evolutionary—the state evolved from the family, with the head of state the equivalent of the family's patriarch or matriarch.
- Force—one person or group of people brought everyone in an area under their control, forming the first government.
- Divine Right—certain people were chosen by the prevailing deity to be the rulers of the nation, which is itself created by the deity or deities.
- Social Contract—there is no natural order. The people allow themselves to be governed to maintain social order, while the state in turn promises to protect the people they govern. If the government fails to protect its people, the people have the right to seek new leaders.

Influences of philosophers on political study

Ancient Greek philosophers Aristotle and Plato believed political science would lead to order in political matters, and that this scientifically organized order would create stable, just societies.

Thomas Aquinas adapted the ideas of Aristotle to a Christian perspective. His ideas stated that individuals should have certain rights, but also certain duties, and that these rights and duties should determine the type and extent of government rule. In stating that laws should limit the role of government, he laid the groundwork for ideas that would eventually become modern constitutionalism.

Niccolò Machiavelli, author of *The Prince*, was a proponent of politics based on power. He is often considered the founder of modern political science.

Thomas Hobbes, author of *Leviathan* (1651), believed that individual's lives were focused solely on a quest for power, and that the state must work to control this urge. Hobbes felt that people were completely unable to live harmoniously without the intervention of a powerful, undivided government.

John Locke published *Two Treatises of Government* in 1689. This work argued against the ideas of Thomas Hobbes. He put forth the theory of *tabula rasa*—that people are born with minds like blank slates. Individual minds are molded by experience, not innate knowledge or intuition. He also believed that all men should be independent and equal. Many of Locke's ideas found their way into the Constitution of the United States.

The two French philosophers, Montesquieu and Rousseau, heavily influenced the French Revolution (1789-1799). They believed government policies and ideas should change to alleviate existing problems, an idea referred to as "liberalism." Rousseau in particular directly influenced the Revolution with writings such as *The Social Contract* (1762) and *Declaration of the Rights of Man and of the Citizen* (1789). Other ideas Rousseau and Montesquieu espoused included:
- Individual freedom and community welfare are of equal importance
- Man's innate goodness leads to natural harmony
- Reason develops with the rise of civilized society
- Individual citizens carry certain obligations to the existing government

David Hume and Jeremy Bentham believed politics should have as its main goal maintaining "the greatest happiness for the greatest number." Hume also believed in empiricism, or that ideas should not be believed until the proof has been observed. He was a natural skeptic and always sought out the truth of matters rather than believing what he was told.

John Stuart Mill, a British philosopher as well as an economist, believed in progressive policies such as women's suffrage, emancipation, and the development of labor unions and farming cooperatives.

Johann Fichte and Georg Hegel, German philosophers in the late eighteenth and early nineteenth centuries, supported a form of liberalism grounded largely in socialism and a sense of nationalism.

Political orientations

The four main political orientations are:
- Liberal—liberals believe that government should work to increase equality, even at the expense of some freedoms. Government should assist those in need. Focus on enforced social justice and free basic services for everyone.
- Conservative—a conservative believes that government should be limited in most cases. The government should allow its citizens to help one another and solve their own problems rather than enforcing solutions. Business should not be overregulated, allowing a free market.
- Moderate—this ideology incorporates some liberal and some conservative values, generally falling somewhere between in overall belief.
- Libertarian—libertarians believe that the government's role should be limited to protecting the life and liberty of citizens. Government should not be involved in any citizen's life unless that citizen is encroaching upon the rights of another.

Principles of government

The six major principles of government as outlined in the United States Constitution are:
- Federalism—the power of the government does not belong entirely to the national government, but is divided between federal and state governments.
- Popular sovereignty—the government is determined by the people, and gains its authority and power from the people.
- Separation of powers—the government is divided into three branches, executive, legislative, and judicial, with each branch having its own set of powers.
- Judicial review—courts at all levels of government can declare laws invalid if they contradict the constitutions of individual states, or the US Constitution, with the Supreme Court serving as the final judicial authority on decisions of this kind.
- Checks and balances—no single branch can act without input from another, and each branch has the power to "check" any other, as well as balance other branches' powers.
- Limited government—governmental powers are limited and certain individual rights are defined as inviolable by the government.

Powers delegated to the national government

The structure of the US government divides power between national and state governments. Powers delegated to the federal government by the Constitution are:
- Expressed powers—powers directly defined in the Constitution, including power to declare war, regulate commerce, make money, and collect taxes
- Implied powers—powers the national government must have in order to carry out the expressed powers
- Inherent powers—powers inherent to any government, not expressly defined in the Constitution

Some of these powers, such as collection and levying of taxes, are also granted to the individual state governments.

Federalism

The way federalism should be practiced has been the subject of debate since writing of the Constitution. There were—and still are—two main factions regarding this issue:
- States' rights—those favoring the states' rights position feel that the state governments should take the lead in performing local actions to manage various problems.
- Nationalist—those favoring a nationalist position feel the national government should take the lead to deal with those same matters.

The flexibility of the Constitution has allowed the US government to shift and adapt as the needs of the country have changed. Power has often shifted from the state governments to the national government and back again, and both levels of government have developed various ways to influence each other.

Federalism has three major effects on public policy in the US:
- Determining whether the local, state, or national government originates policy
- Affecting how policies are made
- Ensuring policy-making functions under a set of limitations

Federalism also influences the political balance of power in the US by:
- making it difficult, if not impossible, for a single political party to seize total power
- ensuring that individuals can participate in the political system at various levels
- making it possible for individuals working within the system to be able to affect policy at some level, whether local or more widespread

Branches of the US government

The following are the three branches of the US Federal government and the individuals that belong to each branch:
- Legislative Branch—this consists of the two Houses of Congress: the House of Representatives and the Senate. All members of the Legislative Branch are elected officials.
- Executive Branch—this branch is made up of the President, Vice President, presidential advisors, and other various cabinet members. Advisors and cabinet are appointed by the President, but must be approved by Congress.
- Judicial Branch—the federal court system, headed by the Supreme Court.

The three branches of the Federal government each have specific roles and responsibilities:
- The Legislative Branch is largely concerned with law-making. All laws must be approved by Congress before they go into effect. They are also responsible for regulating money and trade, approving presidential appointments, and establishing organizations like the postal service and federal courts. Congress can also propose amendments to the Constitution, and can impeach, or bring charges against, the President. Only Congress can declare war.
- The Executive Branch carries out laws, treaties, and war declarations enacted by Congress. The President can also veto bills approved by Congress, and serves as commander-in-chief of the US military. The president appoints cabinet members, ambassadors to foreign countries, and federal judges.
- The Judicial Branch makes decisions on challenges as to whether laws passed by Congress meet the requirements of the US Constitution. The Supreme Court may also choose to review decisions made by lower courts to determine their constitutionality.

US citizenship

Anyone born in the US, born abroad to a US citizen, or who has gone through a process of naturalization is considered a citizen of the United States. It is possible to lose US citizenship as a result of conviction of certain crimes such as treason. Citizenship may also be lost if a citizen pledges an oath to another country or serves in the military of a country engaged in hostilities with the US. A US citizen can also choose to hold dual citizenship, work as an expatriate in another country without losing US citizenship, or even to renounce citizenship if he or she so chooses.

Citizens are granted certain rights under the US government. The most important of these are defined in the Bill of Rights, and include freedom of speech, religion, assembly, and a variety of other rights the government is not allowed to remove. A US citizen also has a number of duties:
- Paying taxes
- Loyalty to the government (though the US does not prosecute those who criticize or seek to change the government)
- Support and defense of the Constitution
- Serving in the Armed Forces when required by law
- Obeying laws as set forth by the various levels of government.

Responsibilities of a US citizen include:
- Voting in elections
- Respecting one another's rights and not infringing on them
- Staying informed about various political and national issues
- Respecting one another's beliefs

Bill of Rights

The first ten amendments of the US Constitution are known as the Bill of Rights. These amendments prevent the government from infringing upon certain freedoms that the founding fathers felt were natural rights that already belonged to all people. These rights included freedom of speech, freedom of religion, the right to bear arms, and freedom of assembly. Many of the rights were formulated in direct response to the way the colonists felt they had been mistreated by the British government. The first ten amendments were passed by Congress in 1789. Three-fourths of the existing thirteen states had ratified them by December of 1791, making them official additions to the Constitution. The rights granted in the Bill of Rights are:
- First Amendment—freedom of religion, speech, freedom of the press, and the right to assemble and to petition the government
- Second Amendment—the right to bear arms
- Third Amendment—Congress cannot force individuals to house troops
- Fourth Amendment—protection from unreasonable search and seizure
- Fifth Amendment—no individual is required to testify against himself, and no individual may be tried twice for the same crime
- Sixth Amendment—right to criminal trial by jury, right to legal counsel
- Seventh Amendment—right to civil trial by jury
- Eighth Amendment—protection from excessive bail or cruel and unusual punishment

- Ninth Amendment—prevents rights not explicitly named in the Constitution from being taken away because they are not named
- Tenth Amendment—any rights not directly delegated to the national government, or not directly prohibited by the government from the states, belong to the states or to the people

In some cases, the government restricts certain elements of First Amendment rights. Some examples include:
- Freedom of religion—when a religion espouses illegal activities, the government often restricts these forms of religious expression. Examples include polygamy, animal sacrifice, and use of illicit drugs or illegal substances.
- Freedom of speech—this can be restricted if exercise of free speech endangers other people.
- Freedom of the press—laws prevent the press from publishing falsehoods.

In emergency situations such as wartime, stricter restrictions are sometimes placed on these rights, especially rights to free speech and assembly, and freedom of the press, in order to protect national security.

> **Review Video:** The Bill of Rights
> Visit *mometrix.com/academy* and enter **Code: 585149**

Constitutional rights of criminals

The US Constitution makes allowances for the rights of criminals, or anyone who has transgressed established laws. There must be laws to protect citizens from criminals, but those accused of crimes must also be protected and their basic rights as individuals preserved. In addition, the Constitution protects individuals from the power of authorities to prevent police forces and other enforcement organizations from becoming oppressive. The fourth, fifth, sixth and eighth amendments specifically address these rights.

Equal protection under the law for all individuals

When the Founding Fathers wrote in the Declaration of Independence that "all men are created equal," they actually were referring to men, and in fact defined citizens as white men who owned land. However, as the country has developed and changed, the definition has expanded to more wholly include all people. "Equality" does not mean all people are inherently the same, but it does mean they all should be granted the same rights and should be treated the same by the government. Amendments to the Constitution have granted citizenship and voting rights to all Americans regardless of race or gender. The Supreme Court evaluates various laws and court decisions to determine if they properly represent the idea of equal protection. One sample case was Brown v. Board of Education in 1954, which declared separate-but-equal treatment to be unconstitutional.

Civil liberty challenges addressed in current political discussions

The civil rights movements of the 1960s and ongoing struggle for the rights of women and other minorities have sparked challenges to existing law. In addition, debate has raged over how much information the government should be required to divulge to the public. Major issues in today's political climate include:
- Continued debate over women's rights, especially regarding equal pay for equal work
- Debate over affirmative action to encourage hiring of minorities
- Debate over civil rights of homosexuals, including marriage and military service

- Decisions as to whether minorities should be compensated for past discriminatory practices
- Balance between the public's right to know and the government's need to maintain national security
- Balance between the public's right to privacy and national security

Civil liberties and civil rights

While the terms "civil liberties" and "civil rights" are often used synonymously, in actuality their definitions are slightly different. The two concepts work together, however, to define the basics of a free state:
- "Civil liberties" defines the role of the state in providing equal rights and opportunities to individuals within that state. An example is non-discrimination policies with regards to granting citizenship.
- "Civil rights" defines the limitations of governmental rights, describing those rights that belong to individuals and which cannot be infringed upon by the government. Examples of these rights include freedom of religion, political freedom, and overall freedom to live as one chooses.

Thirteenth, Fourteenth and Fifteenth Amendments

The Thirteenth, Fourteenth and Fifteenth Amendments were all passed shortly after the end of the Civil War:
- The Thirteenth Amendment was ratified by the states on December 6, 1865. This amendment prohibited slavery in the United States.
- The Fourteenth Amendment overturned the Dred Scott decision, and was ratified July 9, 1868. American citizenship was redefined: a citizen was any person born or naturalized in the US, with all citizens guaranteed equal protection by all states. It also guaranteed citizens of any race the right to file a lawsuit or serve on a jury.
- The Fifteenth Amendment was ratified February 3, 1870. It states that no citizen of the United States can be denied the right to vote based on race, color, or previous status as a slave.

> **Review Video:** The 13th Amendment
> Visit *mometrix.com/academy* and enter **Code: 867407**

> **Review Video:** The 14th Amendment
> Visit *mometrix.com/academy* and enter **Code: 928755**

> **Review Video:** The 15th Amendment
> Visit *mometrix.com/academy* and enter **Code: 102009**

Reconstruction

The three phases of Reconstruction are:
- Presidential Reconstruction—largely driven by President Andrew Johnson's policies, the Presidential phase of Reconstruction was lenient on the South and allowed continued discrimination against and control over blacks.
- Congressional Reconstruction—Congress, controlled largely by Radical Republicans, took a different stance, providing a wider range of civil rights for blacks and greater control over

Southern government. Congressional Reconstruction is marked by military control of the former Confederate States.
- Redemption—gradually, the Confederate states were readmitted into the union. During this time, white Democrats took over the government of most of the South. In 1877, President Rutherford Hayes withdrew the last federal troops from the South.

Carpetbaggers and Scalawags

The chaos in the south attracted a number of people seeking to fill the power vacuums and take advantage of the economic disruption. Scalawags were southern Whites who aligned with Freedmen to take over local governments. Many in the South who could have filled political offices refused to take the necessary oath required to grant them the right to vote, leaving many opportunities for Scalawags and others. Carpetbaggers were northerners who traveled to the South for various reasons. Some provided assistance, while others sought to make money or to acquire political power during this chaotic period.

Transcontinental railroad

In 1869, the Union Pacific Railroad completed the first section of a planned transcontinental railroad. This section went from Omaha, Nebraska to Sacramento, California. Ninety percent of the workers were Chinese, working in very dangerous conditions for very low pay. With the rise of the railroad, products were much more easily transported across the country. While this was positive overall for industry throughout the country, it was often damaging to family farmers, who found themselves paying high shipping costs for smaller supply orders while larger companies received major discounts.

Immigration limits

In 1870, the Naturalization Act put limits on US citizenship, allowing full citizenship only to whites and those of African descent. The Chinese Exclusion Act of 1882 put limits on Chinese immigration. The Immigration Act of 1882 taxed immigrants, charging fifty cents per person. These funds helped pay administrative costs for regulating immigration. Ellis Island opened in 1892 as a processing center for those arriving in New York. 1921 saw the Emergency Quota Act passed, also known as the Johnson Quota Act, which severely limited the number of immigrants allowed into the country.

Nineteenth century changes in agriculture

Technological advancements
During the mid 1800s, irrigation techniques improved significantly. Advances occurred in cultivation and breeding, as well as fertilizer use and crop rotation. In the Great Plains, also known as the Great American Desert, the dense soil was finally cultivated with steel plows. In 1892, gasoline-powered tractors arrived, and were widely used by 1900. Other advancements in agriculture's toolset included barbed wire fences, combines, silos, deep-water wells, and the cream separator.

Government actions

Four major government actions that helped improve US agriculture in the nineteenth century are:
- The Department of Agriculture came into being in 1862, working for the interests of farmers and ranchers across the country.
- The Morrill Land-Grant Acts were a series of acts passed between 1862 and 1890, allowing land-grant colleges.
- In conjunction with land-grant colleges, the Hatch Act of 1887 brought agriculture experiment stations into the picture, helping discover new farming techniques.
- In 1914, the Smith-Lever Act provided cooperative programs to help educate people about food, home economics, community development and agriculture. Related agriculture extension programs helped farmers increase crop production to feed the rapidly growing nation.

Inventors and inventions

Major inventors from the 1800s and their inventions are:
- Alexander Graham Bell—the telephone
- Orville and Wilbur Wright—the airplane
- Richard Gatling—the machine gun
- Walter Hunt, Elias Howe and Isaac Singer—the sewing machine
- Nikola Tesla—alternating current
- George Eastman—the Kodak camera
- Thomas Edison—light bulbs, motion pictures, the phonograph
- Samuel Morse—the telegraph
- Charles Goodyear—vulcanized rubber
- Cyrus McCormick—the reaper
- George Westinghouse—the transformer, the air brake

This was an active period for invention, with about 700,000 patents registered between 1860 and 1900.

Gilded Age

The time period from the end of the Civil War to the beginning of the First World War is often referred to as the Gilded Age, or the Second Industrial Revolution. The US was changing from an agricultural-based economy to an industrial economy, with rapid growth accompanying the shift. In addition, the country itself was expanding, spreading into the seemingly unlimited West. This time period saw the beginning of banks, department stores, chain stores, and trusts—all familiar features of the modern-day landscape. Cities also grew rapidly, and large numbers of immigrants arrived in the country, swelling the urban ranks.

> **Review Video:** The Gilded Age: An Overview
> Visit *mometrix.com/academy* and enter **Code: 684770**

Suffrage and franchise

Suffrage and franchise both refer to the right to vote. As the US developed as a nation, there was much debate over which individuals should hold this right. In the early years, only white male landowners were granted suffrage. By the nineteenth century, most states had franchised, or granted the right to vote to, all adult white males. The Fifteenth Amendment of 1870 granted suffrage to former slave men. The Nineteenth Amendment gave women the right to vote in 1920, and in 1971 the Twenty-sixth Amendment expanded voting rights to include any US citizen over the age of eighteen. However, those who have not been granted full citizenship and citizens who have committed certain crimes do not have voting rights.

Changes in voting process

The first elections in the US were held by public ballot. However, election abuses soon became common, since public ballot made it easy to intimidate, threaten, or otherwise influence the votes of individuals or groups of individuals. New practices were put into play, including registering voters before elections took place, and using a secret or Australian ballot. In 1892, the introduction of the voting machine further privatized the voting process, since it allowed complete privacy for voting. Today debate continues about the accuracy of various voting methods, including high-tech voting machines and even low-tech punch cards.

Political parties

Different types and numbers of political parties can have a significant effect on how a government is run. If there is a single party, or a one-party system, the government is defined by that one party, and all policy is based on that party's beliefs. In a two-party system, two parties with different viewpoints compete for power and influence. The US is basically a two-party system, with checks and balances to make it difficult for one party to gain complete power over the other. There are also multi-party systems, with three or more parties. In multiparty systems, various parties will often come to agreements in order to form a majority and shift the balance of power.

George Washington was adamantly against the establishment of political parties, based on the abuses perpetrated by such parties in Britain. However, political parties developed in US politics almost from the beginning. Major parties throughout US history have included:
- Federalists and Democratic-Republicans—these parties formed in the late 1700s and disagreed on the balance of power between national and state government.
- Democrats and Whigs—these developed before the Civil War, based on disagreements about various issues such as slavery.
- Democrats and Republicans—the Republican Party developed after the Civil War, and the two parties debated issues centering on the treatment of the post-war South.

While third parties sometimes enter the picture in US politics, the government is basically a two-party system, dominated by the Democrats and Republicans.

> **Review Video:** Political Parties
> Visit *mometrix.com/academy* and enter **Code: 640197**

Functions of political parties

Political parties form organizations at all levels of government. Activities of individual parties include:
- Recruiting and backing candidates for offices
- Discussing various issues with the public, increasing public awareness
- Working toward compromise on difficult issues
- Staffing government offices and providing administrative support

At the administrative level, parties work to ensure that viable candidates are available for elections and that offices and staff are in place to support candidates as they run for office and afterwards, when they are elected.

Process for choosing political candidate

Historically, in the quest for political office, a potential candidate has followed one of the following four processes:
- Nominating convention—an official meeting of the members of a party for the express purpose of nominating candidates for upcoming elections. The Democratic National Convention and the Republican National Convention, convened to announce candidates for presidency, are examples of this kind of gathering.
- Caucus—a meeting, usually attended by a party's leaders. Some states still use caucuses, but not all.
- Primary election—the most common method of choosing candidates today, the primary is a publicly held election to choose candidates.
- Petition—signatures are gathered to place a candidate on the ballot. Petitions can also be used to place legislation on a ballot.

Citizen participation in political process

In addition to voting for elected officials, American citizens are able to participate in the political process through several other avenues. These include:
- Participating in local government
- Participating in caucuses for large elections
- Volunteering to help political parties
- Running for election to local, state, or national offices

Individuals can also donate money to political causes, or support political groups that focus on specific causes such as abortion, wildlife conservation or women's rights. These groups often make use of representatives who lobby legislators to act in support of their efforts.

Campaign funding

Political campaigns are very expensive. In addition to the basic necessities of a campaign office, including office supplies, office space, etc., a large quantity of the money that funds a political campaign goes toward advertising. Money to fund a political campaign can come from several sources including:
- The candidate's personal funds
- Donations by individuals
- Special interest groups

The most significant source of campaign funding is special interest groups. Groups in favor of certain policies will donate money to candidates they believe will support those policies. Special interest groups also do their own advertising in support of candidates they endorse.

Free press and the media

The right to free speech guaranteed in the first amendment to the Constitution allows the media to report on government and political activities without fear of retribution. Because the media has access to information about the government, its policies and actions, as well as debates and discussions that occur in Congress, it can keep the public informed about the inner workings of the government. The media can also draw attention to injustices, imbalances of power, and other transgressions the government or government officials might commit. However, media outlets may, like special interest groups, align themselves with certain political viewpoints and skew their reports to fit that viewpoint. The rise of the Internet has made media reporting even more complex, as news can be found from an infinite variety of sources, both reliable and unreliable.

Maps and Data in Social Studies

Analysis of areas of human population

In cities, towns, or other areas where many people have settled, geographers focus on distribution of populations, neighborhoods, industrial areas, transportation, and other elements important to the society in question. For example, they would map out the locations of hospitals, airports, factories, police stations, schools, and housing groups. They would also make note of how these facilities are distributed in relation to the areas of habitation, such as the number of schools in a certain neighborhood, or how many grocery stores are located in a specific suburban area. Another area of study and discussion is the distribution of towns themselves, from widely spaced rural towns to large cities that merge into each other to form a megalopolis.

Cartographers and maps

A cartographer is a mapmaker. Mapmakers produce detailed illustrations of geographic areas to record where various features are located within that area. These illustrations can be compiled into maps, charts, graphs, and even globes. When constructing maps, cartographers must take into account the problem of distortion. Because the earth is round, a flat map does not accurately represent the correct proportions, especially if a very large geographical area is being depicted. Maps must be designed in such a way as to minimize this distortion and maximize accuracy. Accurately representing the earth's features on a flat surface is achieved through projection.

Map projections

The three major types of projection used in creating world maps are:
- Cylindrical projection—this is created by wrapping the globe of the Earth in a cylindrical piece of paper, then using a light to project the globe onto the paper. The largest distortion occurs at the outermost edges.
- Conical projection—the paper is shaped like a cone and contacts the globe only at the cone's base. This type of projection is most useful for middle latitudes.
- Flat-Plane projections—also known as a Gnomonic projection, this type of map is projected onto a flat piece of paper that only touches the globe at a single point. Flat-plane projections make it possible to map out Great-Circle Routes, or the shortest route between one point and another on the globe, as a straight line.

Four specific types of map projections that are commonly used today are:
- Winkel tripel projection—this is the most common projection used for world maps, since it was accepted in 1998 by the National Geographic Society as a standard. The Winkel tripel projection balances size and shape, greatly reducing distortion.
- Robinson projection—east and west sections of the map are less distorted, but continental shapes are somewhat inaccurate.
- Goode homolosine projection—sizes and shapes are accurate, but distances are not. This projection basically represents a globe that has been cut into connected sections so that it can lie flat.
- Mercator projection—though distortion is high, particularly in areas farther from the equator, this cylindrical projection is commonly used by seafarers.

Map elements

The five major elements of any map are:
- Title—this tells basic information about the map, such as the area represented.
- Legend—also known as the key, the legend explains what symbols used on a particular map represent, such as symbols for major landmarks.
- Grid—this most commonly represents the Geographic Grid System, or latitude and longitude marks used to precisely locate specific locations.
- Directions—a compass rose or other symbol is used to indicate the cardinal directions.
- Scale—this shows the relation between a certain distance on the map and the actual distance. For example, one inch might represent one mile, or ten miles, or even more depending on the size of the map.

> **Review Video:** Elements of a Map
> *Visit mometrix.com/academy* and enter **Code: 437727**

Equal area map and conformal map

An equal area map is designed such that the proportional sizes of various areas are accurate. For example, if one land mass is one-fifth the size of another, the lines on the map will be shifted to accommodate for distortion so that the proportional size is accurate. In many maps, areas farther from the equator are greatly distorted; this type of map compensates for this phenomenon. A conformal map focuses on representing the correct shape of geographical areas, with less concern for comparative size.

Consistent scale map and thematic map

With a consistent scale map, the same scale, such as one inch=ten miles, is used throughout the entire map. This is most often used for maps of smaller areas, as maps that cover larger areas, such as the full globe, must make allowances for distortion. Maps of very large areas often make use of more than one scale, with scales closer to the center representing a larger area than those at the edges.

A thematic map is constructed to show very specific information about a chosen theme. For example, a thematic map might represent political information, such as how votes were distributed in an election, or could show population distribution or climatic features.

Relief map

A relief map is constructed to show details of various elevations across the area of the map. Higher elevations are represented by different colors than lower elevations. Relief maps often also show additional details, such as the overall ruggedness or smoothness of an area. Mountains would be represented as ridged and rugged, while deserts would be shown as smooth.

Elevation in relief maps can also be represented by contour lines, or lines that connect points of the same elevation. Some relief maps even feature textures, reconstructing details in a sort of miniature model.

Mountains, hills, plains, and valleys

- Mountains are elevated areas that measure 2,000 feet or more above sea level. Often steep and rugged, they usually occur in groups called chains or ranges. Six of the seven continents on Earth contain at least one range.
- Hills are of lower elevation than mountains, at about 500-2,000 feet. Hills are usually more rounded, and are found throughout every continent.
- Plains are large, flat areas and are usually very fertile. The majority of the Earth's population is supported by crops grown on vast plains.
- Valleys lie between hills and mountains. Depending on their location, their specific features can vary greatly, from fertile and habitable to rugged and inhospitable.

Plateaus, deserts, deltas, mesas, basins, foothills, marshes, and swamps

- Plateaus are elevated, but flat on top. Some plateaus are extremely dry, such as the Kenya Plateau, because surrounding mountains prevent them from receiving moisture.
- Deserts receive less than ten inches of rain per year. They are usually large areas, such as the Sahara Desert in Africa or the Australian Outback.
- Deltas occur at river mouths. Because the rivers carry sediment to the deltas, these areas are often very fertile.
- Mesas are flat, steep-sided mountains or hills. The term is sometimes used to refer to plateaus.
- Basins are areas of low elevation where rivers drain.
- Foothills are the transitional area between the plains and the mountains, usually consisting of hills that gradually increase in size as they approach the mountain range.
- Marshes and swamps are also lowlands, but they are very wet and largely covered in vegetation such as reeds and rushes.

Bodies of water

- Oceans are the largest bodies of water on Earth. They are salt water, and cover about two-thirds of the earth's surface. The five major oceans are the Atlantic, Pacific, Indian, Arctic, and Southern.
- Seas are generally also salt water, but are smaller than oceans and surrounded by land. Examples include the Mediterranean Sea, the Caribbean Sea, and the Caspian Sea.
- Lakes are bodies of freshwater found inland. Sixty percent of all lakes are located in Canada.

- Rivers are moving bodies of water that flow from higher elevations to lower. They usually start as rivulets or streams, and grow until they finally empty into a sea or an ocean.
- Canals, such as the Panama Canal and the Suez Canal, are manmade waterways connecting two large bodies of water.

> **Review Video:** Bodies of Water
> *Visit mometrix.com/academy and enter Code:* **463122**

Communities

Communities, or groups of people who settle together in a specific area, typically gather where certain conditions exists. These conditions include:
- Easy access to resources such as food, water, and raw materials
- Ability to easily transport raw materials and goods, such as access to a waterway
- Room to house a sufficient work force

People also tend to form groups with others who are similar to them. In a typical community, people can be found who share values, a common language, and common or similar cultural characteristics and religious beliefs. These factors will determine the overall composition of a community as it develops.

Cities

Cities develop and grow as an area develops. Modern statistics show that over half of the world's people live in cities. That percentage is even higher in developed areas of the globe. Cities are currently growing more quickly in developing regions, and even established cities continue to experience growth throughout the world. In developing or developed areas, cities often are surrounded by a metropolitan area made up of both urban and suburban sections. In some places, cities have merged into each other and become a megalopolis—a single, huge city.

Cities develop differently in different areas of the world. The area available for cities to grow, as well as cultural and economic forces, drives how cities develop. For example, North American cities tend to cover wider areas. European cities tend to have better developed transportation systems. In Latin America, the richest inhabitants can be found in the city centers, while in North America wealthier inhabitants tend to live in suburban areas.

In other parts of the world, transportation and communication between cities is less developed. Recent technological innovations such as the cell phone have increased communication even in these areas. Urban areas must also maintain communication with rural areas in order to procure food, resources, and raw materials that cannot be produced within the city limits.

Fine Arts

Visual Arts

Basic elements of art

There are five basic elements of art: line, shape, space, texture and color. Each has a specific function; each must be understood to truly appreciate the objet d'art being studied. The following definitions are composed from the American Heritage College Dictionary:
- Line is a continuous path made by a moving pen, pencil or brush that makes a real or imaginary mark in relation to a point of reference.
- Shape is the characteristic outline or contour of an object that is distinguished from its surroundings by its distinctive form.
- Space is a three-dimensional empty area with a specific outline that is reserved for a particular purpose.
- Texture is a surface of elements woven together that has distinctive or identifying characteristics.
- Color is the appearance of objects caused by different qualities of reflected light that involves hue, lightness, darkness, value and purity.

Light and dark

In western culture, the reaction to light and dark arouses strong, primitive emotions. Light suggests goodness, intelligence and wholeness. Dark expresses mystery, ignorance and evil. Contrasting these opposites in a work of art helps convey feelings and has a powerful psychological impact. Light and dark can also depict space and enhance form in two and three dimensional art. On a two dimensional surface, the effects of light and shadow can be very dramatic. When light is blocked by different parts of a form and casts a shadow, the figures in a painting seem to come alive. This technique is called chiaroscuro.

Light and shadow on sculpture and architecture define the form of the piece. As the contour fades away, the light grows dimmer causing changes in contrast and tonal value on the surface, which makes the object seem to swell and recede while enhancing the drama of its structural composition.

Basic principles of art

In art, there are five basic principles: balance and harmony, proportion and unity and variety. Each has a unique function and needs to be understood to appreciate the artist's vision whether it is shown in a painting, sculpture or a piece of architecture. The following definitions are composed from the American Heritage College Dictionary:
- Balance and Harmony is a state of equilibrium between parts that creates a pleasant arrangement in the whole and depicts a difference in dimension between opposing forces or influences.
- Proportion is the pleasing symmetry between objects or their parts with respect to comparative size, quantity or degree.

- Unity is the state of being in accord and having a continuity of purpose or action. Its partner is Variety, which is diversity in a collection that has specific characteristics.

Art forms

The following definitions are taken from The American Heritage College Dictionary.
- A painting is a picture or design created in oil or water based paint.
- Literature is a body of creative writing that helps define a language, period or culture.
- Music is sounds arranged to produce a unified composition that has melody, rhythm and timber.
- A sculpture is an object created by chiseling marble, molding clay or casting in metal into a real or abstract figure.
- Theater is dramatic or comedic literature or other such material performed by actors impersonating characters through dialogue and action.
- Drama is verbal literature composed of serious subject matter written specifically to be performed by actors in the theater or on television, radio or film.
- Comedy is humorous or satirical verbal literature depicting funny themes, situations or characters that is written to be performed by actors in the theater or on television, radio or film.

Subject matter within a painting

The following terms relate to subject matter within a painting:
- background – the part of the scene intended to be the most distant from the perspective of the viewer
- foreground – the part of the scene intended to be nearest the viewer
- horizon – the line where sky and earth meet; also referred to as "ground line"
- landscape – a view of a section of country – applicable to outdoor scenes only
- middle ground – the area between the foreground and the most distant part of a scene
- vertical lines – lines that are painted straight up and down
- horizontal lines – lines that are painted across the picture (90 degrees from straight up and down)
- point-of-view – the angle from which the viewer is observing the work
- negative space – the space behind and around an object; in two-dimensional art it is often synonymous with background
- overlapping – occurs when one object partially covers another; usually done for compositional purposes
- design – the arrangement of the elements of a picture

Aesthetic awareness

The act of appreciating visual art is, in its simplest form, one of simply deriving satisfaction or pleasure from observing the beauty given to it by its creator. Research has shown that a capacity for appreciating (or, alternatively, creating) aesthetically pleasing art appears to be present within every individual although it does seem to vary in terms of degrees. For most people, innate abilities remain untrained or underdeveloped – not so much in terms of the possession of individual tastes and opinions or in terms of an ability to find something beautiful, but rather in an ability to recognize artistic mastery with respect to technique or style. Education can reconcile such a deficiency.

Therefore, anyone can truly appreciate art, but true "art appreciation" requires some understanding of the creative process involved in production, or perhaps, some particular insight into the thoughts and feelings of the creator. Ideally, art is best appreciated when one considers both dimensions.

Wood carving and engraving

Wood carving is an ancient art which has changed very little in its history. The process is relatively straightforward. After selecting a suitable wood, most carving is done with a limited set of tools to create works which don't typically exhibit an abundance of fine detail.

Engraving is a more refined version of carving and is sometimes a preliminary step in other artistic activities such as printmaking where fine detail and exacting shapes are desired. Several varieties of wood can be used successfully by the engraver although boxwood is a preferred type for its favorable characteristics. The wood is sawn cross-grain which results in a block with both a tighter grain and better shape-holding ability.

Due to its exacting nature, engraving often requires tools similar to those used by copper and steel workers. The tools are arranged into groups such as gravers, tint tools, scorpers, spit stickers, and small chisels. A typical beginning set includes flat, round, burin and lozenge, as well as both large and small U and V cutters.

Pastels

Pastels are chemically pure pigments gently bound by gum or resin and are much softer than their harder chalk crayon cousins. Due to the nature of the pigment cohesion, durability is a primary concern when using them. The ability to correct mistakes is also severely limited. For this reason, pre-planning a work is crucial.

A fairly recent addition to the arts, pastel work was pioneered mostly by French artists in the 18th century. Notable pastel artists of the era included Quentin de la Tour, Jean-Baptiste Perroneau and Jean-Baptiste Chardin. More recent artists include Odilon Redon and Mary Cassatt.

Having never gained the popularity of other forms such as oils and watercolor, pastels remain one the less regarded mediums within the artistic community.

Pen and ink

Pen and ink is one of the least demanding art forms in terms of equipment requirements. Pen and ink artists simply need the addition of virtually any kind of paper to produce their work.

Historically, medieval monks employed pen and ink on prepared animal skins such as goat, sheep, calf, lamb or kid using the quills of goose feathers.
Pen use continued during the Renaissance and along with mixed media such as white highlighting, crayon and watercolors it flourished as an art form. It gained even more widespread use during the Post-Renaissance era by such artists as Rubens and Van Dyck. Hogarth is considered an exemplary penman of the 18th century while the advent of magazines and the mass production of books in the 19th century provided an outlet for notables such as Charles Keene and George du Maurier.

By the 20th century, pen and ink luminaries included Matisse, Pascin and Picasso.

Sculpture design

Mass – This is perhaps the most influential element in sculpture that, when manipulated, can have a dramatic effect upon interpretation, light reflectivity and symmetry.

Space – Space in a multi-piece sculpture is an element that can be manipulated to effect interpretation by yielding clues with respect to the relationship between individual pieces.

Plane – An element with two dimensions – length and width; plane thickness is typically minimized to provide the most dramatic differentiation between plane and volume

Line – Line lends an element of space to a sculpture; vertical lines belie support and strength lending a monumental quality while horizontal lines have a somewhat less dramatic effect. Convex lines can create tension while concave lines often indicate either real or implied forces.

Movement – generally an implied effect; often a function of reflected light that can be altered through the manipulation of the sculpture's mass. Some sculptors, such as Alexander Calder, employ actual movement in their work through mobiles or similar effects.

Scale – the relative size of the work; often a product of the manipulation of other elements such as mass

Texture – the surface quality of the work; primarily manipulated to either enhance or diminish light reflectivity and shadowing

Color – achieved through a variety of effects; can often add a sense of realism or a particular quality, such as age, to a work

Perspective

Perspective is a system of creating the illusion of three dimensions on a two-dimensional surface. There are two basic categories of perspective – aerial and linear. Aerial perspective refers to atmospheric effects on objects in space and can be seen as diminishing tones for objects which are receding from view. Put simply, linear perspective describes a process of seeing lines on objects from various angles converge and diverge.

The position from which an object is seen and drawn is called the station point or point of sight. The horizon is represented by the eye level or horizon line. Ground plane refers to the horizontal plane where the artist is standing. The center of vision is the point on the horizon immediately opposite the eye. Vanishing points occur where parallel lines converge.

Shape, form and proportion

Shape is an aspect of form which constitutes the individual masses, groupings or aesthetics that the artist uses to render the overall work. It is form, combined with content, which constitutes the basis of the art work itself.

Proportion refers to the symmetrical three-dimensionality or solidity of a work. In representational art, the intent is to create an illusion of reality by rendering a work which is convincing in form.

The mathematical concept known as the "Golden Mean" is often employed, either purposefully or incidentally, when rendering proportion. Put simply, it is the precept that the proportion of the smaller part to the larger part of a whole is equal to that of the larger to the whole.

Perhaps the most well-known demonstration of the "Golden Mean" is the 1509 Leonardo da Vinci work titled "Divine Proportion".

Protective apparel

Protective apparel such as gloves, long sleeves, long pants and boots or shoes rather than sandals help prevent contact of chemicals with the skin. The garments should be dedicated for use in the studio or work area and washed frequently in a separate load from other laundry.

If skin contact does occur, flush immediately with soapy water or other suitable cleaners. Avoid the use of solvents or bleach to clean the skin as these will often absorb and enter the blood stream where they can accumulate in internal organs.

If splashes or flying debris are concerns, goggles should be worn in the work area. Ear protection is generally advised when working with noisy equipment for extended periods. Wear a properly fitted respirator or dust mask if vapors or dust are present.

Refrain from wearing jewelry when working and tie long hair back to prevent it from being caught in tools and equipment.

Do not work when fatigued and always wash hands before drinking, eating or smoking.

Materials to avoid

Numerous materials specially designed for children are available commercially. Adult supervision is also advisable when children are working with art materials. All adult materials should be avoided as these may contain toxic chemicals, including solvents, thinners, shellacs, acids, alkalis, bleaches, rubber cement and permanent markers.

Materials which must be sprayed such as paints, fixatives, adhesives and airbrush paints should be avoided as well as pottery glazes, copper enamels, stained glass and pastels.

Also, any materials requiring solvents for clean-up such as oil paint or oil-based printmaking inks should be substituted for water-based alternatives when available.

It is often best to limit the amount or quantity of material given to very young children to reduce the risk should ingestion occur. Children should also be taught to wash their hands thoroughly after working with the materials.

Places to view art and architecture

The architecture of home construction is one obvious place. Although many newer areas around cities lack compelling diversity and creativity, there are almost always exceptions. This is particularly true of older areas with established traditions.

Churches are another excellent place to discover art. The relationship between religion and art is as old as most religions themselves. Christianity is certainly no exception. Modern churches frequently have collections of paintings and sculpture consistent with the beliefs of their own individual congregations.

For those fortunate enough live in Europe or in the Eastern United States, numerous older churches are accessible. Many of these are exemplary works of art in themselves.

A number of businesses, particularly large corporations, have substantial art collections in their common areas, many of which are accessible to visitors. Shopping centers, banks government buildings (particularly with respect to sculpture) are often rich resources for art seekers.

Color terminology

- Hue – any specific color
- Shade – a color made by adding black to a hue
- Tone – a color made by adding grey to a hue
- Value – the degree of light or darkness
- Achromatic – black, white and grays; artwork executed without color
- Black – the complete absence of light
- Chroma – the intensity, strength or purity of a color
- Complementary Colors – colors which appear opposite one another on a color wheel
- Secondary colors – orange, violet, green; each is midway between the Primaries from which it can be mixed
- Shade – using a mixture of black mixed with a color to make it darker; the opposite of shade is tint
- Spectrum – colors that are the result of a beam of white light that is broken by a form of prism into its hues
- Tint – the opposite of shade; combining white with a color to make it lighter
- Value – shadows, darkness, contrasts and light

Carving, casting, collage, drypoint, engraving, and etching

These definitions are from the New York City Public Library Desk Reference, Second Edition.

Carving means to cut hard material such as stone, wood or marble to create a form.

In Casting, the sculptor pours plaster or molten metal into a mold and lets the substance harden into the desired form.

A Collage is made of separate pieces of various materials and other objects glued to a surface.

Drypoint is an engraving technique that uses a sharp steel needle to create a rough edge, which produces soft, velvety lines.

Engraving is the art of carving, cutting or etching a design on a wood or metal surface then adding ink so the design can be printed.

Etching is the art of cutting into a metal or glass surface then bathing the surface in acid, adding ink to the plate, and printing the design.

Frieze, lithography, modeling, and polyptych

These definitions are from the New York City Public Library Desk Reference, Second Edition.

In architecture, a frieze is a horizontal band of painted or sculpted decoration usually found at the top of a wall between the molding and the cornice.

Lithography is a printing process in which a stone or metal plate has been treated with an oily substance so that the desired design retains ink while the rest of the surface is treated to repel ink. When a sculptor uses clay or wax to build up a form, it is called modeling. Using color and light to create the illusion of a three dimensional plane in drawing and painting is also known as modeling.

A polyptych is multiple scenes hinged together. A diptych has two panels; a triptych has three panels.

Relief, stenciling, still life, and woodcut

These definitions are from the New York City Public Library Desk Reference, Second Edition.
In architecture when a form sticks out from the background, depending on how far it protrudes, it is known as high relief or low relief (bas-relief). In painting or drawing, if an object appears to project out from the flat surface suggesting three dimensions, it is called relief.

Stenciling is the technique of applying paint or ink to forms cut out of cardboard, metal, plastic or other flat materials to create letters, numbers and other images and designs.

A still life is a study of ordinary objects in an every day setting in a painting, drawing or photograph. A still life can also be created on a tabletop or in a bookcase or a shadow box.

Woodcutting is the art of carving an image on a wood block then using ink or paint to print the design.

Music

Creative Expression
Being creative means the ability to produce or bring into existence a work of art (music, painting, sculpture, comedy, drama, and literature) that is original and imaginative. To express something is to convey an idea, an emotion or an opinion, or to depict a direct or indirect representation of an idea, an emotion or an opinion. The idea, emotion or opinion can be shown in words, pictures, gestures, signs and symbols. A person with creative expression has the burning need to bring forth a unique manifestation of his or her understanding and interpretation of mankind's primal desires.

A soaring music score by Beethoven, a memorable scene by Grandma Moses, a gentle poem by Emily Dickinson, a moving performance by Sir Laurence Olivier are all examples of individual creative expression by artists of uncompromising vision.

Classifications of music

The style of music showcases not only the time and political or spiritual mood of the period, but also the composers and the mindset of the people. Music is meant to be listened to and, as such, can be repeated, expounded upon through different media, appreciated in different ways at different times, accepted as an individualistic part of the hearer, respected as a demonstration of a culture or belief system, and touted as a societal bragging right. Music offers these different abstract feelings, but its primary purpose and people's eternal fascination falls back on the fact that music is created for people's enjoyment. The styles of music are usually classified into chronological sections and referred to as Renaissance, Baroque, Classical, Romantic, and Twentieth Century.

Quality of music

Music is difficult to label as good and bad since the biggest deciding factor of the quality of music is the listener. Defining any greatness in art by comparing the positive and negative aspects limits the artistic voice of the creator and the imagination of the audience. Critics have been in the business of defining the quality of art for centuries and have often made poor calls because of their inability to accept a new style or the enduring aspect of the composer and the audience reception of that style . For any musician to become accepted, he or she must master a particular style or technique and perform or compose with a kind of genius that inspires others. To be considered great, music must be able to stand the test of time as being an indispensable example of a kind of work for the period, country, or composer.

Symphony

As a work for an orchestra with multiple movements or multiple parts in one movement, the symphony contained three movements of fast-slow-fast and was named for the Italian opera *Sinfonia*. Performed with strings and winds, these musical pieces were enjoyed at private gatherings in palaces, monasteries, and residences, as well as civic functions and public concerts. The foundation for the symphony genre comes from Sammartini whose works used the three-part movement with both strings and winds. As the Classical Period developed, the symphonic format increased to four parts or movements with an even greater transition in the third movement. After being expertly worked by Haydn, the symphony became a more celebrated style of music that allowed for great freedom in composition and features.

Relation of tonal characteristics to their use in orchestration

The orchestrator uses the tonal characteristics of the different instrument families to meticulously layer each sound into a collective whole. The strings tend to have a rich tonal quality and form the basis of many orchestral textures. Strings have a variety of sounds and techniques and can easily function as melody, supporting harmony, or rhythmic texture. High brasses have a clear, focused tonal quality and many times are used melodically or as a crisp rhythmic flourish. Low brasses tend to provide bass lines as well as rhythmic motives. Woodwinds have held various roles within the orchestra and can easily function as melody, supporting harmony, or rhythmic texture, similar to strings. Percussive instruments have historically held a rhythmic role in orchestral writing, but have also been used as melodic interest through the marimba, timpani, and other melodic percussion instruments.

How sound is produced

Brass instruments
Brass instruments typically produce sound through the buzzing of the player's lips as the air travels through a tubular, expanding metallic wind instrument. The lips act as a vibrating valve that produces oscillating air and pressure. As the air vibrates through the tubular instrument, some of the energy is lost as viscous and thermal energy, while the rest emerges from the instrument as sound. Almost all brass instruments consist of a tube that gets larger towards the end of the tube called the bell. The tube is often coiled so that the instrument is easier for the player to hold. Brass instruments resonate at certain frequencies more easily than others, so to produce other tones, players can change the length of the instruments through valves or slides. Narrower, more cylindrical brass instruments like the trumpet and the trombone produce sharp and clear sounds, while wider, larger-belled brass instruments like the French horn and euphonium produce warmer, darker sounds.

Stringed instruments
Stringed instruments produce sound through the vibrations of the strings on a resonating body usually made of wood. The strings, made of nylon, steel, or silk, can be set in motion by plucking, bowing, or striking. As the string sets the surrounding air in motion, it also vibrates the soundboard through the bridge as the resonant vibrator and the audible tone effuses out of the instrument through a sound hole. Pitches on a stringed instrument are modified by string tension, thickness, and length: the higher the tension, the higher the pitch; the thicker the string, the lower the pitch; and the longer the string, the lower the pitch. Strings can be parallel to the soundboard as in the lute, guitar, violin, piano, and dulcimer, or at a right angle to the soundboard as in the harp.

Woodwind instruments
Woodwind instruments produce sound through vibrations in an enclosed tube. The vibrations can be set into motion by blowing through single or double reeds, across an opening, or through an opening. Single-reed woodwind instruments produce sound when air is blown through a reed that vibrates against the mouthpiece. Single-reed instruments include the clarinet and the saxophone. Double-reed woodwind instruments produce sound when air is blown through two reeds that are tied together and vibrate. Double-reed instruments include the oboe, bassoon, and sarrusophone. Woodwinds that produce sound when the player blows across an opening are the transverse flutes, which are held sideways. Woodwinds that produce sound when the player blows directly into an opening are the whistle and the recorder. Players change the pitch of an instrument by shortening or lengthening the air column through covered holes or keys.

Percussion instruments
Percussion instruments are instruments that produce sound by being hit, scraped, or shaken. Certain percussion instruments such as drums produce sound through the vibration of a membrane around a resonating body. Also known as membranophones, the membrane on these instruments can be struck by hands or mallets, as well as rubbed and scraped. Other percussion instruments produce vibrations without the aid of air, string, or membranes; these musical instruments are known as idiophones and include concussion idiophones, percussion idiophones, rattles, scrapers, and friction idiophones. Concussion idiophones are two objects that are struck together; examples include rhythm sticks, castanets, and claves. Percussion idiophones are those struck by mallets and include marimbas, bells, gongs, and xylophones. Rattles are shaken, such as a maraca. Scrapers are

stroked across a notched surface, such as washboards and guiros. Friction idiophones are played by rubbing and include the musical saw and the glass harmonica.

Baroque style vs. Classical style

While the stylistic choices for music differ between Baroque and Classical, the integrity and depth of composition evident in both. Music requires a certain kind of simplicity for comprehension, and the simpler styles of the Classical Period did not take away that complexity. While Bach may create incredible musical feats on his polyphonic style, he incorporated a lucid design in his work. The surface sounds of works by Haydn and Mozart may appear simple but are in actuality incredibly organized and conceived, using a great amount of material and genius in that simplicity. The Baroque composers sought to express magnificence and grandeur in their music, while the Classical composers adopted an unpretentious format of hiding deep feelings. Baroque gave us the motet and opera, but from the Classical Period came the symphony, string quartet, and sonata.

Most celebrated composers

Probably the three most celebrated composers from the history of music are Bach, Mozart, and Beethoven. Each changed the course of music as it affected audience members from their time to now. Bach's style of music with all its groundbreaking reverberations and genius became outdated within his lifetime, and his own reputation was tarnished by his limited scope when it came to moving on with the period. Mozart remained true to his period and is viewed as the supreme example of musical perfection with an unimagined future if he had lived longer. Beethoven was the real revolutionary, a then-modern rock star, who used the rigors of the genre to explode in individualistic expression amidst his completely disciplined musical control.

Johann Sebastian Bach
Born into an extraordinary musical family in Eisenach, Germany, in 1685, Johann Sebastian Bach influenced the entire musical world with his works and his genius. Starting on violin, Bach spent most of his childhood playing music on the organ under the tutelage of his brother. After singing in the church choir in Lüneburg, Bach stayed on as the church harpsichordist and violinist. A self-taught composer, Bach accepted a position as organist at St. Boniface church in Arnstadt and would include variations in his hymns. With several publications, Bach moved on to Mülhausen in 1706 before accepting a position as court organist and then concertmaster for Duke Wilhelm Ernst of Weimar. While arranging and copying parts of Vivaldi pieces for performances, Bach combined his German style with the Italian energy and rhythm. Bach became Kapellmeister to Prince Leopold in Cöthen and concentrated on secular music for court.

Bach fathered 20 children with wives Maria Barbara, who died after birthing the seventh, then Anna Magdalena Wülken. His children acted as assistants and copyists as well as musicians in their own right. Early Bach pieces written under the patronage of Prince Leopold include The Well-Tempered Clavier and Inventions, but Bach's organ pieces were often too difficult for most organists to perform. All Bach's work is religious-based with a foundation of the Lutheran hymn or chorale, and even secular pieces are dedicated to God. The pieces themselves are vocal pictures, such as "Wie zittern un wanken" from the cantata Herr, Gehe nicht ins Gericht (Lord, go not in judgment) where the oboe repeats the same phrase and there is no bass or foundation for the piece. Bach mastered the art of polyphony and counterpoint and is celebrated for his fugues and canons such as "Jesu, Joy of Man's Desiring."

Wolfgang Amadeus Mozart

Though most of his most important works occurred at the end of his life, Wolfgang Amadeus Mozart started his musical career as a child prodigy. Able to raise the standard for good music, Mozart was considered by Haydn to be the greatest composer ever heard. Mozart's father, Leopold Mozart, a minor composer with the local court and a published violin teacher, was a strict but remarkable teacher who taught him about the music of his predecessors and current composers. Mozart composed symphonies, operas, and quartets based on his own talent and his absorption of the different styles he studied. All of Mozart's work had a defined style and determined procedure. He did not try to break through the boundaries set forth with Classical music but used those guidelines to affect music's future.

Ludwig van Beethoven

With a tyrant as a father, Ludwig van Beethoven was forcibly introduced into the world of music, so that he could achieve the notoriety of Mozart. Beethoven was instructed by Neefe to play Bach fugues and preludes to learn the discipline and stamina of the period and to develop. Known for his improvisation, Beethoven was often hired to teach noblemen's children and became appreciated by the more sophisticated crowds. He studied music with Haydn, Italian vocal composition with Salieri, and counterpoint with Albrechtsberger. All the teachers saw the genius but the incomparable stubbornness and ego in the pupil. While his early pieces such as *Symphony No. 1* were conservative, his middle works such as the *Pathétique Sonata* showed his developing fire. His later pieces showcased the more Classical sense of order.

Jazz

Influencing different types of music, jazz started as an African-American creation of principally instrumental music combined with elements of the church, story telling, vocal inflections, and the call-and-response technique. Jazz combined the strong tonality, instrumentation, and rhythms of the American marching band music, ragtime, piano music of Debussy, American popular music, and Latin-American dance music. As technology played a bigger part in music creation, jazz also incorporated the electronic innovations of rock and soul. New Orleans was the birthplace of jazz, where all the cultural icons converged between 1890 and 1910. Jazz offered many opportunities for improvisation and development, and the different wind, brass, and percussion instruments allowed for different combinations and rhythms. Jazz gave rise to swing in the 1930s and 1940s.

Musicals

The musical theater of the twentieth century was popularly expressed through musicals, which were mainly developed in America and England. The structure and basic style are similar to the European operetta, combining spoken dialogue with developing dramatic situations that are susceptible to the inclusion of dance, song, and ensemble performance. With a melodic and harmonic format similar to the Tin Pan Alley period of songwriting, musicals developed from the minstrel and vaudeville shows of the 1800s. Irving Berlin created his songs and acts based on ragtime and dance rhythms and syncopation. The musical show form itself became fully defined in the 1920s with librettos combining dialogue and music with contemporary or urban settings. Many composers and songwriters gained popularity through this venue.

Rock 'n' Roll

Popular music of the 1950s, Rock 'n' Roll was founded on the tenets of African-American music and rhythm. Rock pieces by such artists as Bill Haley and the Comets, Elvis Presley, Jerry Lee Lewis,

Chuck Berry, Little Richard, and Fats Domino were disseminated worldwide with great success. The appeal of rock transcended racial and cultural lines and attracted lovers of the music of Tin Pan Alley, country and western, and black popular music. As a form of rhythmic blues, rock pieces are written in some variation of the 12-bar blues form with instrumentation of electric guitars, saxophones, and a rhythm section of piano, drums, and bass. With a fast-paced tempo, rock music lyrics are usually about sex while the dynamic level is high with rough and raucous musical stylings. The genre originally was splintered to include rhythm and blues while the writing and arranging followed the same pattern.

Intervals

As the basis for any discussion of melodic or harmonic relationships, the interval refers to the measurement from pitch to pitch. The half step or semitone is the smallest movement and is the distance from one key to the next in the chromatic scale, such as C to C#. The whole step or tone refers to a full movement in which the notes are 2 keys apart, such as from C to D. The half step and whole step act as the basis of measurement for intervallic discussions. These intervals are defined by quantity and quality. The quantity, or numeric value assigned to the note, is established by the musical arrangement, such as C D E F G A B. Any interval created with C and G will always be a fifth, regardless of any sharps or flats.

Scales

A musical scale is the sequenced arrangement of notes or pitches that are located within the octave. Both major and minor scales have seven different notes or scale degrees, and each scale degree is indicated by the Arabic number showing the position of the note as it appears in the scale. Each major scale has two similar units of four notes, or tetrachords, that are separated by a whole step where each tetrachord has two whole steps and one half step.

Minor scales are classified as natural, harmonic, and melodic and all start with the same minor tetrachord of 1-2- b3-4 with variations occurring on degrees 6 and 7 in the upper tetrachord.

Dynamics in music

Dynamics is the degree of loudness or softness of a musical piece. Certain terms can indicate this degree, as well as specific abbreviations and symbols used within the music and at specific places. Dynamic marks can also indicate a change in volume or sound quality and usually suggest the character of the piece to be observed during its performance. Usually written in Italian, dynamic marks are often abbreviated and range from very soft pianissimo (pp) to mezzo piano (mp) to mezzo forte (mf) to fortissimo (ff) which is very loud.

Gradual changes in volume can be represented by a < or the word crescendo for increasing in volume and by a > or the words diminuendo or decrescendo for decreasing in volume. These marks for the changing of volume can be several measures long or just a span of a few notes.

Tempo

The tempo or speed of the piece of music can be designated by specific tempo marks as well as certain Italian words that describe the speed and also the character of the piece. The words used include grave for very slow and serious, largo for broad, lento for slow, adagio for slow and with ease, andante for steadily moving, moderato for moderate, allegretto for fast, allegro for fast and cheerful, vivace for lively, presto for very fast, and prestissimo for as fast as possible. Other relative changes in tempo can be described with the words ritardando, or rit., for slowing, as well as accelerando for quickening and più mosso for faster. The tempo marking are a guide for the performance and can be interpreted differently by different conductors.

Rhythm

As the pattern of movement in a particular time, rhythm has referred to both the flow of a piece and the ability of the piece to maintain or uphold the pulse. Rhythm can be generally assigned to cover any aspect of music that is not related to pitch, although it has also been used as another factor for consideration with melody and harmony. As an equal partner to meter and tempo, rhythm can describe a pattern of stresses and retreats that are defined by a particular tempo or meter and are composed of hazy pitches or subtle harmonies as well as percussive bursts. For rhythm to sustain, the stresses and retreats should be frequent enough to maintain the melodic or harmonic thought and have defined articulation.

Acoustics

Acoustics refers to the study of the production and perception of sound within a particular room or area. By producing musical sound, musicians create mechanical vibrations from the stretching of strings or membranes, movement of wooden parts, and the oscillatory movement of air columns. This sound action affects the air, which carries the energy of the vibrations from the musician to the audience member. The sound is transmitted through to the brain where it is deciphered and interpreted. The perceived sound is referred to as a pure tone and has a frequency of full oscillations occurring each second. The human ear can perceive 20 to 20,000 cycles per second, or cps, and the corresponding frequency of the pure tone determines the pitch.

Educator's role

Any educator of children is in a position to exert remarkable control and influence over these young lives. As such, educators are responsible in making that influence a positive one, so that the child can reach his or her fullest potential. All teachers should seek out ways to prepare for curriculum planning and designing instructions that are appropriate for the child's particular educational level. Music combines with all developmental, cognitive, language, physical, emotional, and social arenas of education and makes the music educator one of the most fundamental of teachers. Training is necessary for any teacher dealing with children; it is especially important for teachers dealing with children who are still young enough to be easily influenced. Music educators should be able to guide children in their musical experiences and encourage their progress as it occurs.

Importance of singing and chanting

Young children explore their world with a different perspective than adults do, and the sense of touch is especially important when learning new things. Percussion and other simple instruments allow children to see and feel how an accented beat corresponds to music and the words in songs. Rhythmic songs and chants are important for children to understand the combination of sounds and beats and apply that process to their own sensory perceptions. When music educators participate in the singing or chanting, they can interact with the children, and show them how much fun moving to music and creating music can be for all ages. Through this type of exercise, children can learn how words work together and how they should sound by following the example of the music educator.

Breathing warm-up

Before beginning any choral rehearsal, it is essential for the director to prepare the singers both physically and mentally. One important aspect of warming up a choral ensemble is the breathing warm-up. Breathing warm-ups engage the diaphragm for supported singing and help to warm the vocal chords for singing. Not only will the breathing exercises physically prepare the lungs and vocal mechanisms for singing, they will also mentally center the singer to be mindful of breath during the rehearsal. One choral breathing warm-up consists of taking in a deep breath over as many counts as possible, holding the breath, and then slowly letting out the air on an "s" sound, over as many counts as possible. Another choral warm-up consists of having the singers exhale on a pulse with an open mouth "ha."

Instrumental and choral warm up

Warming up serves several important physical and mental functions for the group ensemble. Mentally, it has the effect of centering and adjusting the ensemble to an appropriate mental state for performance and establishing proper physiological cues for posture, breathing, etc. Warm-ups serve as a unifying tool for all members of the ensemble to begin listening to each other as a musical entity and adjusting sound according to the group. Physically, the warm-up promotes blood flow to the entire body, making every member ready to respond to the physical demands of making music. Though easy to overlook, the warm-up serves an important function for the instrument as well as the body. Whether a brass, woodwind, string, percussion, or vocal instrument, every instrument should be properly warmed and its mechanisms stretched and lubricated. Without a proper warm-up, singers could damage their vocal mechanisms, and the tonal quality of instrumentalists could suffer.

Correct use of breath in singing

For any singer, the breath plays an essential role in producing a controlled, robust tone while keeping the vocal chords in good health. To begin any breath, the singer must inhale first; the inhalation should be deep and initiated by the contraction of the diaphragm, the muscle and tendon that runs along the bottom of the ribcage. As the diaphragm contracts and is actively engaged, it creates a vacuum in the lungs, which begins the intake of oxygen. After the intentional inhalation, the singer must control the rate of exhalation, as the flow of air through the vocal chords results in sound. The singer must use great care not to allow the chest to collapse while managing the rate of airflow by engaging the abdominal muscles to achieve a steady stream of air through the trachea and larynx.

Long tones for brass players

Long tones are a critical practice for brass and woodwind players. The benefit of the exercise lies in removing other aspects of performance such as reading, fingering, and so on. This allows the player to singly direct his or her focus towards the production of those aspects that create a pleasing tone. The definition of "pleasing tone" may vary according to the personal preference and the idiom of performance; however, long tones allow the performer to scrutinize and adjust pitch, timbre, vibrato, etc. Although the exercise has the additional benefit of increasing stamina and strength of the muscles involved, maximum duration of the held note should not be the sole or primary focus of long-note practice. Instead, the performer's attention should focus on the quality of the note through the coordination of the entire system that produces the note: diaphragm, throat, oral and sinus cavities, embouchure, and the instrument.

Teaching songs

Music educators must determine the best way to teach young children the words of songs, especially when those children cannot read and must learn songs by rote. The music educator can sing the same song repeatedly or incorporate different methods of participation for the children . Folk songs and nursery rhymes are easy to teach to children, since they are usually written in the limited vocal range of children and are composed of small segments. Parents may also be able to sing these songs with their children. Folk songs are usually specific to a culture or area and would probably be shared across generations. Music educators can also sing to children in order to teach them a new song that may be too complex for their abilities as yet or to show them how much fun music is.

Creative and synchronized movement

Movements that are associated with music and performed as dance or exercise by young children are classified as either creative movement or synchronized movement. Creative movement gives children a freer avenue for expression and allows them to improvise and enjoy the physical act itself. Synchronized movement follows an established routine and is choreographed to the rhythm and beat of the selected music. Synchronized movement helps children work as a group and realize the importance of teamwork, while creative movement allows them to freely express themselves to song. Both types of movement allow children to develop their listening skills and focus on what they are hearing. Focused listening is also considered perceptive or active listening.

Creative movement involves a child's interpretation of the song without paying attention to the beat. Before a child can be expected to move freely, he or she must have a repertoire of movements already learned, and must feel comfortable choosing from that list. Before being allowed to move creatively, children should be familiar with walking, marching, running, galloping, dancing, clapping, hopping, sliding, and jumping to music. Music educators can help children expand their basis even more by suggesting imagery exercises, such as asking children to show how an ice cube melts or how a wind-up doll moves. Young children can also watch how older children and adults move and then attempt to duplicate those movements.

Benefits of music education

Combining music education with other facets of education improves the overall educational experience for children in many ways. One benefit is allowing them to learn about the use of symbols in different formats. Music education allows students to see the application of math in different subjects, learn the fulfillment of self-expression while developing a personal creativeness, and discover the fundamentals of self-image and self-discipline through music practice. Students of music education find their problem-solving skills becoming more advanced, as well as experiencing the intellectual satisfaction of sharing in the work required for a performance and of completing the challenge. Students do not suffer from music education and often broaden their own experiences with activities that are uplifting and wholesome.

Inclusion of music

Music should be included in the basic curriculum for several reasons. As a topic and area of expression, music is worth learning about since it tells a lot about people and culture. Every person has the potential for musical abilities, as is evidenced in the elementary classrooms, and school is the perfect place for a child to explore that possibility. By learning about music and how different voices depend on each other, students can view the interdependence of people of various backgrounds and cultures. The study of music improves other studies, especially for students who may have difficulty in some subjects. The hearing and creating of music inspires the listeners and the performers.

Increased focus on music and the arts

Music currently stands as a sideline to the major focus of science, math, and language regardless of the studies that show how music education can improve students' whole educational experience. An increased focus on music and the arts could motivate students to learn more in other areas, and all educational encouragement avenues should be considered for the changing student body. More researchers and educators are beginning to recognize music as a form of intellectual development along the same lines as Howard Gardner's multiple intelligence theory that encompasses linguistic, spatial, intra-personal, bodily-kinesthetic, logical-mathematical, inter-personal, naturalistic, musical, and possibly existential intelligences. These theoretical systems support the inclusion of music in the basic curriculum and argue that teaching music is only the first step to teaching all other subjects students must learn. Any learning that occurs can be fortified in other areas.

Goals of music education

Music educators, parents, other teachers, and other adults have witnessed an improvement in children who participate in instrumental and choral music education and practice, not only in their musical abilities, but also in their social skills and teamwork. These children learn about self-discipline while improving their self-esteem and enhancing their self-expression and creativity. The basic foundations of learning an instrument and then mastering that instrument to play a beginner piece and eventually an advanced piece serve to instill within the child a sense of accomplishment that correlates to improved self-image and a greater confidence in an ability to complete other tasks and to persevere even when those tasks appear daunting. The goal, then, of music education should be to foster a sense of purpose and self-worth in the student.

Renaissance music

While there is debate about the inception of Renaissance music, most authorities will agree 1430 is an approximate beginning so as to match the accepted date for the historical Renaissance period. The ars nova, or new art, of de Machaut and Dufay allowed music to evolve into a newer style which was communicated to other parts of Europe through the travels of minstrels. Composers of the time did not feel that any work over 40 years old was adequate for their audience and sought to create a new birth, or renaissance, of music by connecting music and social aspects of culture such as humanism. These composers sought to explore chromatic and enharmonic styles of ancient music, set popular folk tales to music, rediscover the meter and rhythm of ancient music as in musique mesurée, and allow the syntax and pronunciation of words to be as prominent as the meaning.

Recognizing rhythm

Once young children have grasped the concept of reading the rhythm and are comfortable with the musical notation, the music educator should lead them in the clapping of the beats for songs that are familiar, such as "Twinkle, Twinkle, Little Star." This exercise will allow children to associate their lesson on rhythm with music they know. Music educators can also clap a measure or phrase and have the children clap the same pattern back. This will involve the children in the motor skills exercise of clapping with the perceptive listening of the rhythm and the particular emphasis as it is placed on the first note or another accented note within the phrase.

Opera

Operatic works are centered around the recitative or singing that serves as a speech or declamation, which follows the natural rhythms of the written text. The harmony is used to give the audience the suggestion of changing moods and increase or decrease in tension. Since the opera is primarily sung, it differs from other theatrical productions and dramatic pieces where the music is used as an occasional accompaniment to the story. The musical accompaniment for an opera could include a full orchestra or just a small ensemble depending on the scope of the work and the composer's preferences. While madrigals would perform mostly for their own amusement, operas are performed for live audiences and can be written by either playwrights or dramatists before being set to music or written by the music composer.

Twentieth century composers

From 1900 on, composers of all nationalities were searching for a different kind of expression that would be new and exciting. Claude Debussy created the whole-tone scale after studying Eastern music, and Arnold Schoenberg worked with atypical harmonies created by using different tonal schemes. The Nationalist movement was still strong with Hungarians like Béla Bartók, who combined the newer tonal schemes with the more traditional folk song. Manipulation of rhythms was explored in addition to melodic schemes, and the modified symphony drew the attentions of Mahler and Dmitri Shostakovich. While many composers, such as Igor Stravinsky, worked with changing tonal structure and balance, , other composers such as Giacomo Puccini and Sergei Rachmaninoff sought to enhance the musical advancements made by previous composers. The foreign-sounding tonal structures have waned in popularity since the 1960s.

Technological change

With different inventions and increases in technology, the music of the twentieth century and modern music can be shared on a grander scale and in more different formats than at any time before 1900. Whereas the music of the previous centuries was expressed from one person or ensemble to another person or audience, the twentieth century saw music disseminated to larger groups of people through radio and television broadcasts, as well as through pre-recorded sessions on other media. There has also been developments in the field of electronically-produced music.

Rise and fall of music

America has seen different styles of musical expression rise and fall within 100 years. The African-American styles of ragtime, blues, and jazz appealed to listeners, just as the folk and classical traditions of music entertained audiences years before. Western popular culture and Rock 'n' Roll have permeated musical preferences worldwide. While composers of earlier periods had to please their audience to continue creating music, the Modern composers could alienate audience members since some will listen to music because of a popular trend. The composers from non-Western countries have also affected Western composers, so that Modern music may hearken to a traditional mode but incorporate the more rhythmic pulses of monophonic Indian music. With a larger choice for musical style, modern musicians have become better able to play many different styles and have improved their own techniques and performances. This expansion has allowed for more prominent composers than any other musical period.

Reading measures

Music is written in measures within the staff. To introduce young children to the concept of the measure, the music educator should have the children count the measures or sections separated by bar lines. Much of today's sheet music provides a count for the measure so that professional musicians can follow along when they are not playing or so that the conductor can call attention to a particular part of the music. Music educators can ask children to count the measures and to locate a specific measure of the music. Once children are comfortable with the basic format for musical notation, they can be instructed more effectively on how to interpret other musical notations, such as the time signature or the rhythm.

Reading time signatures

Music educators can show children how each measure contains a specific number of beats and how that is indicated at the beginning of the first measure with the time signature. Music educators can show students that the top note of the time signature tells how many beats occur in the measure and the bottom note shows which note gets one beat. The music educator can explain how a 4/4 time signature shows that there are four beats in each measure, counted as 1, 2, 3, 4. Contrasting that with a 3/4 time signature, the music educator can show that there are only three beats in each measure, and can then ask students what other time signatures would show. Eventually, music educators can show students the mathematical relationship between quarter notes and half notes, whole notes, and sixteenth notes.

Reading rhythm

The bottom number of the time signature becomes important when music educators try to teach children how to read rhythm. The bottom number shows which note gets one beat. In the 4/4 time signature, the quarter note gets one beat and is counted as 1, 2, 3, 4 within the measure. A mathematical explanation of how the bottom number relates to other notes can be incorporated into the lesson, and children can see how two half notes are counted as 1, 3 while eight eighth notes are counted as 1 &, 2 &, 3&, 4&. This exercise combines a study of math with the basic fundamentals of music, and music educators can lead the children toward reading combinations of the notes and playing or clapping those rhythms.

National Music Education Standards

The National Music Education Standards as outlined for music educators instructing students in grades K-4 as they read and notate music involve the following abilities:
- Ability of each child to read whole, half, dotted half, quarter, and eighth notes and rests in time signatures of 2/4, 3/4, 4/4, and others
- Ability of each child to incorporate the use of a system to determine basic pitch notation within the treble clef as it relates to major keys

- Ability of each child to identify traditional terms and symbols and differentiate their meanings in regards to articulation, dynamics, and tempo while correctly interpreting these symbols during Visual and Performing Arts
- Ability of each child to incorporate the use of standard symbols to indicate meter, pitch, rhythm, and dynamics in easy phrases as presented by the music educator

Improvising or singing new songs

As children get older, there is an increase in their vocabulary and in their ability to add experiences and movements to their personal repertoire. Music educators can assist children in their ability to improve their motor skills while improvising or singing new songs. Children between five and nine enjoy games that involve rhythm and rhyme, so jump rope rhymes or chants are a great way to show children that music can be fun and entertaining. The music educator can show children a simple or even age-specific complex rhyme or chant, and the children can add clapping or stomping as they become more familiar with the rhyme and feel comfortable enough to improvise. Such rhymes include "Teddy Bear, Teddy Bear" and "The Lady with the Alligator Purse."

Music education at home

To continue a child's musical education outside of school, music educators should encourage parents to involve their children in music outings, such as free concerts or performances in outdoor theaters where children can listen to the music as well as to the sounds of the outdoors and the audience members. Parents can even plan to attend with other families, so that the children can enjoy the outing socially as well as musically. Music educators can also help parents locate musical instructors who would be willing to provide lessons for the children. As a limited option, music educators could create a marching band take-home box for parents that includes books on the music of marching bands or even composers like John Philip Sousa, CDs of marching band songs, index cards describing how to make small instruments, and party hats to remind the parents and children that music is fun.

Rests

Music is an important skill for music educators and parents to teach, and different children will be focused on certain sounds or the volume of those sounds. Silences or rests within the music can be the most difficult to teach young children who are interested in playing or singing continuously. Based on the same concept as the whole, half, quarter and eighth note beats, rests are set up with a corresponding count and also adhere to the restrictions put in place by the time signature. Children should be introduced to the symbols used to indicate rests and instructed how to count each rest. When interspersing beats with rests, some music educators find that clapping the beat and then turning the palms out for the rest is an easy way to show children how the rests function in relation to the beat.

Attitude

Music educators should always approach any musical assignment or practice with children with the right attitude of patience and exploration in order for the children to get the most out of their musical experience. The best equipment and the most up-to-date books will not guarantee that children have a good experience with musical instruments and music appreciation in general, so the attitude of the music educator is paramount to the children's success. Children learn best in a classroom and musical environment that includes structure even while fostering an individualized, creative movement format of learning. Music educators should adopt a philosophy of how to introduce children to music successfully that is based on core values and life experiences.

Self-consciousness

Not all children between six and nine are comfortable dancing and moving in front of other children or the music educator unless they have been doing so since they were much younger. One of the easiest ways to foster an environment of acceptability is to sing and dance alongside the children, so that they can see others behaving in a particular way without being ostracized or ridiculed. Music educators could also provide areas for creative movement that have higher walls or are separated and somewhat shielded from the rest of the room. The music center can include headphones so that children do not feel they are encroaching on others' quiet time for homework. Room dividers combined with rugs and drapes can also provide some basic soundproofing.

Equipment

Music classrooms for children of all ages include different types of materials that are appropriate for the development of the children. Besides large instruments such as pianos and large or small keyboards, the music classroom will also include rhythm instruments, percussion instruments, string instruments, Orff instruments, Montessori sound cylinders and bells, guitar, and autoharp. Optional hardware includes tape recorders, headphones, tapes, CDs, players, and a karaoke machine. Some music educators like to provide specific furniture for the classroom, such as containers or shelving systems for storage, tables, tents, and rocking chairs. Music boxes are a nice addition to smaller sections, and computer software may be more appropriate for older children. Music-related pictures can be hung around the room as well as unbreakable mirrors for children to watch their own movements.

Music educators may have to create simple instruments or may find the children are creative enough to benefit from a more hands-on experience so as to appreciate this part of the work. The construction materials used in a music classroom may include paper, glue, and paint, as well as rubber bands, shoe boxes, and milk cartons of different sizes. Regular household items such as paper or disposable plastic plates, cans with lids, plastic bottles, toilet paper tubes, mailing tubes, and wrapping paper tubes act as containers and can be filled with such items as rocks, rice, beans, sand, or seeds. The containers can be further enhanced with guitar strings, bells, or brass pipes in different lengths. Scarves and ribbons can help with movement visualization, and drum heads and sandpaper samples can introduce different textures. As always, music educators can employ whatever materials imaginable to teach children about sound.

History of singing

The voice can be used as a musical instrument through singing or humming. With a strong link to community relations predating recorded history, singing has been a task of the priest, healer, actor, poet, and entertainer. Greatly popular during the Middle Ages and the Renaissance, singing became less popular with the progression of instrumental music. Vocalists were encouraged to pursue musical instruction in how to use the voice as a musical instrument and not in the folk traditions enjoyed by previous audience members. As a result, music was composed to show off the vocal ranges of singers, and it was expected that vocalists would ornament their vocal pieces the same way instrumentalists would ornament theirs. Popular music and jazz have allowed singers to develop their voices more independently than the composers of the Romantic period did.

Theatre and Dance

Similarities in form and expression

<u>Between dance and music, and between dance and visual art</u>
As art forms, dance and music enjoy an unusually tight affinity. The two intersect mainly in their use of time, force, and energy. Each manipulates the elements of beat, tempo, rhythm, meter, syncopation, and sequence (through the form of canon, for example) to create a particular mood or feeling. Force and energy are varied in phrasing and dynamics in both forms. Additionally, improvisation is featured as a means of creative, spontaneous expression in certain styles of each art form.

Although dance is a dynamic (moving) art form and visual arts are mainly static (excepting kinetic sculptures and some other types), the two areas overlap in their use of space and design elements. Shape, form, dimension, plane, and other fundamental concepts of visual art also serve as basic elements in the development of choreography. Both forms also explore the pull between spatial tension and visual balance, negative and positive space, asymmetry and symmetry, and curves and straight lines.

<u>Among dance, mime (pantomime), and theater</u>
Dance, mime, and theater are dynamic, expressive arts. Their common goal is to express ideas and feelings through action. Each form has borrowed specific skills from the others to further develop its own capabilities.

Pantomime and dance are both essentially wordless forms of communication. Mime's vocabulary is limited to gestures and facial expressions, whereas dance vocabulary can be more abstract and varied. The two have been intertwined throughout history, with mime used to promote enhanced understanding of many Romantic and Classical-period ballets.

Although staging and expressive concerns can be quite different for actors and dancers, theater and dance still share many of the same logistical concerns when performed onstage. These include completing entrances, exits, and transitions; responding to cues; hitting the correct mark on the stage plot; and adequately projecting the performers' energy into the audience. Dance has adopted many theatrical production elements, such as lighting, makeup, set design, and props.

Skills that the pursuit of dance can instill and foster

Obviously, daily dance training can shape a dancer's body into a strong, flexible, coordinated machine, and years of physicality offer a deep understanding of the human body. The study of dance can also cultivate many other valuable mental and emotional attributes.

Because dance is a demanding field of study both physically and mentally, and because it is not traditionally well-supported by educational or industrial institutions, dancers gain attributes related to mental "toughness," such as self-reliance and self-discipline. They "do it for the love of the dance."

Dance also promotes skills related to mental agility, such as memorization and the ability to shift movements or sequences in space and time. Making choices among endless improvisation or choreographic options hones creative problem solving skills. Ensemble work (especially contact) cultivates open-minded cooperation, communication, and collaborative skills.

Additionally, the particular demands of dancers' daily schedules tend to make them highly organized and efficient.

Contact improvisation

In the contact improvisation form of modern dance, partners react spontaneously to each other's movements, often in close contact. Unfamiliar orientations of limbs and bodies are used. Contrary to ballet partnering, where one partner supports the other while both remain mostly upright, contact improvisation requires partners to distribute their collective weight to achieve, maintain, or transition through shapes and movements. This form allows partners to use each other as a support, ballast, launchpad, mat, ladder, blanket, etc.

Because contact improvisation is a mental moving exercise—practitioners are constantly learning to simultaneously balance the objectives of responding to movement, creating movement, and adjusting tempo, pressure, and expectations—it has proven useful for generating fresh choreography. Often, contact exercises will present a concept or task that aligns with the choreographer's intentions for a dance piece, and promising movement culled from the exercise will be repeated and manipulated to become set choreography.

Judson Church dancer Steve Paxton originated the practice of contact improvisation in the 1970s, focusing on the physical and energetic points of contact between two or more dancers and the way they could initiate movement through the dancers' responses. These responses could vary in terms of weight, energy, and momentum. The form can be practiced by people with a range of physical abilities or physical limitations, as the form's main emphasis is on sensitivity to the movements and energy of other dancers, as well as on inventive ways of creating movements by using the perceived information.

Begun as a subset of post-modern dance, contact improvisation has become its own distinct form with diverse manifestations. It is used by some as a meditative movement practice, by others as a specialized form of social dance, by others as a means of movement research to generate choreographic material, and by the highly skilled as a form of dance suitable for performances in concert settings.

Imagery

The human brain comprehends and assimilates familiar images more readily than analytical information or technical instruction, especially in a quick-moving environment such as a dance class or a rehearsal, where dancers must continually adjust and "think on their feet." Additionally, since dance is an expressive form of movement which seeks to communicate meaning through physical images, it follows that making visual, kinesthetic, or emotional images part of the student's learning process will elicit more evocative and expressive movement from the student. Teachers can take advantage of the natural human affinity for mimicry, and can present students with images to mimic that will embody the qualities of the desired movement.

Imagery connects the unfamiliar with the familiar, allowing a dancer to understand and feel the movement being performed. Following are some examples of imagery that could be used to improve technique, and their desired effects.
- To improve balance: The image of sand slowly falling and accumulating (as in an hourglass) to fill up a standing leg
- To prolong lift in a leap: The image of a gazelle leaping and remaining suspended for a second before landing
- To achieve deeper abdominal contraction: The image of a snail curling deep into its spiraling shell
- To sharpen angular movement and shapes: The image of skyscrapers that are full of hard lines and acute angles
- To soften tension in port de bras: The image of a soft blanket gently gliding over the skin, or of gentle waves washing the arms
- To accelerate attack in an assemblé: The image of stepping on a dollar bill before someone else gets it
- To better employ plié in preparation for jumps: The image of a floor made out of springs

Comparing the use of time (tempo, rhythm, accent, etc.) in ballet and tap

Usually choreographed with an existing work of music in mind, ballet closely reflects the rhythms of the western classical (symphonic) music to which it is most often performed. Balletic movement usually begins on the first count of a standard eight-count measure, makes use of multiple instrument voicings that correspond with the movements of different groups, and mimics note length to produce corresponding movement. Examples of the latter are repetitive changement jumps during eighth-note triplets and adagio extensions during whole-note legato sections.

In tap dance, the rhythm made by the feet upon the floor is paramount, whether the rhythm is in concert with or counter to the rhythm of the accompanying music, or the dance is performed a cappella, with no musical accompaniment at all. In keeping with tap's spirit of rhythmic play, tap dancers emphasize accent in their rhythms, and often employ syncopation to vary rhythmic patterns and keep things interesting.

Syncopation and polyrhythm

Syncopation is placing an accent on a normally weak beat, or "between" beats. It can also refer to the absence of an accent on an expected strong beat. Because a listener's or viewer's attention is given to beats that are accented, the use of syncopation can serve to "spice up" a regular rhythm of music or movement. Syncopation is often used in tap dance and jazz, where there is a strong emphasis on improvisation and personal style.

The term polyrhythm refers to simple, multiple, and different rhythm patterns played at the same time. The layering of rhythms over each other can create sensations of gathering, complexity, urgency, overwhelming force, and even—ironically—unity. Developing a dance to polyrhythmic music can afford a choreographer the opportunity to create several movement motifs (and possibly characters) to correspond with each rhythm, to single out one rhythm or a few rhythms, or to ignore the rhythms completely. Each choice creates its own effect.

Physical characteristics and movement philosophies of classical ballet

Classical ballet technique revolves around a dancer's lifted, contracted torso. To provide stability, strength in the core muscles of the body is needed. The limbs are elevated from the core. Arms are typically extended away from the body in "airy" postures. The legs perform movements in a position rotated or "turned out" from the hips, requiring flexibility in the muscles of the hips and legs. Balances are often held upon the tips of the toes, known as "en pointe."

The majority of movement is done in upright positions—balanced, locomoting upon, or jumping/leaping and landing upon the feet. This requires both flexibility and strength in the legs and feet. Movement is largely directed away from the floor, as the ballet dancer continually strives to create the illusion of weightlessness and effortlessness. The ultimate visual goal is elevation and elongation of the "lines" of the body, and of movement.

Technical features of modern dance

Although part of the heritage of modern dance rests upon the freedom of each dancer to find a personal way of moving, nearly all styles of modern dance share certain features. These include:
- Parallel Foot Positioning → Feet are situated in alignment under the hips, and the toes point forward.
- Flexed Feet → This is comparable to the pointed toe of ballet. It communicates humanity, capability, locomotion, defiance, homeliness, or comedy, or it can be used to add another angle to the visual design of a dance.
- Groundedness → This is an affinity for the floor and the force of gravity that takes a dancer there. It allows for the use of momentum in swings, and for "pushing into" the floor to gain greater height in jumps and extensions.
- Weight Sharing in Contact Work → Partners distribute their combined weight in optimal proportions to make shapes and movements while in close contact.

Tap dancing

Rhythm tap focuses on the musical (acoustic) aspect of tapping, in which dancers express themselves through the rhythms they create. This style tends to be grounded into the floor to focus on the feet. Rhythm tap dancers are called "hoofers," and consider themselves part of the jazz musical tradition. The origins of both forms can be traced back to nightclubs, when rhythm tappers would set the tempo for jazz bands. Famous "hoofers" include Bill "Bojangles" Robinson, Sammy Davis Jr., Gregory Hines, and Savion Glover.

Broadway, or show, tap focuses on the design and dance (aesthetic) aspect of tapping, and incorporates elements of modern, ballet, jazz, and social dances. Hallmarks of this style include the use of choreographed movements of the arms and torso as well as the legs and feet, and a lighter, more lyrical style than rhythm tap. Noted Broadway tappers include Fred Astaire, Gene Kelly, and Ann Miller.

Jazz dance

Like tap from which it evolved, jazz maintained a strong interplay with the accompanying music, but shifted emphasis upward from the feet to the hips, spine, limbs, and head. This created a more sensuous and expressive response to the often syncopated rhythms. Elements of ballet, theatrical, social, and ethnic dance injected a sense of physical prowess into this expression of the cultural climate.

Like modern dance, jazz does not emanate from a system of codified steps. It is more a style of "physical slang," conveying attitude and nonchalance. Over the years, a canon of movements contributed by its practitioners has developed. Improvisation and embellishment are hallmarks of the form, as are movements done in syncopation.

Physically, jazz is embodied in a looseness and fluidity of movement punctuated by sharp rhythmic features and dramatic shapes created by the use of isolations, which involves moving body parts independently of—and often deliberately against—the whole.

Origins of jazz dance

Jazz dance began to emerge in America in the 1940s, beginning as an offshoot of tap dancing and sharing its close attention to the syncopated musical rhythms of jazz music. By the 1950s, it had left behind tap's necessity of creating audible rhythms, and had evolved into its own distinct form by incorporating elements of ballet, theatrical dance, social dances, and ethnic traditional dances from many countries. In this way, jazz dance, like America itself, became a "melting pot."

As the influences on jazz broadened, so did its movement style. Increasing numbers of dancers from various backgrounds were attracted to the form, diluting its mainly African American origins and further expanding the form's vocabulary and expressive capabilities. The post-World War II boom created a nervous energy in the country that was perfectly portrayed by the isolations, syncopation, and attitude of jazz.

Staging a play

Staging a play is the process of determining where actors should physically be located at various points in the play. The aim of this exercise is to ensure that the position of the actors achieves the desired visual focus. The actors, props, set and lighting need to all work together to focus the audience's attention to the right place at the right time. Staging a play also involves blocking, which is pinpointing where the actors should be situated on stage. Staging a play also involves coordinating stage business, which is any activity that takes place on stage during a performance. For example, an actor may answer a telephone as part of a scene.

Stages

Most simply, a stage is the space where a dramatic production takes place. There are currently three major types of stages in use:
1. Theatre in the round or the arena stage allows the audience to surround the stage, which provides a much different dramatic experience for both players and audiences alike. Originally, this form of stage was used in classical theatre in Greece and Rome, and is widely used today in smaller experimental theaters around the world.
2. The apron or thrust stage seats audiences on the sides of a platform. Less commonly used today, Shakespeare's Globe Theatre was an early form of the apron stage.
3. The most common stage in current use is the proscenium stage where the audience sits in front of a stage framed by the acting space. This form is very common in drama, opera, and musical presentations.

The type of stage used affects the action of the dramatic work, and each offers a unique experience to the audience.

Stage areas

↔BACKSTAGE AREA↔

Stage Right	Up Stage Center	Stage Left
Center Stage Right	Center Stage	Center Stage Left
Down Stage Right	Down Stage Center	Down Stage Left

↔AUDIENCE SEATING↔

Set design

Tools for modeling
Modern set designers are able to utilize a variety of modeling software to create set designs and layouts, but design software can be costly and difficult to learn. More primitive methods that are still very common include *renderings*. A rendering is a free-hand drawing of a set based on the first impressions of the designer or director. The renderings rarely ever represent a complete idea and are changed throughout preproduction. Designers may also create a set using a ground plan, which is a drawing of the set design from above the stage looking directly down. This allows the designer to gauge the space between items on the stage. Set designers may also use three-dimensional models and thumbnail sketches. Scale drawings of the set are called *elevations* and are commonly used in set design.

Mise-en-scene

Mise-en-scene is a French term that translates as "put in the scene." The term refers to everything that is placed upon a stage to be filmed or shown as part of a performance. The term can refer to actors, scenery, lighting and costumes. It can refer to the manner in which the performance space is utilized or to the movements of the actors in relation to the scenery. It is a very all-encompassing term. Scholars agree that the term can take on various meanings and some feel that mise-en-scene is better defined as the emotional tone of a film.

Costume designing

The costume designer's role is very important in helping to achieve the director's vision. The costumes should contribute to the tone and style of a production and the time period in which the play is set must be taken into account. It is important to consider the many facets of a character's personality and lifestyle, including their job and social status. The costumes also serve to differentiate or unify certain characters. For example, a play in which the characters are divided between servants and the aristocracy should involve two distinct costuming groups. Costumes must also be practical for the actors, allowing them to move freely and change quickly. It is important for costume designers to consult with the director in order to ensure that the costume designs will be consistent with the theme of the production.

Lighting

Lighting in theatre can be used in several ways. The most basic purpose of theatre lighting is to allow the audience to see what is happening on stage. Lighting is also useful for providing depth to the stage and actors. The use of highlights and shadows, called *modeling*, creates a three-dimensional effect. Lighting can serve an overall compositional purpose by helping to create a series of connected imagery that brings the director's interpretation to life. It can be used to give information about the setting of a play, pinpointing the time of day, the season and location. Light can also be used to focus the audience's attention on a particular element of the production or to create a mood for a play. The proper lighting can reflect the emotional content of a performance lending to a cohesive and balanced production.

Elements controlled by lighting designers
Light has six primary qualities that can be controlled by lighting designers: intensity, color, direction, distribution, texture and movement. *Intensity* is the light that is reflected by a performer and the background. It can be controlled by use of dimmers, colored gels and the type of light source used. *Color* is the color of the light reflected by the actor and background. It can be controlled through use of colored gels, lamp temperatures and dimmers. *Direction*, the angle of the light, determines the size and direction of shadows. *Light placement* is crucial in controlling direction and *distribution* refers to the part of the stage that will receive lighting. Distribution is controlled by the type of lighting, the focus of the light, masking devices and the direction of the light source. *Texture* refers to the degree of diffusion or clarity in a light source. Texture is determined by the type of light, diffusion gels and screening devices. Intensity and color can be greatly affected by costumes, makeup and props. *Movement* refers to changes in intensity, direction, distribution, color and texture.

Properties of light
The properties of stage lighting include intensity, color, direction, distribution, texture and movement. Each function of stage lighting can be achieved in various ways through the manipulation of the properties of light. Visibility can be altered by the use of intensity, color and direction. Intensity and distribution determine the focus of stage lighting. Modeling is primarily achieved through the manipulation of light direction. Information, like visibility, can be achieved by the use of intensity, color and direction. For example, daytime scenes have brighter lighting than nighttime scenes. The mood of a play can be altered through use of the light properties of intensity, color, direction and distribution. The overall mood of a comedy is often best projected in warm, bright light while tragedies have darker lighting. The manipulation of all these functions and properties determines the success of the composite function of lighting, which serves to create a coherent production.

Types of lights
The profile spot, also called the ellipsoidal reflector spotlight, provides a hard-edged beam of light. Profile spots offer a beam that has a fixed size with a high intensity and very little stray light. Templates or stencils called *gobos* can be inserted into profile spots to cast a specific image or affect. The Fresnel spot offers a soft-edged beam with controllable size. Soft-edged lights like the Fresnel spot are used to light adjacent stage areas because the soft edges allow the lighting to overlap without creating any hard edges. The pebble-convex offers a semi-hard-edged beam. Like

profile spots, pebble-convex lights have little or no stray light. The par is used when an intense and fixed beam of light is needed. Pars can be compared to the headlights of a car. The floodlight is used to flood a large area with light.

Profile spotlight: The profile spot works by reflecting a lamp's light and then passing the light through a gate. A plano-convex lens is used to focus the light and the gate has four shutters that can be moved in order to shape the light beam. Gate runners are built into the light to allow for irises and gobos to be inserted. Irises are devices that control the circular size of the light beam. Gobos are stencils that create patterns of light and shadow. For example, a gobo could be inserted to cast the image of a windowpane. The intensity of the light depends on the size of the beam, with narrow beams producing the highest intensity. The light can be *flat-field* or *peak*. Flat-field means that the light is evenly distributed throughout the beam. Peak refers to the higher concentration of light at the center of the beam. Profiles often have two lenses, one of which can be adjusted to control the size of the beam, while the other is adjusted to control the focus.

Floodlights: Floodlights are used to flood an area with light. There are three types of floodlights: *evenly spread*, *bottom concentration* and *battens*. Evenly spread floodlights provide light to a large area with every part of the beam emitting the same amount of light. Floodlights that are concentrated on the bottom emit a heavier light in the lower part of the beam, achieved by shaping the reflector part of the floodlight with an epitaxial lamp. Battens are created when floodlights are attached in long strips and used to light specific areas. Battens that are set up on the stage floor are called ground rows, those used on the front edge of the stage are called footlights and battens suspended from the ceiling are called border lights or magazine battens.

Health and Fitness

Health

Quite simply, health is the state of being sound in mind, body, and spirit. According to the World Health Organization, health is not only the absence of disease, but the presence of physical, mental, and social well-being. When assessing an individual's health, a professional is likely to examine him or her from a physical, psychological, spiritual, social, intellectual, or environmental standpoint. Although every individual has his or her own standard of health, it is common for people to recognize the following characteristics as healthy: an optimistic outlook in life, the ability to relax, a supportive home life, a clean environment, a satisfying job, freedom from pain and illness, and the energy necessary to enjoy life.

Wellness

Health professionals refer to the highest state of health as wellness. Wellness has a number of definitions: it may mean enjoying life, or having a defined purpose in life and being able to work towards it, or it may mean deliberately taking the steps necessary to avoid disease and maximize health. Wellness is different from health in that it means actively enhancing health, not just maintaining good health. Total wellness depends on psychological, physical, and social factors. In the general model for wellness, all of these factors combine to produce the individual's complete level of wellness. Indeed, part of the reason why health professionals promote the idea of wellness is to show people that all the areas of their lives depend on one another.

Psychological health

In order to achieve psychological health, you must have an accurate and favorable impression of yourself. Having healthy self-esteem does not mean overestimating your talents and value; it means feeling good about your role in life and expecting that you will have the personal resources to deal with any adversity. A person who has a reasonable concept of themselves will be able to tolerate the faults of others, based upon the knowledge gained from self-reflection. Part of establishing a realistic but positive view of the world is accepting that there are many things that you will be unable to change in life, and that rather than making yourself miserable about them, you can direct your attention to those things that are under your control.

Physical education

The meaning of the phrase "physical education" may seem obvious at first glance, but it is quite possible for individuals to have very distinct ideas of what physical education entails. Physical education, by most accounts, is composed of exercise (the use of the body), play (the action generated by the exertion of the body), games (competitions of any kind), leisure (freedom from the responsibilities of work), recreation (any activity that refreshes the mind and body after work), sport (physical activities performed for pleasure or achievement), and athletics (organized, competitive activities). So, a general definition of physical education might be that it is the process whereby an individual improves his or her physical, mental, and social skill through physical activity.

Personal fitness

Personal fitness is particular to the individual. Some people may be considered fit when they can run for a mile without stopping, while others may be athletic enough to accomplish that feat without really being in shape. Most people will acquire a sense of their own fitness only after spending a great deal of time exercising, setting fitness goals, and working to achieve them. However, those who want more objective data on their physical condition may submit to testing at a sports medicine laboratory. There, they will have their muscular and cardiovascular endurance measured on a treadmill, their body fat measured in a submersion tank, and their flexibility tested through a variety of trials.

Cardiovascular fitness

An individual's cardiovascular fitness is the ability of his or her heart to pump blood through the body at the necessary rate. Proper cardiovascular fitness can be achieved through aerobic exercise: that is, any activity during which the amount of oxygen taken into the body is equal to or more than the amount the body is using. Jogging, walking, or riding a bike are all examples of aerobic activity. The heart also gets an excellent workout during anaerobic exercise, in which the body takes in less oxygen than it needs to maintain the activity. Sprinting or swimming fast can be anaerobic exercises, if they leave the person breathless. Nonaerobic exercise, like bowling or golf, does not challenge the heart and lungs and therefore will not improve cardiovascular fitness.

Muscle strength and endurance

Developing healthy muscles is not simply a matter of lifting the heaviest possible object. The ability to use your muscles over and over without getting tired is also an important part of physical fitness. Developing muscular strength and endurance will help make body tissue firmer and more resilient. Well-maintained muscles tend to work more efficiently, and they can withstand more strain. Furthermore, muscular development aids in circulation, with the result that the whole body absorbs and makes use of nutrients in the blood more quickly. Strength and endurance training has also been shown to be one of the most effective ways to lose weight, as developed muscles burn more calories than does fat.

Exercising muscles

Muscles are in a constant state of change. If muscles are not used, they will atrophy and weaken; on the other hand, if they are regularly exercised, they will grow stronger and possibly larger. Muscles are best exercised when they are overloaded or asked to do more than they usually do. When you are training your muscles, you will need to gradually increase the amount of the weight or the number of repetitions to ensure that your muscles are always receiving a challenge. Many fitness professionals contend that a good muscular workout will be somewhat painful because muscles can only be developed by exceeding their normal requirements. However, not every kind of pain is profitable for a muscular workout, and individuals should be careful to distinguish muscular fatigue from injury, particularly when they are lifting heavy loads.

Recreation safety laws

A number of laws exist to ensure the safety of individuals when they engage in recreational activities. For instance, an individual may not be intoxicated while driving a boat. There are also laws governing the use of jet-skis, wave runners, snowmobiles, and all-terrain vehicles. The federal government cites these last vehicles as particularly dangerous for young, untrained, or intoxicated drivers. A set of regulations governs the use of the national and state parks, eg, restrictions on the building of fires. The federal government recently reported a sharp increase in the number of in-line skating and skateboarding injuries; skaters are now denied access to many recreational areas because of the increased safety risk.

Vital signs

Every individual should be able to identify the vital signs and know how to measure them. The four common measures considered to be vital signs are body temperature, blood pressure, pulse rate, and respiration rate. Body temperature can be taken with a thermometer and should register between 96º and 99.9º Fahrenheit, depending on the time of day and sex (women tend to have slightly higher temperatures). Measuring blood pressure requires some equipment; a normal blood pressure is between 120/70 and 140/90, depending on age and sex. A normal pulse rate is about 72 beats per minute. A normal respiration rate is between 15 to 20 breaths a minute.

Warming up and cooling down

There are important reasons for warming up before and cooling down after exercise. For one thing, performance is always enhanced by warming up. Muscles tend to work more effectively when their temperature has been slightly raised; they are also more resistant to strains and tears at a higher temperature. Warming up directs the blood to working muscles and gives the heart time to adjust to the increased demands of the muscles. Warming up also stimulates the secretion of synovial fluid into the joints, which makes them less likely to suffer wear and tear. Warming up should include slow stretching and low-impact cardiovascular exercise. Cooling down is important for easing the body's transition to a normal resting condition. By stretching and slowly decreasing cardiovascular workload, the heart is aided in its readjustment.

Recreation versus competition

One of the perennial issues facing physical educators is whether activities should be promoted as forms of recreation or as competition. If competition is to be the dominant feature, then activities must have explicit rules, a formal way of keeping score, and identifiable winners and losers. When students are taught activities for competition, the emphasis will be on practicing specific skills, and avoiding mistakes as much as possible. When sports are taught as recreation, participation is the most important factor for students. Each student should get an equal amount of experience and performance time, regardless of his or her skill level. Although score is typically not kept in strictly recreational activities, students may receive certificates for good sportsmanship or diligent participation.

Health education as a community service

In a general sense, all of health education can be seen as community service. By teaching positive health behaviors and promoting good health to students, health teachers are improving the quality of life for everyone in the community. More specifically, though, the Center for Disease Control has recommended that health educators use their special training to improve health through work outside of school. Many health educators participate in fundraising for health charities, give speeches on health related topics, or work in the community to generate enthusiasm for exercise and nutrition. According to the Code of Ethics for health educators, it is imperative for those with knowledge and skills to advance positive health behaviors whenever possible and, thus, help their community.

Aerobic fitness

A minimum of aerobic fitness has been achieved when you are able to exercise three times a week at 65% of your maximum heart rate. The easiest means of achieving this level of fitness is by running for 30 minutes three or four times a week. Moderate aerobic fitness is achieved by exercising four or more times a week for at least 30 minutes at a heart rate that is 75% or more of maximum. This level of aerobic fitness is appropriate for athletes who are seeking to play vigorous sports like football or tennis. Maximum aerobic fitness can only be achieved by working close to maximum heart rate several times a week and by exercising vigorously almost every day. In order to achieve this level of fitness, you must consistently work beyond your anaerobic threshold. A good way to do this is having interval training or brief, high-intensity workouts.

Skeletal system

The skeletal system is composed of about 200 bones which, along with the attached ligaments and tendons, create a protective and supportive network for the body's muscles and soft tissues. There are two main components of the skeletal system: the axial skeleton and the appendicular skeleton. The axial skeleton includes the skull, spine, ribs, and sternum; the appendicular skeleton includes the pelvis, shoulders, and the various arm and leg bones attached to these. There are few differences between the male and female skeleton: the bones of a male tend to be a bit larger and heavier than those of the female, who will have a wider pelvic cavity. The skeleton does not move, but it is pulled in various directions by the muscles.

Lymphatic system

The lymphatic system is connected to the cardiovascular system through a network of capillaries. The lymphatic system filters out organisms that cause disease, controls the production of disease-fighting antibodies, and produces white blood cells. The lymphatic system also prevents body tissues from swelling by draining fluids from them. Two of the most important areas in this system are the right lymphatic duct and the thoracic duct. The right lymphatic duct moves the immunity-bolstering lymph fluid through the top half of the body, while the thoracic duct moves lymph throughout the lower half. The spleen, thymus, and lymph nodes all generate and store the chemicals which form lymph and which are essential to protecting the body from disease.

Nervous system

The nervous system collects information for the body and indicates what the body should do to survive in the present conditions. For instance, it is the nervous system that administers a bad feeling when the body is cold, and then sends a more positive message when a person warms up. These important messages are sent by the nerves, which vary in size and cover the entire body. The central nervous system is composed of the brain and spinal cord, and the peripheral nervous system is composed of the rest of the body, including those organs which a person does not voluntarily control. The peripheral nervous system is divided into sympathetic and parasympathetic systems, which counterbalance one another to allow for smooth function.

Digestive system

The digestive system is composed of organs that convert food into energy. This process begins with the teeth, which grind food into small particles that are easy to digest. Food is then carried through the pharynx (throat) and esophagus to the stomach. In the stomach, it is partially digested by strong acids and enzymes. From there, food passes through the small and large intestines, the rectum, and out through the anus. On this journey, it will be mixed with numerous chemicals so that it can be absorbed into the blood and lymph system. Some food will be converted into immediate energy, and some will be stored for future use; whatever cannot be used by the body will be expelled as waste.

Muscular system

The muscles of the body are attached to the skeleton by tendons and other connective tissues. Muscles exert force and move the bones of the body by converting chemical energy into contractions. Every muscular act is the result of some muscle growing shorter. The muscles themselves are composed of millions of tiny proteins. Muscles are stimulated by nerves that link them to the brain and spinal cord. There are three types of muscles: cardiac muscles are found only in the heart and pump the blood through the body; smooth muscles surround or are part of internal organs; skeletal muscles are those a person controls voluntarily. Skeletal muscles are the most common tissue in the body, accounting for between 25 and 40% of body weight.

Endocrine system

The endocrine system creates and secretes the hormones that accomplish a wide variety of tasks in the body. The endocrine system is made up of glands. These glands produce chemicals that regulate metabolism, growth, and sexual development. Glands release hormones directly into the bloodstream, where they are then directed to the various organs and tissues of the body. The endocrine system is generally considered to include the pituitary, thyroid, parathyroid, and adrenal glands, as well as the pancreas, ovaries, and testes. The endocrine system regulates its level of hormone production by monitoring the activity of hormones; when it senses that a certain hormone is active, it reduces or stops production of that hormone.

Circulatory system

The circulatory system is composed of the heart, the blood vessels, and the blood. This system circulates the blood throughout the body, giving nutrients and other essential materials to the body cells and removing waste products. Arteries carry blood away from the heart, and veins carry blood back to the heart. Within body tissues, tiny capillaries distribute blood to the various body cells. The heart takes oxygenated blood from the lungs and distributes it to the body; when blood comes back bearing carbon dioxide, the heart sends it to the lungs to be expelled. Other organs not always considered to be a part of this system (for instance, the kidneys and spleen) help to remove some impurities from the blood.

Hormone system

Hormones are the chemicals that motivate the body to do certain things. They are produced in the organs that make up the endocrine system. With the exception of the sex organs, males and females have identical endocrine systems. The actions of the hormones are determined by the hypothalamus, an area of the brain about the size of a pea. The hypothalamus sends messages to the pituitary gland, which is directly beneath it. The pituitary gland turns on and off the various glands that produce hormones. Hormones, once released, are carried to their targets by the bloodstream, at which point they motivate cells and organs to action. Hormones can influence the way a person looks, feels, behaves, or matures.

Cartilage

The areas of bones that are close to joints are covered in a shiny connective tissue known as cartilage. Cartilage supports the joint structure and protects the fragile bone tissue underneath. Cartilage is susceptible to injury because it is subject to gravitational pressure as well as pressure born of joint movement itself. Long-term stress to cartilage can result in rheumatoid arthritis and osteoarthritis. There are no blood vessels in cartilage; nutrients are delivered by the synovial fluid, and from nearby blood vessels. Cartilage contains a huge number of spongy fibers because it needs to absorb a great deal of shock. Especially resilient cartilage, known as fibrocartilage, is found between the vertebrae and in the knees, among other places.

Ligaments

Ligaments are dense bundles of fibers running parallel to one another from one bone in a joint to another. Ligaments are a part of the joint capsule, although they may also connect to other nearby bones that are not part of the joint. Ligaments are not like muscles; they cannot contract. Instead, ligaments passively strengthen and support the joints by absorbing some of the tension of movement. Ligaments do contain nerve cells which are sensitive to position and speed of movement, and so ligaments can hurt. One function of this pain is to alert the person to an unnatural or dangerous movement of the joint. Ligaments may also be strained or rupture if they are placed under unnecessary or violent stress.

Muscle tissue

Muscle tissue is made up of bundles of fibers which are held in position and separated by various partitions. These partitions range from large (deep fascia, epimysium) to small (perimysium, endomysium), and often extend beyond the length of the muscle and form tendons connecting to a bone. Each muscle cell is extremely long and has a large amount of nuclei. Every muscle cell contains a number of smaller units called sarcomeres; these contain thick filaments of the protein myosin and thin filaments of the protein actin. Muscle tissue contracts when a nerve stimulates the muscle and the thin filaments compress within the sarcomere, causing a general muscle contraction.

Fat

Fats are divided into two main categories: saturated and unsaturated. Saturated fats are mostly found in meat, lard, butter, coconut, and palm oil. Doctors consider these fats to be the most hazardous to health because they increase the risk of heart disease and certain kinds of cancer. Unsaturated fats include sunflower oil, corn oil, olive oil, and canola oil. The last two oils are called monounsaturated fats and are particularly good for the body because they lower cholesterol. Recent research has concluded that the most harmful kinds of fats are trans fats, which are formed when liquid vegetable oil is processed to make table spreads and cooking fats. Trans fats have been consistently shown to create buildup in arteries, a process which can impair heart health.

Many fats can increase cholesterol, a substance in the body which has consistently been linked with heart disease. Cholesterol has many positive uses in the body, like helping the liver operate and helping to form many hormones, but if cholesterol becomes too abundant, it can build up in the arteries and impede the flow of blood. Research has shown that saturated fats cause a more significant buildup of cholesterol than unsaturated fats or other foods that contain cholesterol. In order to minimize cholesterol in the diet, individuals should cut back on fats altogether, but especially limit their intake of saturated fats. Monounsaturated fats, like canola and olive oil, are a good, low-cholesterol source of fat.

Fiber

Whole grains, fruits, and vegetables are all excellent sources of fiber. Fiber can be either insoluble or soluble. Insoluble fibers (cellulose and lignin, for example) speed digestion and can reduce the risk of colon cancer and heart disease. Wheat and corn bran, leafy vegetables, and fruit and vegetable skins are all great sources of insoluble fiber. Soluble fibers (pectins and gums, for example) lower cholesterol levels and help manage the level of blood sugar. They can be found in the pulp of fruits and in vegetables, oats, beans, and barley. Doctors warn that most Americans do not eat nearly enough fiber. However, increasing fiber in your diet should be done gradually, as a sudden increase in fiber can result in bloating, cramps, and diarrhea.

Water

A person should drink 7 to 10 average sized glasses of water daily. Water is probably the most important substance a person can consume. Water carries nutrients throughout the body and regulates body temperature. Water lubricates joints, aids digestion, and helps speed waste matter out of the body. Losing even 5% of the body's water causes immediate physical symptoms, like dizziness, fatigue, and headache; losing 15% of the body's water can be fatal. The normal daily loss is between 64 and 80 ounces of water a day, which is equal to about 9 large glasses of water. Many fruits and vegetables contain helpful water, but people should still consume the recommended amount of water each day. People who are active, live at a high altitude, or travel a great deal should be sure to drink even more water.

Water supply

Even though Americans have generally been able to rely on the water supply, in recent years some concerns have been raised about the prevalence of potentially dangerous chemicals in water. Fluoride, which has greatly improved dental health by strengthening teeth since it was added to the water supply, may be damaging to bone strength if it is consumed in great volume. Chlorine, which is often added to water to kill bacteria, may increase the risk of bladder cancer. One of the most dangerous chemicals that can affect water is lead, which is known to leach from pipes and enter the drinking supply. High amounts of lead in the body can cause serious damage to the brain and heart.

Setting goals

Individuals who are most likely to make positive permanent changes in their health set realistic goals along the way. When setting goals, individuals should identify what resources (time, money, and effort) are available to achieve them. Individuals should also identify the potential barriers to success and consider ways to minimize or remove these problems. It is always better to set a number of small, attainable goals rather than goals that may be difficult to achieve.

Physical fitness

Physical fitness is the body's ability to perform all of its tasks and still have some reserve energy in case of an emergency. People who are physically fit can meet all of their daily physical needs, have a realistic and positive image of themselves, and are working to protect themselves against future health problems. Physical fitness has three main components: flexibility, cardiovascular fitness, and muscular strength or endurance. Some other factors, like agility and balance, are also often considered when assessing physical fitness. The benefits of pursuing physical fitness throughout life are not only physical but mental and emotional; regular exercise is proven to reduce the risk of disease and increase life expectancy.

Flexibility

A person's flexibility is his or her range of motion around particular joints. An individual's flexibility will vary according to age, gender, and posture. Some individuals may be less flexible because of bone spurs, and some individuals may be less flexible because they are overweight. Typically, an individual's flexibility will increase through childhood until adolescence, at which point joint mobility slows and diminishes for the rest of the individual's life. Muscles and the connective tissue around them (tendons and ligaments) will contract and become tighter if they are not used to their potential. Lack of flexibility can lead to a buildup of tension in the muscles and can increase the risk of injury during exercise.

Heart, lungs, and bones

Maintaining physical fitness has a number of advantages besides improving personal appearance. It has been shown time and again that habitual exercise is the best way to prevent coronary death. In fact, individuals who don't exercise are twice as likely as active individuals to die of a heart attack. Exercise makes the lungs more efficient, as they are able to take in more oxygen and make better use of it. This provides the body with more available energy. Exercise also benefits the bones. Individuals who do not exercise are more likely to have weak or brittle bones, and they are more prone to osteoporosis, in which bones lose their mineral density and become dangerously soft.

Mood, disease prevention, and body weight

The benefits of regular exercise are both physical and mental. It is well documented that frequent exercise improves a person's mood, increases energy, focus, and alertness, and reduces anxiety. In fact, long workouts cause the release of mood-elevating chemicals called endorphins into the brain. Exercise also reduces the risk of disease. By aiding in the proper digestion, exercise reduces the risk of colon and rectal cancers. Studies have also indicated that women who exercise are less likely to develop breast cancer. Finally, exercise is beneficial because it helps people lose weight and keep it off. The body's metabolism remains elevated for a prolonged period after exercise, which means food is processed more quickly and efficiently. In addition, regular exercise helps suppress the appetite.

Nutrition and exercise

For most people, the balanced diet depicted in the USDA's MyPlate will supply all the nutrients the body needs to maintain a program of physical fitness. However, individuals who are seriously testing their endurance by exercising for periods of more than an hour at a time will need to increase their intake of complex carbohydrates, which keep the level of blood sugar stable and increase the amount of available glycogen. Contrary to popular thought, heavy workouts do not require a diet high in protein, and in fact, consuming too much protein can put a severe strain on the kidneys and liver. Similarly, most health experts discourage the use of dietary supplements and body-building foods unless under supervision because these products can easily result in nutritional imbalances.

Water and exercise

Water is the most important thing for a person to consume before, during, and after exercise. On hot days, active people can sweat up to a quart of water. If you become dehydrated, your heart will have a difficult time providing oxygen and nutrients to muscles. Even sports drinks cannot provide the hydrating effect of cool water because the sodium, sugar, and potassium in them delay their absorption into the body. Salt tablets should be avoided as well; they are potentially dangerous and unnecessary. Although people do lose a bit of sodium when they sweat, this is more than offset by the huge amount of salt in the average American diet.

First-aid tips and supplies

Since it is necessary to act fast when an emergency happens, it is a good idea to think ahead and have a plan in place. If you are in a public place, you may want to begin by shouting for help to see if a doctor is available. Someone should immediately dial 911. Do not attempt any resuscitation techniques unless you are trained. If you have a car and it is appropriate, you should immediately take the victim to the nearest hospital. Furthermore, every home should have some basic first-aid supplies. A good first-aid kit will include bandages, sterile gauze pads, scissors, adhesive tape, calamine lotion, cotton balls, thermometer, ipecac syrup (to induce vomiting), a sharp needle, and safety pins.

Physical addiction to smoking

Nicotine is consistently shown to be far more addictive than alcohol; whereas only one in ten users of alcohol will eventually become alcoholics, approximately eight of ten heavy smokers will attempt and fail to quit. The method that nicotine uses is similar to that of other addictive substances: it creates an immediate positive feeling when taken; it will cause painful withdrawal symptoms if it is not taken; and it stimulates powerful cravings in the user even after it is removed from the system. Nicotine addiction can become so strong that a heavy smoker will experience withdrawal symptoms a mere two hours after smoking. Persistent tobacco use will also lead to an increased tolerance for nicotine, and so the user will have to consume more and more to achieve the pleasure or avoid the pain.

Alcoholism

The National Council on Alcoholism and Drug Dependence considers alcoholism as a disease that is influenced by social, environmental, and genetic factors. The common features of alcoholism are the inability to control consumption, continued drinking despite negative consequences, and distorted thinking patterns (like irrational denial). It is important to note that alcoholism is not simply the result of a weak will but is a physiological state that requires medical treatment so that it can be controlled. Many individuals may have a problem with alcoholism but not realize it if they are still functioning well overall and only drink in social situations. Alcoholics tend to be those who, even when they aren't drinking, place an undue amount of psychological emphasis on alcohol.

Avoiding alcohol abuse

There are a few guidelines students should know so that they can avoid chronic alcohol abuse. First, never use alcohol as a medicine or as a way to escape personal problems. Always drink slowly, and if possible, alternate alcoholic and non-alcoholic beverages. It is a good idea to eat both before and during drinking so that less alcohol rushes into the bloodstream. Drinking should never be the primary reason for a social function, though individuals should try to avoid drinking alone, as well. At a party, it is a good idea to avoid mixed drinks, as it is often difficult to tell just how much alcohol they contain. Finally, and most importantly, every person should have the self-control to say "no" to a drink without feeling guilty or rude.

Drug abuse

A drug is any chemical substance that changes the way a person acts or feels. Drugs may affect a person's mental, physical, or emotional state. Though many drugs are taken to improve the condition of the body or to remedy personal problems, drugs can also undermine health by distorting a person's mind and weakening a person's body. According to the World Health Organization, drug abuse is any excessive drug use that is not approved by the medical profession. The use of some drugs in any quantity is considered abuse; other drugs must be taken in large quantities before they are considered to have been abused. There are health risks involved with the use of any drug, legal or illegal, insofar as they introduce a foreign substance into the balanced system of physical health.

Psychological and physical dependence on drugs

A psychological dependence on drugs may begin as a craving for the pleasurable feelings or relief from anxiety that the drug provides. However, this craving can soon turn into a dependency on the drug in order to perform normal mental operations. A physical dependency, on the other hand, is said to occur when the individual requires increasing amounts of the drug to get the desired effect. Many drugs, like marijuana or hallucinogens, do not cause withdrawal symptoms; others, like heroin or cocaine, may be extremely painful to stop using. Individuals with a severe chemical dependency will eventually use a drug like this simply to avoid experiencing the effects of withdrawal. Typically, an individual with a severe dependency will try to stop many times without success.

Smog

Smog is the informal name given to the combination of smoke, gases, and fog that accumulates in major industrial or metropolitan areas. Most smog is created by motor vehicles, wood-burning stoves, industrial factories, and electric utilities plants. Gray smog, which is mainly sulfur dioxide, is common in the eastern United States because of the high concentration of industry. This kind of smog acts like cigarette smoke on the lungs, impairing the ability of the cilia to expel particulates. Brown smog comes from automobiles and is mainly composed of nitrogen dioxide. Ozone, one of the other components of brown smog, can impair the immune system. Automobiles are also known to produce carbon monoxide, which diminishes the ability of the red blood cells to carry oxygen.

Pollution

Many people do not consider pollution a personal health issue, but polluted air and water can affect every aspect of a person's life. Scientists define pollution as any change in the air, soil, or water that impairs its ability to host life. Most pollution is the byproduct of human acts. Some of the common health problems associated with pollution are nasal discharge, eye irritation, constricted air passages, birth defects, nausea, coughing, and cancer. Environmental agents that change the DNA of living cells are called mutagens, and they can lead to the development of cancer. Pollutants that can pass through the placenta of a woman and cause damage to an unborn child are called teratogens.

Appetite

The feeling of hunger can be caused by up to 12 different hormones and areas of the brain. There is even some speculation that the size of an individual's fat cells may cause him or her to feel hungry. The appetite is the physiological desire to eat, and though it is thought to be the body's means of avoiding failure, it can also be stimulated when the body does not really need food. Humans tend to stop eating when they reach the point of satiety, in which they are no longer hungry and feel full. Scientists have advanced the set-point theory of appetite, which contends that each individual has an internal system that is geared to regulate hunger and satiety so as to keep body fat at a certain rate.

Exercise and weight loss

Despite the appeal of quick solutions to obesity, exercise remains the best way to reduce weight and maintain weight loss. Many people think that increasing exercise will make them want to eat more; in actuality, frequent exercise tends to reduce the appetite, and since it raises the rate of metabolism, it also helps keep weight off. There are numerous other advantages to exercise in regard to weight; exercise burns off fat reserves and increases muscle mass. Since muscle tends to use calories more quickly than fat, this means it will be more difficult for the individual to put on pounds of fat. In study after study, individuals who exercise regularly are shown to be more likely to lose weight and keep it off.

Communicable and non-communicable diseases

Communicable diseases are those that are caused by microorganisms and can be transferred from one infected person or animal to a previously uninfected person or animal. Although some diseases are passed on by direct contact with an infected individual, many can be spread through close proximity: airborne bacteria or viruses account for most communication of disease. Some examples of communicable disease are measles, smallpox, influenza, and scarlet fever. Some communicable diseases require specific circumstances for transmission; for instance, tetanus requires the presence of infected soil or dirt. Any disease that cannot be transferred from one person or animal to another is considered non-communicable.

Infectious and non-infectious diseases

Infectious diseases are those that are caused by a virus, bacterium, or parasite. Infectious diseases are distinguished from non-infectious diseases in that they stem from biological causes, rather than from physical or chemical causes (as in the case of burns or poisoning). An infectious disease will always have an agent (something that has the disease and spreads it to others) and a vector (a way of transmitting the disease). In the case of malaria, for instance, a parasite contains the disease, and it is introduced to the body when a mosquito carrying it places it in the bloodstream. The vector of an infectious disease does not need to be biological; many diseases are transmitted through water, for example.

Immune system

The body uses a number of different weapons to try to defeat infections. Most obviously, the skin repels most invaders. Many substances produced by the body (like mucus, saliva, and tears) also fight against infection. When these methods are ineffective, however, the immune system goes to work. The immune system consists of parts of the lymphatic system, like the spleen, thymus gland, and lymph nodes, and vessels called lymphatics that work to filter impurities out of the body. The spleen is where antibodies are made, as well as the place where old red blood cells are disposed. The thymus gland fortifies white blood cells with the ability to find and destroy invaders. The lymph nodes filter our bacteria and other pathogens.

Whenever an antigen, or infecting substance, enters the body, the immune system immediately goes to work to defeat it. To begin with, the T cells fight the antigen, assisted by macrophages (cells that scavenge for foreign or weakened cells). While this battle is raging, the B cells create antibodies to join in. Many pathogens will be transported to the lymph nodes, where a reserve store of antibodies will eliminate them. It is for this reason that the lymph nodes often become swollen during cold and flu season. If the antigens find some success, the body will rush a greater blood supply to the infected area, enriching the supply of oxygen and nutrients. In the event that the pathogens are able to contaminate the blood stream, the infection becomes systemic and much more dangerous.

Allergies

An allergy is a hypersensitivity or overreaction to some substance in a person's environment or diet; it is the most common kind of immune disorder. There are many different symptoms of an allergic reaction, but the most common are sneezing, hives, eye irritation, vomiting, and nasal congestion. In some extreme cases, the person may collapse and even die. Allergic triggers, or allergens, can be anything from peanuts to pollen, from insect bites to mold. Although there is no way to reverse or eliminate a personal allergy, science has made progress in treating the allergic reaction. These days, it is possible to be treated for an allergic reaction without becoming drowsy or sluggish.

Immunizations

Despite the overwhelming evidence supporting the use of immunization in preventing potentially life-threatening diseases, many Americans still neglect to get the basic immunizations. At present, the American Academy of Pediatrics recommends that every child be immunized against measles, mumps, smallpox, rubella, diphtheria, tetanus, and hepatitis B. Some vaccinations will need to be repeated on a certain schedule. Basically, a vaccination is the intentional introduction of a small amount of an antigen into the body. This stimulates the immune system to learn how to fight that particular antigen. There are certain vaccinations that a pregnant woman should not get, and a person should never be vaccinated if he or she is sick.

Common cold

The common cold is one of the most pesky and irritating of viruses, though it is rarely a great risk to long-term health. One reason the cold is so difficult to fight is that there are over 200 varieties of the virus, so the body is never able to develop a comprehensive immunity. The cold virus is typically spread through the air or through contact. There is no completely effective medical treatment, either. Indeed, doctors warn that taking aspirin and acetaminophen may actually suppress the antibodies that the body needs to fight the infection and may therefore contribute to some symptoms. There is also no conclusive evidence to support taking vitamin C in large doses. Antihistamines, which many people credit with relieving the symptoms of the common cold, may make the user drowsy.

Cancer

Cancer is the uncontrolled growth and spread throughout the body of abnormal cells. Cancer cells, unlike the regular cells of the body, do not follow the instructions encoded in the body's DNA. Instead, these cells reproduce themselves quickly, creating neoplasms, or tumors. A tumor may be either benign, when it is not considered dangerous, or malignant (cancerous). Unless they are stopped, cancer cells continue to grow, crowding out normal cells in a process called infiltration. Cancer cells can also metastasize, or spread to the other parts of the body by entering the bloodstream or lymphatic system. The gradual overtaking of the body by these cancer cells will eventually make it impossible to sustain human life.

Every cancer has some characteristics in common with other cancers, but it may be more or less treatable depending on its particular nature. The most common forms of cancer are carcinoma, sarcoma, leukemia, and lymphoma. Carcinoma is the most common kind of cancer; it originates in the cells that line the internal organs and the outside of the body. Sarcomas are those cancers that develop in the connective and supportive tissues of the body, namely bones, muscles, and blood vessels. Leukemias are cancers that originate in the blood-creating parts of the body: the spleen, bone marrow, and the lymph nodes). Lymphomas are cancers that originate in the cells of the lymph system where impurities are filtered out.

By now, most Americans should be aware that the risk of developing cancer is increased more by cigarette smoking than by any other single behavior. Not only do cigarettes lead to lung cancer, but they also lead to cancer of the mouth, pharynx, larynx, esophagus, pancreas, and bladder. The risk of developing cancer is not limited to cigarettes: pipes, smokeless tobacco, and cigars all put a person at risk. Second-hand smoke has a similar effect; scientists have shown that individuals who are exposed to environmental smoke for more than 3 hours a day are three times more likely to develop cancer than those not exposed. In addition to tobacco, other acknowledged carcinogens are asbestos, dark hair dye, nickel, and vinyl chloride. Individuals should always try to make certain their living and working spaces are well ventilated to reduce the harmful substances in the air.

Hygiene

Besides helping you maintain an attractive appearance, hygiene is essential for keeping you healthy and free of disease. The body is usually covered with a certain amount of bacteria, but if this number is allowed to grow too high, you may place yourself at risk for disease. Individuals who fail to regularly wash their hair are more likely to have head lice, and those who fail to properly clean their genitals are more susceptible to urinary tract infections. Good hygiene also reduces an individual's contagiousness when sick. Hygiene is especially important when dealing with food: failing to wash everything involved in the preparation of a meal can result in the spread of bacterial infections like E. coli and hepatitis A.

To stay clean and reduce the risk of disease, students should practice daily basic hygiene. Everyone should wash hair and body daily and should wash the hands more frequently than that. Teeth should be brushed between one and three times daily. Always wash hands before eating, avoid spitting or nose-picking, and cover your mouth when sneezing. Try to avoid coming into contact with any bodily fluids, and keep clothes and living space clean. Finally, avoid putting your fingers in your mouth, and try not to touch any animals before eating.

Similarities between basic food preparation and medical hygiene

There are a few basic hygiene habits that every individual should practice when preparing food or performing basic medical procedures. Always clean off the areas where food will be prepared, and wash your hands after touching any uncooked foods. Do not use the same tools to prepare different foods. Always refrigerate foods before and after they are used. Label stored food to indicate when it was produced. Dispose of any uneaten food that cannot be stored. When performing basic medical procedures, always use sterile bandages and any necessary protective clothing, like masks, gloves, or eyewear. Always make sure any medical waste, like used bandages, is disposed of securely.

Family and Consumer Science and Career Development

Time management

Some of the techniques used in time management include setting goals, planning the best way to complete a task, scheduling, prioritizing tasks, making sure that all necessary equipment is easily accessible, and effectively managing one's workload. A successful time management system successfully incorporates all of these techniques, with the end result of accomplishing the most tasks possible in the amount of time given.

Prioritizing activities

One of the most important techniques in time management is prioritizing so that the most important tasks are completed first and the least important tasks are left for when a person has more time available to do them. This system allows people to rank both goals and the corresponding tasks that lead to achieving those goals based on how essential they are to the individual or the organization. An individual, family, or organization can determine what activities are important by first identifying and defining which goals need to be achieved in order to continue functioning. Once this step is completed, people can then decide what tasks are the most crucial for the individual or organization to continue functioning. These tasks should be given the highest priority, while less important tasks, although they also can lead to goal accomplishment, should be considered a lower priority.

Goals and decision-making

A goal is a particular purpose that an individual or organization wants to achieve in the near or distant future. In a corporate setting, for example, a goal could be achieving a specified amount of sales in the next quarter. In a family setting, a goal might be for a teenager in the family to find a job before the end of summer.

Decision-making is the process by which an individual or group attempts to determine what would be the best managerial selection from a set of possible options and/or actions from a managerial perspective, usually for the purpose of achieving a particular goal. For instance, a couple looking for a new home may make a list of the advantages and disadvantages of living in each house they view to help them decide which house to buy.

Goal-setting

Goal-setting is important because it allows individuals and organizations to identify what objectives they seek to accomplish and then determine the best means by which to accomplish those objectives. Goal-setting typically involves establishing a particular timeframe in which a goal should be achieved. Knowing what goals he or she is striving to reach in a set amount of time helps motivate each individual involved to reach that ultimate objective. Goals also provide the individual or organization with a means of measuring the amount of effort—or lack thereof—that each individual puts into obtaining those goals. In a corporate setting, goals can also provide the organization with a way to measure its overall success, which in turn can be important in determining what future actions the organization will need to take.

Valid goal

Individuals or organizations attempting to set a goal can follow the common management mnemonic SMART (specific, measurable, achievable, relevant, and time-related) to make sure that their goal is well-defined, valid, and useful when both measuring success and motivating the organization as a whole. Established goals should be specific and well-defined, have some way of being measured accurately, be attainable, and be relevant to the tasks that need to be completed for the success of the organization. The individual or organization should also decide upon an appropriate amount of time that should be spent in achieving a goal not only to make sure that it is achieved in a timely fashion, but also to ensure that the goal can be compared to other goals in the future.

1. A manager of a local retailer that usually does somewhere between $35,000 and $60,000 a week decided that his or her store should set a goal of making $50,000 in sales a week each week for the month of November.

This example demonstrates a completely valid goal, as the goal is well-defined and quantifiable. It can be measured by examining the amount of sales the store has done each week. In addition, the goal is relevant to the store's ability to make a profit within a set amount of time, as the goal of $50,000 is achievable because it falls within the store's normal sales range.

2. The mother of a child who is having difficulty in school has decided that her son needs to improve his grades.

While the goal of improving the child's grades may be achievable and relevant to the success of the child, it is not well-defined enough to be considered a valid, effective goal. Although the goal could be measured, no criteria are established as to what would be satisfactory improvement in the boy's grades. Furthermore, the mother has not established a timeframe in which her son is expected to reach the goal.

Working effectively toward achieving any given goal

Both internal and external factors can have an effect on whether an individual or organization will be able to achieve a particular goal. However, the most important thing for an individual or organization to keep in mind, regardless of the situation, is that everyone involved in the goal-attaining process should remain focused on the goal and the appropriate ways by which to achieve that goal. This means that if a goal is important to the success of the individual or the organization as a whole, people must be committed to giving their best efforts to achieve that particular goal. Any less important or irrelevant goals should not be allowed to distract the individual or the organization from the primary goal; any secondary goals should ultimately be put aside until the primary goal is achieved. From a managerial standpoint, it is important that people are regularly encouraged to recognize that the goal is achievable so that no one gives up before the goal is actually reached.

Decision-making process

The decision-making process is important because understanding the process can aid in the discovery of a future rational and reasonable course of action when an individual or organization is presented with a decision that must be made. Each individual has a unique perspective and therefore a different way of reaching a particular decision; through a combination of intuition, knowledge, and an understanding of how the decision-making process works, a decision that is best suited for the goals of a particular individual or group can be made. Effective, knowledgeable decision making consists of identifying the decision that needs to be made, recognizing the benefits of each choice related to that decision, analyzing the potential drawbacks of making each choice related to that decision, and, finally, actually making a choice. By understanding what specifically needs to be identified at each stage of the decision-making process, an individual or organization will be able to make a more informed decision that will be more likely to lead to the achievement of a particular goal.

An individual who is in the process of making a well-informed decision will often gather as much information as possible from as many reliable sources as possible, list the advantages and disadvantages of each choice, and then compare each choice with the others. In an employment or business situation where finances are involved, an individual may use a mathematical approach and calculate exactly how much money each job choice or each potential new product could offer, as well as how much a poor decision might cost if something goes wrong. A mathematical approach can be an extremely solid strategy when one is attempting to determine what choice might be the most appropriate. Unfortunately, many individuals do not make well-informed decisions because they oftentimes employ faulty methods of decision making. In such instances, they may rely too heavily on the opinions of their peers, gather information from such unreliable sources as erroneous web sites, or even leave the decision to random chance by flipping a coin.

Some of the most common pitfalls that should be avoided when attempting to make a well-informed decision are entering the decision-making process with a preconceived notion that the individual is unwilling to abandon, allowing peer pressure to influence a decision, and overgeneralizing. Entering the decision-making process with a prejudice either for or against a particular idea, source of information, or choice will often lead to the selection of an option that is not the best or most logical choice available. While outside sources should be used to gather information about the decision that needs to be made, no single source should be allowed to pressure the individuals involved in making the decision into making a particular choice. Furthermore, the overuse of generalizations, stereotypes, and attempts to attribute effects to causes that may not have any logical link will often lead to a decision being made that may not be the best course of action.

Some of the most common decision-making strategies that a business or other organization might use when making a decision include the Pareto analysis system, a cost/benefit analysis strategy, a force field analysis strategy, a grid analysis strategy, and a scenario analysis strategy. Because each strategy has its own advantages and disadvantages, businesses and other types of organizations will usually select the system or systems that best support the kind of decision they are attempting to make. For example, a Pareto analysis system can be useful when an organization is attempting to handle a group of related problems that are discovered to be responsible for most of the difficulties that the organization is experiencing. However, a Pareto analysis system will not work as well, if at all, in situations where a large number of problems are caused by completely unrelated factors.

Pareto analysis system

Basically, the Pareto analysis system is a decision-making model which assumes that approximately 80% of the benefits that an organization receives from a particular task are the result of 20% of the effort that the various individuals within the organization put into the task. It also assumes that 80% of the problems that the organization faces are produced by approximately 20% of the factors that may be causing them. The first step necessary in using the Pareto analysis system is to list all of the problems that need to be addressed and/or the choices that are available. Next, each of those problems or choices should be grouped so that the choices offering similar benefits and/or the factors leading to larger related problems are grouped together. Each group is then given a score based on how much that particular group affects the overall organization.

Cost/benefit analysis strategy

Cost/benefit analysis is a decision-making strategy that examines the total estimated cost of each option that is available alongside the total estimated benefit of each option available and then compares the cost with the benefit to determine if the benefits of the option outweigh their cost. Usually, a cost/benefit analysis refers to the financial cost and benefit of a particular decision, but it can actually be used in any situation in which resources are used. For example, if a corporation has two clothing materials, A and B, that both cost the same but material B can be used more efficiently, the cost/benefit analysis would show that material B is the best choice because it allows for the production of the most clothing using the least amount of material. While cost/benefit analysis can be useful when deciding which option will have the greatest benefit, this method also relies heavily on estimation, which makes it not as accurate as other methods of analysis.

Force field analysis strategy

Force field analysis is a decision-making strategy that examines all of the factors that affect a particular situation and identifies those factors as either aiding the organization in achieving a goal or ultimately causing the organization to fall short of reaching its specified goal. Basically, force field analysis is the process of identifying and listing which factors involved with each option help the organization and which ones hurt the organization. The first step of the force field analysis strategy is to make a list of all of the factors involved with a particular option and then identify them as either aiding the organization in moving towards a particular goal or hindering the organization's movement towards that goal. Each factor is then given a rating on a scale of 1 to 5, with 1 being the weakest and 5 being the strongest. If the forces that hinder the organization are have higher numbers, indicating that they are stronger overall, the option is probably not a sensible or realistic choice; however, if the forces that aid the organization have higher numbers, then the option may prove beneficial.

Grid analysis strategy

Grid analysis is a decision-making strategy that takes all of the factors involved with each option, rates each factor, and then gives each factor a weight based on its importance to the overall decision. For example, if the owner of a clothing factory had three materials and was attempting to decide which material would provide the most profit, he or she might consider each material's cost, how much material is wasted during the manufacturing process, and how difficult each material is to use. The owner would then rate the materials using a set scale—from 0 to 5, for example, with 0 being the most expensive or most wasteful and 5 being the least expensive or least wasteful—and rate the cost, waste, and difficulty of each material's use. By using a similar scale, the owner would then assign the factors of each option a weight based on the effect each factor has on the company's overall profit. Finally, the owner would determine a weighted score by multiplying the weight by the rating that each factor received. The material with the highest total score would be the best option.

Scenario analysis strategy

The scenario analysis strategy is a decision-making method whereby individuals or organizations use their experience, knowledge, and intuition to predict what kind of situations may arise from each option if that particular option were chosen. In other words, decision-makers employing the scenario analysis strategy attempt to determine all of the possible outcomes of a particular choice and what effect each outcome might have on the organization or individual as a whole if that choice were made. In some instances, especially in a business setting, each of these potential outcomes might be assigned a score based on how likely it is that each scenario will actually occur. However, anticipating every possible outcome that might occur and accurately predicting what events are most likely to occur in the future can be impossible.

Resources

A resource is anything that can be used to aid either in the daily functioning of an individual or organization or in the achievement of a particular goal. The four primary types of resources are land and natural resources, labor resources, capital and capital goods, and information resources. Land and natural resources consist of anything that comes from the environment, such as water, oil, soil, timber, and the land itself. Labor resources are comprised of the actual effort that various people involved in an organization put into a project, leading to the completion of that project. Capital and capital goods consist of any financial and human-made resources, including money, tools, equipment, buildings, and houses. Information resources are any resources that allow an individual or organization to find, compile, and put to use knowledge that might help in achieving a particular goal.

An individual or organization that is assessing whether enough resources are available for a particular project might begin by determining exactly what the project consists of and researching how much the project will cost in both time and money. After the individual or organization has developed a basic outline of what the project needs, an inventory of what resources are readily available should be conducted. This inventory would include noting such resources as how much money has been allocated for the project, how many people are available to work on the project, what kind of equipment is available to complete the project, and whether workers have sufficient information regarding the project to complete it. If the individual or organization determines that the resources necessary to complete the project are not available, then the project is not realistic.

A family that is attempting to determine the status of its financial resources should first collect all of the financial records from each source of income that it has. The family should then list all of its assets, including the amount of cash the family has on hand, along with the amount of cash it could get by selling any stocks, bonds, mutual funds, and property that it owns. After adding up all of its on-hand assets and potential assets, the family should then list all of its loans, unpaid bills, balances due, and financial obligations and add the numbers together to get the family's total amount of liability. By subtracting its estimated total liability from its estimated total assets, the family will get a good estimation of its financial standing in terms of its net worth.

Consumer rights

Consumer rights consist of a series of protections, usually guaranteed by law, that seek to prevent individuals from being taken advantage of in the marketplace. In the United States, a large number of state and federal laws establish the rights of consumers, rights that are enforced by the consumer affairs departments of each state, the Federal Trade Commission, and the U.S. Justice Department.

Some examples of federal acts that have guaranteed certain rights to consumers are the Equal Credit Opportunity Act, the Fair Housing Act, the Fair Credit Reporting Act, the Fair Debt Collection Practices Act, and the Truth in Lending Act. All of these federal acts and state laws are important because they help prevent consumers from wasting their finances by spending them on products or services that have been sold to them under unethical business practices. Some of these acts also protect the consumer from being discriminated against by businesses or individuals that harbor prejudices against certain consumers.

Time management

Time management is the process of using skills, tools, principles, and practices together in order to most efficiently use the time that an individual or group of individuals has available. The efficiency goal of time management is similar to that of work simplification; however, time management itself does not actually make work easier. Instead, time management involves finding the most proficient way to complete a task at hand in the amount of time given. Time management is extremely important in both business and personal settings, as people often do not have enough time available to complete every single task they face. Planning how to complete the greatest number of tasks possible in the amount of time available allows people to get more value out of their time and efforts.

Using different types of resources

Land resources can be used as locations for homes and businesses or as sites for other natural resources located on a piece of land, such as oil, minerals, soil that can be used for planting, and water for drinking and fishing. Examples of people who can be considered labor resources are marketers who determine the best way to sell a product, salespeople who sell the product to the consumer, factory workers who assemble that product, and anyone else who aids in achieving the end goal of those dealing with the product. Capital refers specifically to money, but capital goods include the machinery that turns raw goods into a finished product in a factory. Information resources may be books or online sites that can be used to learn how to construct a better product or how to better manage a particular organization. All of these resources can be used in a variety of ways, and most projects require a combination of different types of resources.

Importance of non-financial resources to a family during difficult economic times

Non-financial resources, or resources that are not cash or cannot be sold outright and turned into cash, can be extremely useful to a family that is experiencing financial problems. Non-financial resources can often be used to produce income or reduce costs that the family is experiencing. For example, a family that may not want to sell its house can rent out a room to make additional money. A family member who is a seamstress could lower the family's costs by mending everyone's clothing instead of throwing it away and buying new garments. A carpenter in the family could make necessary repairs to the family home, eliminating the cost of paying anyone else for labor. Any skill that a family member possesses can help cut the family's costs, and any service the family can offer to people outside the home can serve as a way of gathering additional income.

Identifying and defining the goals and values before making a decision

Identifying and defining the goals that a family or other organization needs to meet and the moral values that the family or organization wants to uphold can be extremely important prior to any decision because doing so offers a guide as to what options are unacceptable before an incorrect choice is made. By setting well-defined goals to achieve in the future, a family or organization can choose the options that appear to move it closer to the achievement of those goals. Defining the family's or organization's moral values is also important, because doing so aids in eliminating choices that might be directly opposed to what the family or organization considers correct and ethical.

Basic rights that consumer laws protect

The overall purpose of any consumer law is to uphold the three basic rights of the consumer: the right to safety, the right to be informed, and the right to be treated fairly. Federal and state laws are usually designed to protect one or more of these basic rights and may include protections against products that are dangerous, protections against deceptive business tactics or hidden costs associated with a transaction, and protections against certain types of discrimination within the marketplace. Ultimately, state and federal laws are designed to hold businesses accountable for the manner in which they conduct business.

Equal Credit Opportunity Act and the Fair Housing Act

The Equal Credit Opportunity Act is a federal act prohibiting any organization that issues credit to consumers from denying credit to a consumer on the basis of race, gender, age, marital status, religion, national origin, or skin color. The act also prohibits any organization from denying a consumer credit if he or she is receiving federal aid or has previously used another of their rights granted to them by federal law so long as the consumer used that right without malicious intent. If a consumer is denied credit, the organization issuing the denial is required by law to send the denial notification in writing, and the consumer has 60 days to request that the organization send the reason for the denial in writing as well. The Fair Housing Act is a similar anti-discrimination act that prevents a seller or organization offering financing for a home from denying to sell, rent, or finance a residence on the basis of race, color, gender, religion, family status, national origin, or handicap.

Fair Credit Reporting Act

The Fair Credit Reporting Act states that consumer reporting agencies collecting and distributing information about consumers for credit related purposes are required to follow certain guidelines concerning how they maintain and distribute the information they collect. This act requires consumer reporting agencies to follow a series of procedures established by law to verify and correct mistakes on a consumer's credit record if a consumer makes a dispute. Agencies must also keep records confidential and release them only to businesses that have a legitimate need for those records. This act also sets limits as to how long certain negative information can be kept on record. If a negative piece of information is removed through a dispute, that information cannot be added back onto a consumer's record without notifying the consumer in writing within 5 days. This act was later amended by the Fair and Accurate Credit Transactions Act to allow consumers the right to receive one free copy of their credit report from the three major credit reporting agencies each year.

Fair Debt Collection Practices Act

The Fair Debt Collection Practices Act requires third party debt collectors, businesses that collect debts due to other individuals or businesses, to refrain from using abusive or deceptive practices in collecting those debts. This act prohibits such actions as calling consumers at times other than in between 8:00 a.m. and 9:00 p.m. local time and contacting consumers in any manner other than filing a lawsuit if the consumer has given written notice not to contact him or her regarding the debt. This act also prohibits the collection agency from such practices as adding extra fees and charges to the original balance unless allowed by law, threatening consumers with arrest or legal action that is not permissible by law, or reporting false information on a consumer's credit report. This act also requires third party debt collectors to identify themselves as a debt collector to the consumer during every communication and to provide verification of the original debt upon request.

Responsible consumer

Even though state and federal laws exist to protect consumers from unethical business practices, preventing every type of unscrupulous tactic from being used is not always possible. As a result, consumers should be knowledgeable about their rights to avoid being scammed. Many businesses adhere to legal standards and do not employ tactics that are illegal or unethical. However, some businesses choose to do what is profitable instead of what is ethical. Finding loopholes in regulations allows businesses to make claims about their products that may not necessarily be true without being held legally accountable for those claims. Unethical business operations have also been known to find ways to charge consumers additional fees that are legally questionable. In spite of the number of laws designed to protect them, consumers must be diligent about protecting their own interests when making transactions in the marketplace.

Caveat emptor

The Latin phrase "caveat emptor" literally means "let the buyer beware." This expression suggests that a buyer needs to be aware of products or services that may be defective or not as useful as the buyer had anticipated. Some states have laws that create implied warranties regarding certain types of products and allow a consumer the right to return a product that is defective. However, even implied warranties do not protect the consumer from some kinds of defects and protect the consumer only from defects that show up before a certain period of time has passed. If the product or service is not what the consumer thought it was and the seller made no deliberate attempt to defraud the consumer, the seller is typically under no legal obligation to take the product back or refund the consumer's money.

Before making any purchase that requires a financial investment, a consumer should gather as much information as possible about the product or service he or she plans to buy. By finding out what other consumers have said about a particular product and discovering exactly what the product is and is not capable of doing, a consumer can avoid purchasing a product that is defective or less useful than he or she originally thought. A consumer can also research what kinds of problems other consumers have had with the product, as well as compare the quality and uses of similar products to determine if another product would be a better match for the needs of the consumer. Because the seller of a product is not under any obligation to inform a consumer about how the product compares in price, quality, and usefulness to other products, it is the consumer's responsibility to know exactly what he or she is getting when making a purchase.

Wants and needs

A want is anything that a person desires, as opposed to a need, which is anything that a person requires to continue functioning. A plasma television, for example, is a want because it is not necessary to an individual's continued survival. An example of needs would be food and water, both of which are things an individual requires to survive. Because people are inherently different, wants or desires vary from person to person. Typically, a person has more desires than his or her resources can fulfill. Needs, however, are universal because they are everyone's basic necessities and must be met for the continued existence of an individual.

Decision process that a consumer usually goes through to make a purchase

The first step of the decision process for any consumer planning to make a purchase is recognizing that he or she has a need or a want that to fulfill. After the want or need has been identified, the consumer typically gathers information about products or services that will fulfill that need or want by searching online, examining magazines and advertisements, or talking with other people. The consumer will then evaluate the various product or service choices available in order to determine which option will best fulfill that need or want. Once the consumer's options have been evaluated, he or she will decide which product or service is most suitable and make the purchase. After the purchase is complete, the consumer will be able to decide whether or not that product or service really satisfied the initial want or need that initiated the decision process.

Marketing

Marketing is the process of informing as many consumers as possible of the existence of a particular product or service and the benefits of that product or service with the intent of influencing a consumer's purchasing decisions. In other words, marketing is a combination of tactics that includes many different forms of advertising that individuals, businesses, and other organizations use to convince consumers to purchase their products. Marketing is important because it allows businesses to play a large role in what consumers actually purchase. Consumers may have the final say in what products or services they decide to use, but marketing can make certain products seem more appealing, more useful, and of a higher quality than a consumer would normally believe them to be. Marketing can also be useful to consumers by informing them about various useful products within the marketplace; however, consumers should be wary of claims and advertisements made by marketers that may make products seem better than they really are.

Marketing can influence almost every stage of the consumer's purchase decision process, but it has the greatest direct effect on the first three stages of the process. The first stage of the process can be triggered by an advertisement marketing a certain product that the consumer may not normally consider to be necessary. By creating the idea or image that a product or service is something necessary to the consumer, a business can make something the consumer wants appear to be something the consumer needs. Marketing can also directly influence the second and third stages of the decision making process by making a product appear better or more useful than competing products, even though this may not necessarily be true. The marketing process can even indirectly influence the fourth stage of the process; consumers actually purchase the product because they have the preconceived notion that a certain product is better than other similar products as a result of the advertisements that they have seen.

State of the economy

The economy plays an important role in how careful consumers are when using their resources and what they perceive as needs as opposed to what they perceive as wants. When the economy is doing well, unemployment figures are low, which means that people can easily attain their basic necessities. As a result, consumers will are typically more willing to spend their financial resources. Consumers will also be more willing to spend their resources on products and services that are not necessary to their survival, but are instead products and services that consumers enjoy having and believe increase their quality of life. On the other hand, when the economy is in a slump, consumers are much more likely to cut back on their spending because they perceive a significantly higher risk of being unable to acquire basic necessities due to a lack of financial resources.

Private and government agencies that can provide resources to consumers

A number of agencies can provide resources that help inform consumers about the advantages, disadvantages, and even the scams related to certain products and services. Some of the government agencies that are most useful to consumers are the Federal Citizen Information Center, the Consumer Product Safety Commission, the National Fraud Information Center, and the Federal Trade Commission. All of these agencies have extensive information online, as well as available print publications, about many of the most common products on the market. Probably the most well known and useful private agencies to consumers are Consumer's Research, a non-profit agency that publishes the magazine *Consumer Reports*, and the Better Business Bureau, which is a private organization made up of businesses that sets certain standards which its members are expected to follow.

Health care

A consumer who is in need of health care services might take into account the number of complaints and the types of complaints a facility or specific doctor has received and consequently examine the qualifications of the doctors who practice in that facility. These factors are important to a consumer for any health care decision ranging from choosing a physician for a simple examination to choosing a surgeon for a complex surgery because they give the consumer a basic idea of the overall quality and reliability of the doctor and medical facility. By determining the number of complaints and the types of complaints that have been filed against a doctor or facility, a consumer can get an idea of what kinds of mistakes and how many of those mistakes the facility or doctor has made. Experience can also be a key factor in how reliable a particular doctor is and can greatly affect the quality of his or her care, as more experienced doctors are usually better capable of providing more effective care.

Unfortunately, determining the exact number of complaints a physician or facility has had filed against them is difficult because no federal law exists that requires physicians or facilities to disclose or even report information regarding complaints. However, the United States Department of Health and Services does keep track of reported complaints and is a good source of information for a consumer who is attempting to gather information about a specific doctor or medical facility. Despite the lack of federal laws, many states have laws that do require medical facilities to report the number of complaints and the nature of those complaints filed against the facility or doctors employed by the facility. In many of these states, the facility may not be obligated to disclose the information directly to patients, but a consumer can oftentimes access a state database containing the information online.

Child care services

A consumer should consider many factors when attempting to decide which child care service to use. Some of the most important factors include how many children each teacher or caregiver is in charge of, what qualifications the teachers or caregivers have, how long those teachers or caregivers have worked for the facility, and whether the facility is appropriately licensed and accredited. The number of children that a particular caregiver has to care for at one time, as well as how many children attend the facility, can play a large role in how much time a caregiver can devote to each child. A consumer should also verify that not only the facility itself is accredited and licensed, but also that the teachers or caregivers who work with the children have the knowledge and experience necessary to care for them.

While many resources are available to consumers seeking the best child care in their area, one of the best sources of information is usually the child care facility itself. By visiting child care centers under consideration, consumers can gather firsthand information about a particular facility, such as how many children the facility cares for at one time. A consumer should also be able to find information regarding the facility's accreditation while visiting the facility and should later verify that the accreditation is valid and accurate. The Child Care Bureau, which is a subdivision of the United States Department of Health and Human Services, has services available to help consumers locate local organizations that will verify the accreditation of a child care provider. The Child Care Bureau can also be a useful resource for finding additional information about local child care programs.

Elder care services

The first step in the process of choosing a facility to care for an elderly family member is recognizing that the family member needs assistance beyond what the rest of the family can provide. After the family realizes that the elderly individual needs additional care, the second step is to evaluate the needs of the family member. By having a basic idea of what the elderly individual is capable of doing on his or her own and what he or she needs assistance with, a consumer will more effectively be able to research facilities that best suit the needs of the individual. The next step of the process involves gathering information regarding the appropriate facilities for the elderly individual. Finally, the family should choose the facility that appears to best suit those needs.

Knowing the needs of an elderly person and finding the elder care facility that best suits those needs is important because each elderly individual functions at a different level of ability. Because each person has different capabilities and needs, facilities should be evaluated on how well they are able to take care of the individual needs of each patient. Ensuring that an elderly individual is placed in the environment that allows him or her the most freedom and is the closest match to his or her current level of functioning is of utmost importance. For example, a woman who is capable of performing normal activities such as bathing, eating, and moving around on her own should not be placed in a nursing home. However, for a woman who has a high risk of injuring herself due to medical conditions, an assisted living home may be an appropriate option.

A consumer who is examining possibilities for the appropriate care facility for an elderly family member has the option of using resources available from the Administration on Aging. The Administration on Aging is a division of the Department of Health and Human Services that offers resources for locating local care facilities, as well as state and local agencies that monitor those facilities, so that consumers can get a better idea of what kinds of facilities are available. Another source of information available to consumers is the National Institute of Aging, an organization that provides a variety of publications regarding the needs and health concerns of elderly individuals. The National Institute of Aging also offers an online database for finding local care facilities. Regardless of which resources a consumer chooses to use, the best resource is often visiting the facilities in person to see what kind of services they can offer and what problems the facility might have.

Repair services

A consumer who is looking for a nearby repair service can find information about local repair shops, garages, and other repair services providers from the local Better Business Bureau. Each Better Business Bureau is comprised of a number of area businesses that are expected to uphold a certain standard of operation. In return, the Better Business Bureau suggests member businesses in good standing to consumers. If a consumer is considering using a repair service that belongs to a larger chain of stores, he or she might consult a publication such as *Consumer Reports* to discover if the chain has experienced problems or had complaints filed against them in the past. Even if these publications make the chain appear to be a good option, the consumer may still want to check with the local Better Business Bureau, as each store within a chain can often have its own problems and complaints that are separate from the chain itself.

Determining if an automobile, a child's toy, or other product is safe

The best resources that a consumer can use when attempting to determine if a product is safe are *Consumer Reports* magazine, the Consumer Product Safety Commission, and the National Fraud Information Center. In addition to offering a variety of reviews and information regarding the quality of most common products, *Consumer Reports* documents common defects and complaints that consumers have reported about those products. The Consumer Product Safety Commission offers consumers access to a number of publications regarding what to look for when inspecting products for defects. The Consumer Product Safety Commission also features listings of products that have already been recalled or have been shown to have potentially dangerous defects. The National Fraud Information Center can also be an important resource for evaluating the safety of a product, as it provides consumers information about products that businesses may have deliberately hidden or lied about in an attempt to make their products more appealing to consumers.

Creating a family budget

A family that has decided to create a family budget should begin by calculating how much money it has on hand and how much income it receives annually. Next, the family should determine what expenses it has and which of those expenses are necessary and which expenses are for luxuries. Necessary expenses might include housing, food, utilities, child care, health care, transportation, and insurance. Luxuries might include eating at restaurants, going to movies, buying a bigger television, getting manicures and pedicures, and other activities that are not necessary to the family's continued survival. The third step that a family should take when making a budget is to add up all of the total necessary expenses and subtract that total from the family's total annual income to find its total annual income after necessary expenses. Next, the family should decide how much of that money will be applied to the family's savings. Any remaining money can then be budgeted for less necessary items and activities.

Credit

Credit is the ability of a consumer to purchase a product or service now and pay for that product or service at a later time, either in full or in installments. Credit can be useful for consumers because it offers a way for handling larger expenses, such as the purchase of a house, when the consumer does not have enough funds on hand to make the purchase. However, consumers must keep track of the purchases they make with credit and realize that purchases made using credit must be paid back, usually with interest. If consumers fail to pay back the bank or credit card company that loaned them the money for the purchase or does not pay installments on time, their ability to get credit in the future is greatly impacted.

Some tactics that might be useful to consumers attempting to manage their credit more carefully include paying bills on time, avoiding purchases that they cannot afford, keeping track of how much debt they have, and carefully monitoring their credit report. Consumers who avoid making purchases that they cannot afford are much more likely to pay off loans on time, which will help keep their credit in good standing. If consumers make too many purchases, accumulate too much debt, or take out too many loans, they will most likely struggle to pay their bills. Extensive debt often indicates that consumers cannot manage their credit, which adversely affects their credit scores. Consumers should also closely monitor their credit reports so that they can dispute erroneous claims that may be negatively influencing their credit.

Investments and retirement plans

Investment is the process of committing an individual's resources to a particular activity, organization, or fund, with the hope that such a commitment will provide additional resources for the individual in the future. Investing and saving for retirement early in a person's career is important because careful investment planning guarantees that a person's financial resources have the opportunity to grow as much as possible. Individuals may have difficulty maintaining their customary standard of living if they do not have sufficient funds set aside when they retire because living expenses increase yearly. Individuals who do not have enough money set aside when they retire could become a burden to family members, as they may depend on the family to help support them financially.

Some of the factors that an individual or family might consider when making investment decisions are the risk of the investment, the potential return of the investment, and how difficult liquidating the investment would be. The risk of the investment refers to how likely it is that the individual or family will gain some benefit from the investment and how likely it is that the individual or family will lose the resources that they have invested. The potential return of the investment refers to how much money the individual or family will likely earn from the investment's interest or dividends over time. The degree of difficulty in cashing-out the investment is an important factor because different investments have different costs, taxes, lengths of time to mature, and stipulations regarding the access of the money associated with them.

Investments such as checking accounts, savings accounts, and CDs are considered low-risk investments, but they also offer a lower return. These investments are safe because banks guarantee that these accounts will earn a certain amount of interest; however, the rate of interest is relatively low in comparison with other investment options. While CDs are low-risk investments, they do offer slightly higher rates of interest than checking or savings accounts, but they can be liquidated only after they mature over a length of time set by the bank. Mutual funds are usually considered low-risk to mid-risk investments, as people have the potential to lose the resources they have invested, but mutual funds also have the potential to yield a higher return, though not as high as high-risk stocks. Because the stock portfolios that mutual funds are invested in are typically diversified and comprised of many different types of relatively stable stocks, mutual funds are generally regarded to be safe investments.

Families that are selecting what investments to make should first consider the financial goals that they hope to attain from these investments. For example, if a family is investing its resources to send family members to college, the family should estimate how much money it will need to pay for each member who plans to attend college. After a family has determined its financial needs, it can begin researching investment options to determine which investments are likely to yield enough financial gain for the family to reach its goals. Once it has identified which investments best suit its goals, the family should assess how much risk each investment carries. Finally, the family should choose the investment that has the lowest risk but will still meet its financial goals.

An individual who is attempting to determine how much money he or she needs to invest or put aside for retirement should start by adding up how much he or she spends monthly on living expenses, with the exception of health care. That number is then multiplied by 1.5, while health care expenses are multiplied by 2 to determine how much those expenses will increase in ten years. The individual then needs to estimate how many years he or she has before retirement; for every ten years, the health care expenses once again are multiplied by 2 and all other expenses by 1.5. Finally, adding these two results together equals an individual's estimated monthly expenses adjusted for inflation, thereby providing the individual with a rough estimate of how much he or she will need each month to maintain the same standard of living after retirement.

Insurance

The major types of insurance that an individual or family might need are health insurance, homeowner's insurance, life insurance, and car insurance. The reason that a family should have these types of insurance is that a problem in any of these areas can have a significant impact on the financial security of the individual or the family as a whole. Health problems, fire, theft, the death of a provider in the family, or a car accident can all lead to additional expenses that the individual or family may not be able to afford. Having these types of insurance offers individuals and families a way to pay unexpected expenses without significantly impacting their overall financial well-being.

Checking or savings account

An individual or family should consider several factors when opening a checking or savings account: What are the bank's minimum balance requirements? What bank fees are associated with the account? What is the annual interest rate earned by the account? Most banks charge account holders if they have less than the minimum balance required in their accounts. Banks often charge additional fees for ATM use and other services, which makes an account more expensive to the consumer than he or she might realize. If the financial institution charges a significant number of fees without offering a high interest rate on the account, the consumer should move his or her accounts to a different institution. Consumers should also verify that a bank, credit union, or any other institution that they are considering placing money into is insured by the federal government through the Federal Deposit Insurance Corporation (FDIC) or the National Credit Union Administration (NCUA).

Product labels

Product labels are important, and sometimes vital, because they inform a consumer about the ingredients in a product, the materials used in the construction of a product, the appropriate way to use a product, and the hazards that can result from using a product incorrectly. This information can be useful for determining not only which products suit the needs of a consumer, but also if products are safe to use around children and other family members. For example, a label allows a consumer to determine if a particular piece of clothing is made out of a strong enough material for the consumer's intended use or if the material could trigger an allergic reaction in the consumer.

Nutritional needs

Some of the major factors that can affect an individual's nutritional needs include the age of the individual, the individual's gender, and his or her level of activity. The age of an individual plays a major role in the nutritional needs that person has in several ways. As a child grows, for instance, the number of calories the child needs also increases, but after the individual passes a certain age, the number of calories he or she needs decreases. A person's need for specific vitamins and minerals also increases as he or she gets older. Gender can affect an individual's nutritional needs; men typically require more protein and more calories than women do, while women usually require significantly more iron than men. The individual's level of activity also plays a large role in his or her nutritional needs because an individual who is more active will require a larger number of calories than an individual who less active.

Housing

The primary purpose for any type of housing is to act as a form of shelter. Shelter in this context refers to protecting people from harsh weather such as rain, snow, extreme heat, extreme cold, harsh winds, extensive exposure to UV radiation, or any other conditions that might prove unpleasant or harmful. Housing can also provide security by making it more difficult for harmful things, such as animals, insects, unscrupulous individuals, and other threats, to reach people and their belongings. In some cases, housing can also serve as a location for individuals to conduct business in and work from. A house itself can even act as a symbol of the wealth and status of its owners.

The two major types of residential housing are houses and apartments. A house is an entire building with the primary purpose of providing shelter for the individual or family that resides in it. An apartment is a section of a building that has been split into units, and the primary purpose of each unit is to provide shelter for the individual or family that lives in that unit. The major difference between and house and an apartment is that a building is considered a house if the whole building belongs to one individual, family, or several families that share the entire building or at least most of the building. On the other hand, a building is considered to be an apartment building or a complex if it contains separate sections or units that each allow individuals or families to live on their own without sharing a large portion of the building.

The three major types of houses found in the United States are single-family houses, townhouses, and semi-detached houses. A single-family house is any building used for residential use that is separate from any other buildings. Townhouses are a series of buildings where all of the houses share both of their side walls with the buildings on each side, with the exception of the houses at the ends of the row, which only share one wall. Semi-detached houses are two residential buildings that share only a single wall and have empty space on their other side. These three major types of houses are typically determined by how much space is available around the building. A single-family home has space available on all sides, a semi-detached house has space clear in front, behind, and on one side of the house, and townhouses, with the exception of the townhouses on the end of the row, have space only in front and behind the house.

Security

Security can be extremely important for an individual or group that is wealthy, well known, or at high risk of being victimized by thieves or other criminals. A home can provide a wide range of protective measures to help keep people and their belongings safe, including locks on doors and windows, burglar alarms, fire alarms, and carbon monoxide detectors to warn residents of potentially deadly threats. Some homes, especially homes that are located in high-risk areas, might contain a large number of personal assets. Those residences that house individuals who are at high risk due to their social status, political rank, or amount of personal assets, may also have additional security measures in place. These measures include security features such as strong deadbolts locks, security cameras, gates, and checkpoints.

Running a business from home

A number of advantages are associated with running a business from home. Probably the most important advantage of running a home-based business is the fact that individuals or groups can usually significantly reduce their overhead costs as a result of using a single building for both business and living purposes. Overhead costs that can be reduced include expenses related to transportation, business clothing, office furnishings, maintenance, mortgage or rent, taxes, and other similar expenses. Some of the other major advantages of running a home based business are that the individual has a more flexible schedule, has the ability to put most of the time that would be spent commuting to better use, and the individual is readily available to fulfill their domestic responsibilities as well.

For an individual to be able to work successfully and efficiently in any environment, he or she needs a private place to work that is relatively free from distractions. Regardless of what type of business an individual is attempting to run, he or she will also require time to accomplish the work that needs to be done, as well as the necessary equipment to perform that work. Equipment an individual may require for his or her home business includes a computer, printer, fax machine, telephone, and computer programs appropriate to the type of work to be performed. It is also important that an individual is able to find the storage space necessary for any equipment that the business will need to function appropriately.

The single largest problem that home business owners face is the conflict that arises between the needs of the family and the needs of the business. Every business has its own distinct needs, and those needs can be difficult to achieve in a home setting because a conflict can arise between the space, time, and equipment that the family needs and the space, time, and equipment that the business needs. For example, a child or other family member may need the business space or equipment, such as a computer, to complete his or her homework at the same time that the business owner is using the space and equipment for conducting business. On the other hand, the children of the family may not need to use the computer, but instead need the business owner to step into a parental role and feed them or help them with their homework, which distracts the business owner from the tasks he or she needs to complete for work purposes. Any equipment purchased specifically for the business will also require space that the family might have already had dedicated for another purpose in the household.

Status symbol

The major reason that a home can act as a status symbol for an individual or family that lives in it is because of the financial investment necessary to own a home. Regardless of the type of home that someone lives in, purchasing or leasing a home is usually the single largest expense that anyone will take on during his or her life. As a result, the home of an individual or family can act as an indication of the overall wealth that a person or family possesses. This means that the larger and more luxurious a house is, the greater the amount of wealth a person must have had in order to acquire that home. Since wealth is commonly associated with the status of an individual, the type of home that an individual or family lives in acts indicates their social status as well.

Apartments

The most common types of apartments found in the United States are single or multi-bedroom apartments and studio apartments. Single or multi-bedroom apartments are units that have one or more bedrooms that are separated from the rest of the unit. Studio apartments are units that have one large room that makes up the entire unit and performs the functions of a bedroom, living room, dining room, kitchen, and any other rooms that the unit's tenants require. Studio apartments and single or multi-bedroom apartments are usually rented, but it is becoming more and more common for apartments to be sold to consumers as condominiums or cooperatives. Regardless of whether an apartment is rented or purchased, studio apartments are almost always less expensive than multi-bedroom apartments; the price of an apartment increases significantly with each extra separate bedroom attached to the unit.

Condominium and cooperative

A condominium, also known as a condo, is a type of apartment ownership where an individual has purchased complete ownership of a single unit but has shared ownership of certain common areas and common expenses associated with the building. This means that the individual living in the condo owns the unit and is responsible for all of the expenses associated with that unit, but shares the rest of the building and the expenses associated with the remainder of the building. A cooperative, also known as a co-op, is a type of apartment where an individual owns shares in a corporation, and that corporation owns the entire building. An individual who owns the shares has the right to live in a particular unit within the building as long as he or she follows certain guidelines set by the corporation.

The major difference between a condominium and a cooperative is that a condo owner actually owns the unit and shares ownership of the building, while a co-op owner does not actually own the unit or the building, but rather owns part of a corporation and that corporation owns the building. By paying condo fees and discussing problems with a condo association, the owner of a condo directly shares the decisions and expenses related to the upkeep of the building. A co-op owner, on the other hand, is not directly responsible for the expenses and problems of the building as the corporation that owns the building handles these expenses and problems using the funds they gather from the rent or subscription fees paid by the co-op owners.

Renting and purchasing housing

The two most common methods that an individual or family might use to pay for their housing are renting, also known as leasing, and purchasing a house through a mortgage or loan. When an individual does not actually own a house or apartment where he or she resides, but rather pays a monthly fee for the use of that house or apartment, that is renting. People who rent a place to live will never own the property no matter how long they live there and how much rent they pay. In contrast, an individual who takes out a mortgage on a particular type of housing actually purchases that house or apartment using the money acquired from a loan.

The two major advantages of renting housing rather than purchasing housing are that renting is usually less expensive in terms of monthly payments and the individual or family does not have to be concerned with costs associated with maintaining the building. A renter or lessee does not actually own the building and has to pay only whatever fee the building's owner has set for that particular unit, regardless of any work that the rest of the building may require. For example, if a building's plumbing needs work, any cost that is associated with repairing the plumbing is the responsibility of the building's owner and not the responsibility of the apartment's tenant. The major disadvantage of renting is that the individual does not gain any long-term financial advantage from paying rent because each rent payment is not being applied toward the purchase of the property.

The major advantage of purchasing housing rather than renting is that an individual or family actually owns the property and can sell that property or rent it to someone else at a later time. Each monthly payment is applied to paying off the loan that was used to purchase the property, and the owner can decide to sell that property at any point and keep any money that is leftover after paying the bank back. An individual who is renting can leave his or her apartment at any time but will receive no benefit from the money he or she paid while living there. The two major disadvantages of purchasing a home are that the monthly payments are usually higher than what an individual renting a home pays and the individual or family is responsible for all of the expenses associated with maintaining the home.

An individual who is attempting to decide whether to rent or purchase a particular type of housing should base the decision on his or her income. This can be done by estimating how much buying a piece of property will cost the individual per month, how much renting will cost the individual per month, and the individual's monthly income. If the individual has the money available to put a reasonable down payment on a piece of property that he or she is interested in and has the income to make the monthly mortgage payments on the property without a problem, buying is usually the better option. This is because purchasing a piece of property, unlike renting, is an investment that can be sold, usually with some degree of financial return for the original property owner. On the other hand, if an individual cannot afford to make a reasonable down payment and the monthly mortgage payments are more than the he or she can comfortably afford, renting is a better option.

An individual or family that is considering what building to rent or purchase should first determine how much they can afford to spend on housing. Purchasing or even renting housing is always a major investment, and the individual or family needs to make sure that they have the funds available to make the required payments. Next, the individual or family should determine what attributes of the house or apartment are important to them, such as the location of the building, how big the building should be, how much storage space the building has, and how much yard space it includes. Once the individual or family has made a list of all of the things that should be ideal features of their house or apartment, they can then begin looking for houses or apartments that are within their price range and best suit their needs.

Area surrounding a house or apartment

Some of the most important factors regarding the surrounding area of a house or apartment that an individual should consider include the current state of the neighborhood, how accessible the property is, and the quality of local schools and recreational facilities. The current state of the neighborhood refers to factors such as the overall appearance of the neighborhood, the traffic and noise level, the number of children living in the area, parking, zoning or other regulations and restrictions, and the level of police, fire, and community involvement in the neighborhood. The accessibility of a piece of property refers to its location and how close it is to stores, public transportation, major roads and highways, and a resident's place of employment. For active individuals and families with children, quality local schools and recreational facilities are important. Considerations include how close the house or apartment is to these facilities, how well maintained these facilities are, and the reputations of these facilities.

Interior design

Interior design is the process of planning the best way possible to construct a room, a series of rooms, or an entire house. The primary purpose of interior design is to make each room both as functional and as appealing as possible. Interior designers usually consider seven basic elements of design when deciding how to make a particular room appealing: color, texture, pattern, line, shape, form, and mass. Once the interior designer knows the purpose and functional requirements of a room, he or she can then create a floor plan of how the room or rooms will fit into the rest of the house and of how the room itself will be organized to fulfill its intended purpose.

Floor plan

Some of the factors that an individual should consider when designing a floor plan include what size the room or rooms should be, what furniture needs to go in each room, how often each room will be used, and the traffic patterns of the room. The individual should also consider how many electrical outlets the room requires, how much lighting is necessary for the room, and whether the room has any special requirements to fulfill the purpose of the room. For example, a photographer who is planning to add on a darkroom to his house would need a room that is located away from outside walls and windows, lets in virtually no light, has access to a number of electrical outlets and countertops for developing equipment, and has sinks for rinsing film. A well-designed floor plan is important because it allows an individual to eliminate problems such as not enough storage space, not enough room for furniture and equipment, not enough light, and not enough access to power outlets.

Traffic patterns

An individual who is analyzing the traffic patterns of a room should consider the purpose of the room, the location of the room in relation to other rooms, the number of people that will be using the room, and the ease of movement in the room. The traffic patterns of a room refer to how many people are moving into, through, and around that room and how easy it is for them to make those movements. For example, a room that is near the center of a house and connects two rooms on different sides should have a clear, straight path entering and exiting each connecting room. This means that people walking through the room should be able to walk straight through without having to walk around couches, tables, chairs, or other furniture that is blocking their path. A room with a well-planned traffic pattern will allow people to access every part of the room without climbing over or walking around furniture.

Direct and indirect communication

Direct communication occurs when a person who is attempting to convey a given piece of information simply states that information to the person he or she wants to receive the information. Indirect communication, on the other hand, is when the person communicating the information states the information, but not to anyone in particular. For example, if a parent says, "Christine, we need to set the table," that is an example of direct communication because the parent is addressing the person he or she wants to talk to directly. However, if the parent instead simply mutters out loud, "We need to set the table," rather than saying it to someone in particular, that would be an example of indirect communication. Direct communication is far more effective in carrying out the day-to-day functions necessary to maintain a family than indirect communication because various tasks can be assigned directly to a particular individual.

Families with individuals who use direct, clear communication are the most effective. These family members listen to one another, spend more time communicating, respect one another's points of view, and pay attention to the more subtle forms of affective communication. By communicating directly and concisely with other family members, each family member creates a much more effective form of communication than that which would be found in any other setting. If the individuals receiving the information listen to and respect their fellow family members and—more importantly—make the time to listen to them in the first place, the communication between family members will become much stronger. Of course, this communication can be strengthened even further if members of the family are careful to take note of emotional indicators that allow them to identify the feelings of another family member without that person having to verbally express his or her feelings.

Solving any given problem

A well-functioning family would first identify the problem itself and determine the cause of the problem. The family would then develop a list of solutions that could potentially solve the problem, and they would attempt to determine the benefits of each solution. After determining the benefits of each solution, the family would choose the solution that seems to best solve the problem and then, after putting the solution into effect, monitor the solution to make sure that it actually solved the problem. Finally, the family would decide whether the solution worked or not to determine whether it was necessary to try something else. This entire process is important to the functioning of a family because it prevents problems from being misdiagnosed early on and prevents them from getting too far out of control.

Social interaction

Outside social interaction is extremely important for all family members, regardless of age, because it offers an opportunity for each individual to improve his or her social skills, learn about the world around them, and learn more about values that one might not learn from the family alone. This is especially true in the case of children. Research shows that children who have regular outside social interaction, through things such as extracurricular activities, are less likely to rebel or cause problems and more likely to excel in school and relationships. Outside social interaction is also necessary for the children of a family to eventually leave the household and create families of their own, as they need to seek out their own relationships. Therefore, social interaction with individuals outside of the family is necessary not only for the fulfillment of the members of the family, but also to continue the life cycle of the family.

Conflict within a relationship

The many sources of conflict within a relationship are too numerous to mention, but some of the common problems include the following: setting expectations that are too high, not appreciating or respecting the other person in the relationship, not considering the feelings of the other person, being afraid of showing affection or emotion, being overdependent, being inflexible, expecting the other member of the relationship to change, and lacking effective communication. Preventing conflict can be extremely difficult. Preventing it altogether is virtually impossible, but avoiding some or all of these common sources of conflict can greatly reduce the number of conflicts that take place within any given relationship.

A family can successfully resolve a conflict by following steps very similar to those of the basic problem-solving model. First, the family needs to attempt to identify the problem, making sure to maintain open communication while remaining objective and minimizing hostility. After the problem is identified, the family must strive to recognize the various positions that each member has regarding the conflict while again attempting to minimize hostility. After each person involved in the conflict has made his or her position clear, the family must move toward a compromise that will work for everyone. Each step of the conflict resolution process requires that the people involved in the conflict remain as patient and as understanding as possible, which can often be extremely difficult when a solution or compromise cannot be determined immediately.

Divorce

Divorce is the termination of the union created by marriage before the death of either member of the union. It has a significant impact on the stability of the family unit as a whole, and it affects the relationships and well-being of the individual members of the family. Frequently, when the marital couple decides to divorce, there has already been significant stress placed on the entire family from the difficulties the marital couple has been experiencing. However, divorce can often lead to a great deal more stress being placed on the family, especially when children are involved. As a result, individuals within and outside the marital couple may become more withdrawn or hostile as the structure of the family changes. Divorce also allows both members of the marital couple to later remarry, as their legal obligation to each other no longer exists. This can further alter the family structure by adding stepparents to the mix.

Studies indicate that the age at which a couple marries may have a significant impact on whether they remain married for an extended period. Individuals who marry before either member of the couple is 18 will often separate within a few years of their marriage. Individuals who are in the 18–25 range will separate less frequently than those who marry before 18, but they are still at a very high risk for their marriage ending in divorce rather than death. Individuals who marry after both members of the couple are over 25 have a significantly lower risk of divorce than those who marry at younger ages. Ultimately, statistics show that the risk of divorce decreases as the age of each member of the couple at the time of the marriage increases.

There are many factors that may influence the risk of a marriage ending in divorce, including income, education, religion, pregnancy before marriage, and whether the parents of the married couple are divorced. Couples who make over $50,000 a year are at a much lower risk of divorce than couples who make less than that amount. Couples comprised of well-educated individuals who have graduated from high school and have at least some college background also have a much lower risk of divorce than less educated individuals. Couples with no religious background or drastically different religious backgrounds have a much higher risk of divorce than couples who have religious backgrounds that do not conflict. Couples who have a baby prior to being married also have a higher risk of divorce than couples who have children after they are married. Individuals with parents who are divorced also have a higher risk of divorce than individuals from intact families.

Social and economic factors

Social and economic factors affect the overall functioning of a family. In fact, researchers use an index called the socioeconomic status, or SES, to measure the ability of the family to function in a healthy fashion. The SES uses the educational background of the members of the family, the family's total income, and the skill—both actual and perceived—required by the occupations of the individuals who act as providers for the family to measure the family's ability to function. Individuals who are well-educated tend to marry later in life, receive jobs with higher incomes, and have careers with a higher social status, which all add stability to the marriage and stability to the overall functioning of the family. Families that earn a higher income are also less concerned with obtaining basic necessities because the family consistently has the means to obtain them. As a result, there is often less stress experienced by the family.

Affective communication and instrumental communication

The two primary types of communication used by family members are affective communication and instrumental communication. Affective communication is communication in which an individual demonstrates his or her feelings through facial expressions, motions, gestures, or by stating his or her feelings outright. Instrumental communication is when an individual informs another member of the family of a piece of factual information that is necessary to carry out the normal day-to-day functions of the family. An example of instrumental communication is a mother informing her child where he or she can find his or her socks. Families that use both types of communication usually function more effectively than families that use instrumental communication more often than affective communication.

Clear and masked communication

Clear communication occurs when an individual explicitly states the information he or she is trying to convey, and there is no ambiguity as to the meaning of the statement. For example, "I am upset because Daniel is not home from the movies yet" is an example of clear communication because there is no question that the individual making the statement is upset at Daniel for not being home. On the other hand, masked communication occurs when an individual states the information he or she is trying to convey in a vague and somewhat confusing manner. For example, "I am upset" is an example of masked communication because there is no indication as to why the person is upset. As these examples illustrate, clear communication is always more effective in conveying a particular piece of information than masked communication.

Development and education of family members

One of the most important functions a family provides is developing and educating family members. Parents and grandparents pass their heritage and teachings of social norms and acceptable behavior to the children of the family through their customs, traditions, and ultimately their actions. Children learn about their heritage through the traditions of the family and also often learn lessons about the manner in which they are expected to behave by using the behavior of their parents and the rest of the household as a model for how they, too, should behave. Children also learn about the manner in which the world around them functions through the interactions of the members of the family with the world outside the household. This allows the child to understand more complex types of social interaction such as what goods the family needs, where the family must go to fulfill those needs, and what is needed to acquire those necessities (e.g., how much money is required to purchase an item).
1. Behavioral modeling, when related to child development within a family structure, is the manner in which children model their own behavior after the behavior of their parents and other people with whom they interact. Children learn what behavior is socially acceptable by mimicking the behavior of the people around them.

2. Consumer education is the process of teaching a person about the marketplace and its goods and services, the suppliers, and the various considerations associated with searching for goods and services. These concepts are critical for family members to learn so that they can survive in a consumer society.
3. Heritage is anything inherited from one's ancestors, including traditions, customs, or physical characteristics. The family conveys the traditions, customs, and social norms of the previous generation to the generations that follow.

Roles essential to the functioning of a healthy family

There are five major roles that are essential to the functioning of a healthy family. These roles are provision of necessities, development and education, emotional support, management of the family, and satisfaction of the married couple's needs. Individuals within the family need to provide necessities by creating income so that the family has access to food, clothing, and shelter. Family members need to teach not only customs, but also skills that will help the members of the family achieve academically and professionally. Families must provide emotional support for the family members during times of high stress. In addition, the family needs someone to take a leadership role and handle issues such as managing finances and maintaining the roles essential to the family's survival. The married couple has its own requirements, including basic necessities, sexual needs, and emotional needs that must be met for the family to continue functioning normally.

Role, role confusion, and role strain

A role is a collection of social rights, behaviors, and obligations that is assigned to a particular individual. For example, a mother's role might be that of a provider because she is out in the workforce earning an income for the family.

Role confusion occurs when an individual is uncertain of what role or roles he or she should play in a particular situation. For example, a nurse might run into a patient whom she took care of previously while out grocery shopping and be unsure of whether to act in a formal, nurse-to-patient manner or in an informal, friendly manner.

Role strain occurs when an individual is placed in a situation in which carrying out the duties of a certain role will prevent the individual from fulfilling his or her obligations of another role. For example, a working mother might be both caregiver and provider. If her child becomes ill, she cannot carry out both roles; she is forced to choose between working and caring for the sick child.

Marriage

Marriage is a union between two individuals that is often held as a legally binding contract in which the members of the union state their intention to live together and aid each other in maintaining a family. Even though couples who simply live together in the same household can constitute a family under the commonly used definition, the institution of marriage offers a level of stability to the family structure that is not present when an unmarried couple makes up the center of the family. This added stability is primarily a result of the societal, religious, and governmental recognition of the institution of marriage, which creates an expectation that the marriage—and ultimately the family—will remain intact. Although many married couples eventually separate and divorce, it is more difficult for a member of the marital couple to leave the family than it would be for a member of a couple who has no legal or societal obligation to remain together.

The married couple or, in some cases, the couple living together is the core of the family and therefore has a profound effect on the relationships and well-being of the family. If a marital couple is having difficulty in their relationship, and the stress of those difficulties becomes apparent, the rest of the family will most likely exhibit signs of stress. For example, if the marital couple is consistently seen fighting, or even if they just become withdrawn after a fight, other family members may react to the stress and become withdrawn, upset, or even hostile. On the other hand, marital couples who are not experiencing marital difficulties and who appear warm and affectionate will foster the same feelings of warmth and affection in the rest of the family.

Family

The primary purpose of a family is to ensure the survival of the family and to nurture the children. Families facilitate survival by sharing the work and tasks such as earning a living and taking care of the home. Family also provides emotional support to one another during stressful times. The family nurtures the children by offering social and emotional interaction, protecting them from potential danger, and educating them in social norms and customs. The family also provides the basic necessities required for the basic physical development of the children in the household, including food, clothing, shelter, and play.

A family is commonly considered a group of individuals related by birth, adoption, or marriage who reside together, usually for the purpose of raising children. However, a family can refer to any group of people who live together in the same household even if they are not related by blood or legal ties. This means that an unmarried couple who is living together or even a pair of roommates may still be considered a family. A single individual, though, is the opposite of a family because it is a person who lives alone and therefore does not regularly interact with relatives or other individuals within the household.

Family structures

The four major types of family structures are nuclear, extended, single-parent, and blended. Each of these structures is based on the idea that a family is a group of people who participate in raising the next generation. A nuclear family is the traditional concept of a family in which a mother, father, and their children live in the same household. An extended family is an expansion of the nuclear family that includes the mother, father, and their children as well as aunts, uncles, cousins, and grandparents. A single-parent structure is a family in which one parent is the only one in the home caring for the children. A blended family, also known as a stepfamily, is one in which a parent marries or remarries when he or she already has his or her own children, and there is a parent, stepparent, and one or more children living in the household.

The typical family structure in the United States has changed dramatically in recent years as the norm moves away from the nuclear family and toward the blended family. As more people divorce and remarry, blended families are becoming much more common. In this family structure, children are cared for by both biological and stepparents. This increase in the number of blended families, which were unheard of 50 years ago, has resulted in two substructures: simple and complex. In a simple stepfamily, only one of the individuals marrying has children before the marriage. In a complex stepfamily, both parents marrying have their own children before the marriage.

Family life cycle

There are commonly nine stages in the family life cycle. The first five stages are as follows: the bachelor stage, the newly married couple stage, full nest stage I, full nest stage II, and full nest stage III. The bachelor stage is the stage in which the individual is yet to be married, and the family has not yet been established. The second stage is the newly married couple stage in which two individuals have just married but do not have children. The third stage is the beginning of the three full nest stages, when the parents are beginning to raise children. During full nest stage I, the youngest child is under six. The fourth stage, full nest stage II, is when the youngest child is six or over. The fifth stage, full nest stage III, is the stage in which an older married couple has independent children.

The last four stages of the family life cycle are the empty nest I stage, the empty nest II stage, the solitary survivor in labor force stage, and the retired solitary survivor stage. During empty nest I stage, the head of the household is married and still in the labor force, but the couple has no children at home. Empty nest II stage is the same as empty nest I stage except that the head of the household has retired. The next stage, solitary survivor in labor force stage, occurs when one member of the couple has passed away, and the survivor must continue to work to support him or herself. The final stage, the retired solitary survivor stage, is the same as the solitary survivor in labor force stage except that the survivor has retired, and there are no longer any individuals living in the household who are still in the labor force.

Jean Piaget's theory of cognitive development

Jean Piaget's theory of cognitive development theorizes that children will learn more effectively if they are allowed to actively adapt to the world around them through play and exploration rather than being taught skills and knowledge by others. Piaget's theory suggests that there are four major stages that children will go through as they begin to acquire new skills that will aid their ability to learn and process information independently. The four stages of cognitive development that Piaget identifies are the sensorimotor stage, which spans from ages zero to two; the preoperational stage, spanning from ages two to seven; the concrete operational stage for ages seven to 11; and the formal operational stage for ages 11 and up. Piaget's theory is important to the study of child development because it was the first theory that recognized that children can actively and effectively learn on their own rather than being dependent on another person for learning to occur.

The first stage of Piaget's theory of cognitive development, the sensorimotor stage, lasts from birth to age two. This is the period during which a child uses his or her senses of sight, hearing, and touch to learn about and explore elements of the world. Using these senses, children are able to discover new ways of solving simple problems such as using their hands to drop a block into a bucket and then remove it from the bucket. Another example is learning to use their eyes to find an object or person that has been hidden. As a result, it is also at this stage that a child begins to develop hand-eye coordination and the ability to reason out a method of achieving goals.

The second stage of Piaget's theory of cognitive development is the preoperational stage. It spans from ages two to seven. This is the stage in which children begin to use words, symbols, and pictures to describe what they have discovered about particular elements of the world around them. During this stage, children begin to develop an understanding of language, and they can focus their attention on a particular subject or object. Piaget theorized that children at this stage have a faulty sense of logic when attempting to understand certain concepts such as volume, mass, and number when some element is changed. For example, if a liquid is poured into a tall container, and then an equal amount of liquid is poured into a smaller but wider container, the children would believe that the taller container contains more liquid even though this obviously is not the case.

The third stage of Piaget's theory of cognitive development is the concrete operational stage occurring between ages seven and 11. It is the stage in which a child's thinking becomes more logical regarding concrete concepts. In this stage, children are capable of understanding concepts of mass, volume, and number. For example, they can understand that two containers of different shapes that each have the same amount of liquid poured into them still contain the same amount of liquid despite their differences in appearance. The child also begins to identify and organize objects according to shape, size, and color. The child will not be able to understand more abstract concepts such as those found in calculus or algebra, however, until he or she reaches the formal operational stage of development.

The fourth and final stage of Piaget's theory of cognitive development, the formal operational stage, starts at age 11 and continues until the end of an individual's life. During this stage, an individual understands more abstract concepts and develops a logical way of thinking about those concepts. In other words, an individual begins to understand ideas that are less concrete or absolute and that cannot necessarily be backed up by physical evidence or observation such as morality, advanced mathematics, and a person's state of being. It is also within this stage of development that individuals can understand all the variables in a problem and are able to determine most, if not all, the possible solutions to a problem rather than just the most obvious solutions. This stage is never truly completed; it continues throughout a person's life as the individual develops and improves his or her ability to think abstractly.

Later researchers have challenged Piaget's theory of cognitive development because studies indicate that Piaget may have underestimated the abilities of younger children to learn and understand various concepts. Piaget's theory indicates that younger children are unable to understand certain concrete and abstract thoughts early within their development even if another individual teaches the child. However, this notion has been disproved. Research shows that young children can be taught how to handle and understand problems that Piaget believed only older children would be able to comprehend. Researchers have also challenged Piaget's theory because studies indicate that if a younger child is given a task like one an older child might receive, but the difficulty of the task is adjusted to compensate for age, the younger child would actually understand the concept more effectively. Piaget's theory is still important, though, because it presents the importance of active learning in a child's development. Notably, Piaget's theory ignores many of the benefits of adult learning.

Abraham Maslow's hierarchy of human needs

Abraham Maslow theorized that there are five types of human needs that, if arranged in order of importance, form a pyramid. Maslow maintained that individuals would not be able to focus on the upper layers of the hierarchy until they were first able to meet the needs at the lower layers. The first layer of the pyramid represents the physiological needs, which are the basic needs required for an individual's survival such as food, water, breathable air, and sleep. The second layer of the pyramid represents the safety needs, which are the elements that an individual needs to feel a sense of security such as having a job, good health, and a safe place to live. The third layer of the pyramid corresponds to the love and belonging needs, which are needed to form social relationships such as those with friends, family, and intimate loved ones.

The fourth layer of Maslow's hierarchy of human needs is the esteem layer, which represents the individual's need to respect him or herself and be respected and accepted by others. The fifth and top layer of the pyramid is the self-actualization layer. It represents the individual's need for morality, creativity, and trust. Maslow theorized that individuals could survive without reaching the higher levels of the pyramid but that would feel a sense of anxiousness if these needs were not met. Maslow also believed that individuals who reached the higher levels of the pyramid did not receive any tangible benefit from meeting these needs other than a feeling of fulfillment and the motivation to fulfill needs higher on the pyramid.

Maslow later added two additional layers above the self-actualization layer of the pyramid. These are the cognitive layer and the aesthetic layer. The cognitive layer is the layer that represents an individual's need to acquire and ultimately understand both abstract and concrete knowledge. The aesthetic layer, which became the final layer in later versions of the pyramid, is the layer that represents the individual's need to discover, create, and experience beauty and art. Maslow later theorized that if an individual was unable to meet the needs of any given layer of the pyramid, those needs could become neurotic needs. Such needs are compulsions that, if satisfied, would not facilitate the individual's health or growth.

Erikson's theory of psychosocial development

Erik Erikson's theory of psychosocial development breaks the process of human development into eight stages necessary for healthy functioning. The eight stages Erikson identified are infancy, younger years, early childhood, middle childhood, adolescence, early adulthood, middle adulthood, and later adulthood. During each of these stages, individuals must overcome a developmental obstacle, which Erikson called a crisis, to be able to progress and face the crises of later stages. If an individual is not able to overcome one of the crises along the way, later crises will be more difficult for him or her to overcome. Erikson's theory also maintains that individuals who are unable to successfully pass through a particular crisis will likely encounter that same crisis again.

The first stage of Erikson's theory of psychosocial development is infancy, which spans from birth to 12 months. In this stage, a child is presented with the crisis of trust versus mistrust. Although everyone struggles with this crisis throughout their lives, a child needs to be able to realize the concept of trust and the elements of certainty. For example, a child learns that if his or her parents leave the room, they aren't going to abandon the child forever. If a child is unable to realize the concept of trust because of traumatic life events, such as abandonment, the child may become withdrawn and avoid interaction with the rest of society.

The second stage of Erikson's theory of psychosocial development is the younger years stage, which covers ages one to three. In this stage, a child is faced with the crisis of autonomy versus shame and doubt. The child is presented with the need to become independent and learn skills such as using the toilet without assistance. If the child is able to overcome this crisis, he or she will gain the sense of self-pride necessary to continue fostering the child's growing need for independence. If, however, the child is unable to overcome this crisis and cannot establish his or her own independence, the child will develop feelings of shame and doubt about his or her ability to function without assistance.

The third stage of Erikson's theory of psychosocial development is the early childhood stage, spanning ages three to five. In this stage, a child is faced with the crisis of initiative versus guilt. The child is presented with the need to discover the ambition necessary to continue functioning independently. This stage is strongly linked with the moral development of the child as he or she begins to use make-believe play to explore the kind of person he or she wants to become in the future. If children are unable to explore their ambitions or if they are expected to function with too much self-control, they will develop feelings of guilt as they begin to see their ambitions, dreams, and goals as unattainable or inappropriate.

The fourth stage of Erikson's theory of psychosocial development is the middle childhood stage, which covers ages six to 10. In this stage, a child is faced with the crisis of industry versus inferiority and is presented with the need to develop the ability to complete productive tasks such as schoolwork and working in groups. If children are unable to learn how to work effectively, either alone or in a group, they will develop a sense of inferiority as a result of their inability to complete the tasks set before them that their peers are capable of completing. For example, if a child is regularly unable to complete their homework because the child does not understand the material while the rest of the child's peers are not having difficulty, this can lead the child to develop a sense of inferiority.

The fifth stage of Erikson's theory of psychosocial development is the adolescence stage, which covers ages 11 to 18. In this stage, the child is faced with the crisis of identity versus role confusion. During this stage, the child attempts to find his or her place in society and identify future goals and the skills and values necessary to achieve those goals. At this stage, the child also becomes more aware of how people perceive him or her and becomes concerned with those perceptions. If the child is unable to determine what future goals he or she is interested in pursuing, it can lead to confusion about what roles the child will play when he or she reaches adulthood.

The sixth stage of Erikson's theory of psychosocial development is the early adulthood stage, which covers ages 18 to 34. In this stage, the young adult is concerned with the crisis of intimacy versus isolation in which an individual needs to begin establishing intimate relationships with others. If an adult is unable to form intimate relationships with others, perhaps because of disappointing relationships in the past, this person will become more withdrawn and will isolate him or herself from others. Isolation can prove to be a perilous problem in the development of a healthy adult, as it prevents the individual from forming lasting relationships. The lack of social interaction can also lead to severe personality flaws, which may hinder the development of future relationships.

The seventh stage of Erikson's theory of psychosocial development is the middle adulthood stage, occurring between the ages of 35 and 60. In this stage, an adult becomes aware of the crisis of generativity versus stagnation in which the individual is concerned with continuing his or her genetic line before it is too late. Generativity refers to the ability to produce offspring and then nurture, guide, and prepare that offspring for future life. At the same time, however, generativity in this context also refers to any act that gives something of value to the next generation such as teaching children how to read. If an individual is unable to contribute to the next generation in some form, the individual will feel a sense of failure resulting from stagnation, which is simply a lack of accomplishment.

The last stage of Erikson's eight stages of psychosocial development is the later adulthood stage, which is the period that starts at age 60 and extends to the end of one's life. In this stage, an individual is confronted with the crisis of ego integrity versus despair. During this time, an adult begins to examine the course of his or her life by reflecting on the kind of person that he or she has been. If the adult feels that he or she has had a meaningful life and has accomplished something during it, this will lead to a strong sense of integrity. However, if the individual is unhappy with the way he or she has acted, this person will experience despair and will fear death as the absolute end of further achievement.

Familial roles

Fifty years ago, women were the primary caretakers of the family's children, and they were in charge of maintaining the household while men worked to provide for the family. This has changed, however, because of the drastic increase in the number of women entering the workforce since that time. This is partially because it has become more difficult for families to subsist on one income alone. Both members of the marital couple are often forced to work to provide for the family, which can make it difficult when trying to balance the responsibilities of caretaker and provider. Men, who were once the primary providers for the family, are still out in the workforce, but their spouses have joined them, and both individuals have to find ways to make the time to care for the family's children.

Nature versus nurture

The concept of nature versus nurture is the idea that of all a person's traits, some result from his or her genetic heritage, and some result from his or her environment. In this context, nature refers to any trait that an individual is born with, or has acquired through genes. Nurture may be seen as the opposite of nature; it refers to any trait that an individual learns from the environment. Nurture often refers specifically to the environment created by the parents of the child, but it can refer to any environmental condition that affects the development of the child. The concept of nature versus nurture is important because it shows that individuals inherit some of their traits from their parents, but they also develop many of their traits from their environment.

Genetic and environmental traits

Research has shown that some traits that are almost completely genetic include eye color, blood type, and most diseases. In most cases, genetics also determines one's risk of future diseases, vision, and vision impairments. Religion and language, on the other hand, are examples of traits that researchers have proven to be almost completely environmental. These traits are all linked to specific genes or to specific environmental factors, but most traits are actually a result of both environmental and genetic influences. Traits such as height, weight, and skin color are all examples of traits that are influenced by both an individual's genes and his or her environment.

Havinghurst's developmental task concept

The developmental task concept is a theory of human development established by Robert Havinghurst that states that there are certain tasks each individual needs to go through at points during his or her life to continue developing into a happy and successful adult. These tasks, separated into three groups by their causes, are tasks resulting from physical maturation, personal causes, and societal pressures. A child learning to crawl is an example of a task that becomes necessary as the child matures physically. An individual learning basic first aid because he or she is interested in becoming an EMT is an example of a personal cause. An example of a task resulting from societal pressure is a child learning to behave appropriately in a store.

The first three major age periods identified by Havinghurst in his developmental task concept are infancy and early childhood, middle childhood, and adolescence. Infancy and early childhood is the period from ages zero to five, and it consists of tasks such as learning to walk, talk, and eat solid foods as well as learning right from wrong. Middle childhood is the period of development from ages six to 12 that includes tasks such as learning to get along with others, moral values, and skills and knowledge required for day-to-day living. Adolescence is the period from ages 13 to 18, and it requires tasks that include learning how to relate with members of the opposite sex, learning the social role of one's gender in society, and preparing for life after childhood.

The last three major age periods identified by Havinghurst in his developmental task concept are early adulthood, middle adulthood, and later maturity. Early adulthood is the period of life from ages 19 to 29, and it is the age range where tasks such as starting a long-term relationship, finding a career, and starting a family are required. Middle adulthood is the period from ages 30 to 60 that includes tasks such as finding adult recreational activities, achieving in one's chosen career, and helping one's teenage children become healthy and happy adults. Later maturity is the period from ages 61 to the end of a person's life. This period consists of tasks such as adjusting to the death of a spouse, adjusting to the effects of old age, and finding people in one's peer group to interact with.

Early childhood intervention and intellectual giftedness

Early childhood intervention is the process by which children who are experiencing or showing signs of developmental difficulties are diagnosed and treated early to allow them to continue developing in the best manner possible. Early childhood intervention services usually take place before the child reaches school age because studies indicate that the earlier a child who is experiencing difficulties receives special education, the more effective that education will ultimately be.

Intellectual giftedness refers to children who are born with a significantly higher than average IQ and who are capable of learning concepts and information much more quickly than other children their age. Even though intellectual giftedness is an asset to the child, the child often requires education that is adjusted for the speed at which the child can learn. Otherwise, the child will become bored, frustrated, isolated, and may begin to underachieve.

Substance abuse

Substance abuse is a disorder in which an individual begins to overuse or becomes dependent on a particular drug or a group of drugs that ultimately has a negative impact on his or her health and human development. Substance abuse, especially when the individual becomes addicted to or dependent on the drug, can affect the individual's ability to interact both socially and physically. His or her ability to communicate intelligibly or even to complete relatively simple tasks can be severely hindered. After an individual has become chemically dependent on a particular drug, his or her body develops a physical need for the drug, and the individual will experience the effects of withdrawal if he or she is unable to meet that need. However, substance abuse not only affects a person by causing health problems, it also severely hinders an individual's ability for social development, as the individual often has difficulty improving social skills because of his or her inability to control behavior, actions, and even basic speech.

Teenage pregnancy

Teenage pregnancy can be defined as the act of a woman expecting a child prior to her twentieth birthday or, in some areas, prior to her being considered a legal adult. Teenage pregnancy can have a significant number of physical, social, economic, and psychological effects. Studies show that women who become pregnant as teenagers have a significantly higher chance of giving birth to the child prematurely, a higher risk of the child being born at an unhealthy weight, and a higher risk of complications during pregnancy, especially when the mother is under the age of 15. It has also been shown that teenage mothers are more likely to drop out of high school and are even more likely never to finish college. This can make it much more difficult for a teenage mother to find a job, especially if she is the sole caretaker of her child. Also, children born to teenage mothers have been shown to be at higher risk for behavioral problems and often have more difficulty functioning in school.

The two primary ways that the risk of teenage pregnancy can be reduced are through the promotion of contraceptive use or abstinence and through the promotion of social interaction between teenagers and their parents. The best way to reduce the risk of teenage pregnancy is to abstain from intercourse, but the use of a contraceptive, even though it does not guarantee that a teenager will not become pregnant, can greatly reduce the chances of pregnancy when used correctly. Studies have also shown that teenagers who have regular, open communication with their parents are more likely to wait to have intercourse until later in their lives. However, regardless of what precautions are used, the risk of teenage pregnancy cannot be eliminated completely, as there is always the risk of contraceptives failing or the risk that a teenager may become a rape victim.

Maintaining a stable and effective support system before and after a child is born is the most important factor for a teenage mother to function and raise her child in a healthy fashion. Studies have shown that most of the physical effects on the children of teenage pregnancy are a result of malnutrition and poor prenatal care. Both of these factors can be greatly reduced or eliminated if the young mother has help from parents or outside resources that teach her what to eat and where to get appropriate care. Because teenage parents almost always lack the resources and the life experience necessary to both supply and care for the child, a strong support system is essential in helping the mother financially and in raising the child.

Teenage suicide

There are a number of factors that increase the risk of teenage suicide, but studies indicate that a teenager's history, emotional and physical health, social pressures, and access to the methods necessary to carry out a suicide are the most influential factors. If a teenager has attempted suicide, has a history of drug or alcohol abuse, a history of depression or other mental illness, or another family member has committed suicide or been abused, the teenager's risk of suicide increases. Physical illness, religious or cultural pressures, and other suicides in the community can also lead to an increased risk of suicide among teenagers. Finally, if the teenager has access to guns, knives, drugs, or any other means of taking his or her own life, the teenager may be at heightened risk for suicide.

Family and consumer education

Family and consumer education aims to improve a variety of skills that are essential for the day-to-day functioning of an individual and his or her family. Family and consumer education includes specific topics such as family interaction, human development, nutrition, consumer economics, types of housing and housing design, textiles, parenting, and the appropriate cooking and handling of foods. Family and consumer education covers both the physical and the psychological needs of the individual, and emphasizes appropriate social interaction between the individual and the rest of society.

Careers

Family and consumer science skills are useful in food management, financial management, human resources, public relations, tailoring, dress-making, etc. Indeed, regardless of career, an individual always finds a use for these skills in life. An individual in food management needs to know about nutrition and the proper handling and preparation of food. Financial advisors need to know how to assess resources, cut costs, and determine how much an individual needs to save before retirement. Human resource and public relations managers need social skills and training in time and resource management, human development, and psychology. Finally, tailors and dressmakers use their knowledge of textiles and textile design to create better garments.

In order to help students determine their interests and develop their skills, teachers should give them some example descriptions of various careers. Some of these examples may be family and consumer science careers, though it is not necessary for them all to be so. The class should examine a diverse sampling of different careers, especially since family and consumer science skills can be applied to virtually any setting. For example, a construction worker might not need to know about food, textiles, or housing design, but he or she still needs to know various problem-solving techniques. It can also be extremely useful for students to get some hands-on experience applying family and consumer science concepts to the tasks associated with different careers.

Work simplification

Work simplification is the process of discovering and implementing a series of procedures allowing an individual or a group of individuals to complete a task more easily and efficiently. Based on the particular type of task being performed, work can be simplified in a number of ways by determining the best possible way to complete a task without significantly impacting the overall quality of the work. Some of the basic methods used to make any task easier and more efficient include ensuring that individuals have access to necessary equipment, that work areas are organized, and that any steps in the work process that do not directly affect the outcome of the work are eliminated.

Community advisory committees

Community advisory committees can be extremely useful to an education professional who is attempting to determine what areas of the family and consumer science discipline a teaching plan should emphasize because the committees offer insight into the concerns and demographics of the students. Each community has its own problems, concerns, and level of diversity, and it is important that a family and consumer science teacher can recognize and focus on areas of concern in the school's community. For example, a community that is having problems with widespread teenage drug abuse and teenage suicide may want the community's family and consumer science teachers to focus more on the topic of avoiding substance abuse and the methods of handling depression. The goal of a family and consumer sciences educator is to improve the overall quality of life for the students and their families, and the educator cannot do that if he or she does not know what problems need to be addressed.

Some of the functions that community advisory committees perform, other than offering advice to education professionals, include assessing the performance of family and consumer science programs, assessing the performance of students with special needs, and providing equipment, technology, and resources for family and consumer science programs. These resources may include raw materials, textile samples, charts and diagrams, library books, and access to computers and design software. Community advisory committees also help students improve their chances of finding better jobs and careers and act as a public relations liaison for local family and consumer science programs. Ultimately, the primary purpose of a family and consumer sciences community advisory committee is to ensure that a family and consumer sciences program has all of the resources and training necessary to achieve the program's goals.

Balancing home and work roles

It is important that an individual is able to balance his or her work and home roles because it is becoming more and more common for individuals to have to act as both caregiver and provider for the family. The ever more common presence of dual roles in society can be extremely difficult for an individual to balance, as there may be instances where work-related responsibilities and family-related responsibilities conflict with one another. Family and consumer sciences education attempts to teach individuals how to avoid and how to handle these conflicts through the use of successful life management tactics such as time and resources management, problem-solving and decision-making techniques, and effective communication techniques. Family and consumer sciences education also attempts to give individuals a basic understanding of what responsibilities and qualities are necessary for the successful completion of each role so that individuals can set better priorities and find better ways to plan their lives.

Eliminating sexual stereotypes

Eliminating sexual stereotypes is a major concern of family and consumer sciences education. It is important for students to disregard sexual stereotypes and recognize that an individual's gender does not necessarily affect the role he or she plays. In the early- and mid-1900s, women were commonly seen as caretakers of the home and men as providers for the family. However, these roles have changed drastically over the past fifty to sixty years, and are not entirely realistic at this point. As the cost of living increases, it becomes more difficult for a single individual to provide for an entire family. As a result, it is more common for men and women to share the caretaker and provider roles to satisfy the physiological, financial, and psychological needs of the family.

Goals that family and consumer sciences education attempts to accomplish

The Association for Career and Technical Education has identified nine goals commonly associated with family and consumer sciences education. These nine goals include:
1. Improving the overall quality of life for individuals and families.
2. Helping individuals and families become responsible members of society.
3. Encouraging healthy eating habits, nutrition, and lifestyles.
4. Improve how individuals and families manage their resources.
5. Helping individuals and families balance their personal, family, and work lives.
6. Teaching individuals better problem-solving techniques.
7. Encouraging personal and career development.
8. Teaching individuals to successfully function as both consumers and providers.
9. Recognizing human worth and taking responsibility for one's own actions.

Improving the overall quality of life

The first of the nine goals established for family and consumer sciences education is to improve the overall quality of life for individuals and families, which is also the primary mission of all the goals. Family and consumer sciences education teaches people about how individuals, families, and the rest of society interact with each other, along with methods for improving those interactions. These methods include problem-solving techniques, common scams and problems to avoid, methods to stay healthy both physically and psychologically, and the distribution of a variety of other information regarding how the individual, family, and the rest of society function. Ultimately, family and consumer sciences education strives to improve the quality of life by educating individuals and families in the best manner to function on a day-to-day basis. However, this goal is truly accomplished only when the other eight goals of family and consumer sciences education are met as well.

Basic concepts

There are several concepts at the core of family and consumer education, but one of the most important concepts is that families form the basic unit of society. Another important concept of family and consumer education is that individuals need to be life-long learners in order to develop and function successfully. Finally, family and consumer education promotes the idea that individuals and families need to have an understanding of the advantages of experimenting with different decision-making methods and diverse ways of thinking in order to solve any given problem.

Characteristics of occupational family and consumer sciences education

Occupational family and consumer sciences education is a teaching discipline that is similar to the standard discipline of family and consumer education but focuses less on the skills for day-to-day living and more on how those skills can be used in the workplace. Occupational family and consumer sciences education covers information regarding skills that can commonly be applied in fields such as health services, food service, child care, hospitality, fashion design, interior design, and many other similar fields. Occupational family and consumer sciences education places more emphasis on family and consumer skills that directly relate to a career, such as management techniques and ethical businesses practices, than the standard family and consumer education discipline. The occupational family and consumer sciences education discipline ultimately takes the skills that an individual has learned from the standard discipline and shows how those skills can be applied to a career.

Demonstrating family and consumer science concepts

There are a large number of methods that an educator can use to demonstrate concepts related to family and consumer sciences, but the best methods always involve promoting students' active participation. Some examples of active participation include allowing students to use a sewing machine; having students test the qualities of various textiles to see how soft, lustrous, resilient, absorbent, etc. each material is; and requiring students to prepare a meal. Students can also demonstrate active participation with the following activities: comparing advertisements to find the best offer for a particular product, examining common marketing tactics, visiting or working in a local daycare center, and being involved in local community service activities. Many of these activities serve not only as effective ways of teaching students about the important concepts of family and consumer sciences, but also as a means of testing the students' ability to apply the techniques, skills, and information that they have learned.

Professional organizations

Professional organizations such as the American Association of Family and Consumer Sciences, also known as the AAFCS, play an important role in influencing the education of individuals in the methodology and knowledge associated with family and consumer sciences. Many of these local and national professional organizations offer seminars, courses, and publications on a wide range of topics directly to individuals and families to teach them about essential career and management skills, how to be smart consumers, the importance of following nutritional guidelines, and information about a wide range of other topics. These professional organizations also provide publications, advice, and curriculum guides to educational professionals that help these professionals teach and stay informed regarding important changes to the curriculum that result from changes in legislation, society, and the education system itself. These organizations also have a profound effect on family and consumer science education by influencing public policy and gathering support for programs that help educate and protect individuals and families from unsafe habits, business practices, products, and lifestyles.

FCCLA

The FCCLA, which stands for the Family, Career, and Community Leaders of America, is a youth organization for students in family and consumer science education. The FCCLA offers a variety of publications and programs designed to educate people about parenting, relationships, substance abuse, teen pregnancy, and teen violence, among other concerns. By focusing public attention to the problems that young people face, the FCCLA gains support for programs and laws that help protect young people and their families. The FCCLA also shows students how they can improve their family and consumer science skills and apply those skills later in life.

The FCCLA and other similar youth organizations play an important role in influencing national policy related to protecting families and consumers. Additionally, these organizations are important because they support family and consumer science educational programs, which strive to improve the overall quality of life for individuals and families by teaching people skills that will enable them to live better lives.

Legislation

When a new act of legislation is passed, it can often have a profound impact on the types of materials used in family and consumer sciences classrooms, as well as the issues that should be addressed by family and consumer sciences education. It is important that individuals understand the legal protections and rights granted to them by the various acts put into place by state and federal governments. Since laws are constantly changing, family and consumer science educators must be able to adapt quickly and add information regarding new legislation to their curriculum.

Meeting the special needs of a student

The first step an educator should take when determining the best way to meet the special needs of a student is to identify exactly what that particular child's needs consist of, as each student is unique in his or her ability to learn and comprehend. If a student is performing poorly, a teacher must determine the cause of the student's poor performance. Once the cause has been identified, the teacher can then determine how much assistance the student needs. If the student's needs can be met through such techniques as one-on-one attention or special project assignments, this is usually the best course of action. However, if the student has needs that require solutions beyond simple changes in curriculum, including potential psychological or physiological disorders, the educator has an obligation to consult with other educational professionals and to discuss other options with the child's parents.

Affective skill, cognitive skill and psychomotor skill

Affective skill refers to how effectively an individual can recognize, understand, and handle emotions and relationships. Affective skills allow an individual to feel appropriate emotion in response to certain situations or stimuli, and then to respond appropriately.

Cognitive skill refers to an individual's ability to gather and understand information. Cognitive skills allow an individual to comprehend new situations and apply the knowledge that he or she has gathered elsewhere.

Psychomotor skill refers to an individual's ability to coordinate his or her physical movements. In other words, psychomotor skills are a person's control over simple and complex motor functions.

It is extremely important for an individual to be able to use a combination of his or her affective, cognitive, and psychomotor skills together on a day-to-day basis, as each type of skill is essential to the overall functioning of a healthy individual. An individual who has mastered his or her psychomotor skills may be in excellent physical health, but the individual's emotional and intellectual health will suffer if he or she is unable to make effective relationships and understand basic and complex concepts. The situation is the same for individuals who can only maintain effective relationships or who can only understand complex concepts, as it will be significantly more difficult for them to perform everyday functions if they have poor control of their psychomotor skills. For an individual to maintain his or her physical and mental health, along with that of his or her family, the individual must be able to use a combination of different skills.

Some of the factors that can be used to measure how well-developed an individual's affective skills are include determining how well the individual receives emotional stimuli and how well the individual responds to those stimuli. It is also important to determine how easy it is for the individual to acknowledge the worth of a particular situation, relationship, or individual and whether the individual has an organized and well-conceived value system. An individual's ability to receive and respond to emotional stimuli can be measured by how aware the individual is of a particular stimulus, how willing the individual is to acknowledge that particular stimulus, and how focused the individual is on that stimulus. An individual's ability to assign value to a situation and uphold a value system can be measured by how motivated the individual is, how the individual behaves, and how consistent that individual's behavior is. For example, a student that always comes to class and clearly always pays attention may have well-developed affective skills.

Some of the factors that can be used to measure how well-developed an individual's cognitive skills are include determining the individual's ability to retain knowledge, comprehend knowledge, apply knowledge, and evaluate knowledge. An individual's ability to retain knowledge can be measured by testing the individual's ability to remember certain facts and information through exams or simply asking questions. An individual's ability to comprehend knowledge can be measured by an individual demonstrating a concept in a different form, explaining a concept in more detail or simplifying a concept, or predicting a result based on a particular concept. An individual breaking a concept down into individual parts and demonstrating how those parts make up the whole can also show comprehension of a particular concept. An individual's ability to apply knowledge can be measured by an individual demonstrating that they can use a particular concept for a real-life purpose. Finally, an individual's ability to evaluate a particular piece of knowledge can be indicated by the individual showing the value of that knowledge.

Some of the factors that can be used to measure how well-developed an individual's psychomotor skills are include how well an individual performs physical skills and acts, how precisely can the individual perform those skills or activities, and how natural do those activities seem to be for the individual. An individual's ability to use physical skills can be measured simply by how much difficulty the individual has in accomplishing a particular complex physical activity such as climbing a rope or assembling a model. How precisely the individual can perform those skills or activities can be measured by determining the quality of the result of the individual's physical activity and how long it took the individual to reach that result. For example, if the individual has constructed a model plane, does the model look like a plane, are its wings and other parts attached correctly, how long it took to assemble, etc. Finally, an activity is natural for an individual if the individual can perform it without thinking.

Anorexia, bulimia, and obesity

Anorexia and bulimia are very similar disorders, but the one major difference between the two conditions is control. An individual suffering from anorexia is usually already below a healthy weight, still perceives that his or her own weight is unacceptable, and therefore attempts to lower that weight further by limiting food intake. Bulimic individuals, on the other hand, have no sense of control over their eating habits. They instead eat excessively and then attempt to overcompensate for their excessive food intake. In short, individuals suffering from anorexia are usually below what would normally be considered a healthy weight for their age and size and attempt to control their eating to reduce their weight further. Bulimic individuals, however, are usually above a healthy weight as they have no control over their own eating.

Anorexia is an eating disorder in which an individual views his or her own body as being overweight, even though he or she is not, which causes the person to have an extreme, unfounded fear of gaining additional weight. This fear can lead individuals to use desperate and unhealthy methods to reduce their weight below what would normally be healthy. These methods include deliberate vomiting, limiting their food intake, exercising excessively without eating enough food, and using medications to flush their system. Anorexia is commonly found to affect young women, specifically during adolescence. It can pose a serious risk to an individual's health as the obsessive attempts to reduce body weight can affect the health of the heart, brain, immune system, muscles, and other organs. Anorexia can be extremely difficult to treat as it is a complicated psychological condition, but it has been shown that psychotherapy may be able to help the individual overcome the inaccurate perceptions she or he has regarding his or her own body.

Bulimia is an eating disorder, similar to anorexia, in which an individual views his or her own body as being unattractive or overweight, but lacks the ability to control his or her own eating. Bulimic individuals regularly eat an unhealthily large amount of food and then attempt to flush their systems to prevent themselves from gaining additional weight. Some of the methods individuals suffering from bulimia might use to flush food from their systems include deliberate vomiting, excessive exercise, and using diet pills, laxatives, ipecac, and other medications. Bulimia is most commonly found in women, especially younger women from ages 12 to 19, and can have a significant impact on the health of the individual. It can cause problems such as anemia, weakness, muscle and heart problems, dehydration, malnutrition, damage to the stomach, and a wide range of other problems. Bulimia is difficult to treat, but a combination of group psychotherapy and low doses of anti-psychotic medications have been shown to help.

Obesity is a condition of the body where the individual has increased his or her own body weight significantly beyond what is normally considered healthy, usually by excessive eating. Obesity occurs because the individual takes in more food than his or her body can actually use, and the excess food is stored as fat. Overeating is the primary cause of obesity, but obesity can also be tied to family history, genetic factors, stress and lack of sleep, various illnesses and conditions, and many other causes. An individual who is obese is at a significantly higher risk for certain health problems, including problems with the heart, stomach, muscles, lungs, skin, nervous system, and many other areas of the body. The best way to treat obesity is through a well-balanced diet that eliminates excessive food intake and a rigorous exercise program. In extreme cases, individuals may also use medication or even surgery to help lower their weight.

Unfortunately, there is no known way of completely eliminating the risk of an individual developing an eating-related condition such as anorexia, bulimia, and obesity, but it has been shown that some methods may significantly lower the risk of developing these conditions. The best way to reduce the risk of developing eating disorders or becoming obese is for parents to interact more with their children and make sure that they are teaching them good eating habits early on. It is also important that parents attempt to build-up the self-esteem of their children through interactions that show high esteem in both the parents and child. Children who have been taught good eating habits by their parents and who have been taught to have high self-esteem have been shown to eat more carefully, and therefore are at a significantly lower risk of becoming obese or developing eating disorders such as anorexia and bulimia.

Ethics and religion

An individual's religious, moral, and ethical beliefs can play a large part in his or her diet because some beliefs can result in the exclusion of certain foods. Ethical and moral considerations such as preventing animal cruelty or showing disapproval of environmentally unfriendly practices used to acquire certain types of food can lead some individuals to reduce the amount of certain foods they consume, such as meat, or eliminate those foods from their diet completely. For example, many individuals who choose to be vegetarians or vegans usually do so to avoid supporting what they believe to be the unethical slaughter of animals. Religious considerations can also determine a person's dietary choices, as some religions dictate what sort of foods the members of that faith can consume. People practicing Judaism, for instance, can consume only kosher foods, which are foods that conform to a series of guidelines established by the faith and include restrictions related to how an animal was slaughtered, what type of animal was slaughtered, and who prepared the food.

Ethnicity

Ethnicity can play an important role in the foods that an individual includes in his or her diet because people living in different regions of the world usually have different customs regarding the foods that they eat and have different foods commonly available as well. For example, individuals who live in a country like Japan that has easy access to waters suitable for fishing will typically consume significantly more fish than individuals who live in countries that are landlocked. Individuals who have immigrated to another country or who are descendents of immigrants will often include foods in their diet that are traditional foods from their native countries even if those foods are not easily accessible in their new home. People in some regions may include foods in their diets that are not based on how readily available a particular food is, but rather are based on the culture's customary eating habits, as seen in France, where the population as a whole tends to eat foods that are fresh rather than processed.

Food

Food is essential for the health of an individual, because it satisfies an individual's nutritional needs. Additionally, food provides many people some degree of psychological satisfaction as well. Food is a basic necessity for the successful functioning of an individual; therefore, the body makes a person aware of its need for food by creating a feeling of hunger in him or her. When the individual satisfies this hunger by consuming various foods, the body releases hormones that result in the person's feeling a sensation of being full, an indication that the body's need for sustenance has been assuaged. Certain types of foods satisfy an individual's hunger more effectively than other foods. Foods that are high in fiber, protein, and water usually will make an individual feel more satiated, or full. If an individual's body lacks a specific type of nutrient, the body will cause that person to experience a craving for foods that will satisfy that particular nutritional need.

Planning a nutritional meal for a group

Individuals or organizations that are planning to prepare a nutritionally-sound meal for a group of people should first decide what the nutritional goals of the meal are. Once these goals have been established, the individual or organization should continue the planning process by researching which foods will best satisfy these goals without exceeding the available time and resource limits. The individual or organization should then put together a written meal plan that details what foods will be included, the average time it takes to prepare and cook each of these meals, and the cost associated with the preparation of these meals. The individual or organization should then determine the best method of preparing food for these meals, including which foods should be prepared first, the best way to handle or prepare the foods to minimize the risk of illness, and what techniques can be used to reduce the cooking time. Finally, the individual or organization can prepare the meal according to the plan that has been established.

Reducing the amount of time it takes to prepare a meal

Some of the methods that can be used to reduce the time it takes to prepare a meal include keeping the cooking equipment clean and organized, making sure frozen products are thawed ahead of time, preparing foods that have long cooking times beforehand, and preparing foods in order of their cooking times. By keeping the cooking area and the necessary cooking utensils clean, organized, and easily accessible, individuals or organizations can make sure that the time they have available is used as efficiently as possible. Along with thawing products beforehand, preparing foods that require long cooking times ahead of time and re-heating them later can also greatly reduce the amount of time it takes to prepare a meal. Preparing foods according to their cooking times, from longest to shortest, also greatly reduces preparation time because the individual or organization can prepare other foods for the meal while the foods that take the longest are already cooking.

Choosing what foods to prepare for a meal

An individual or organization that is deciding what foods to prepare for a meal should consider the food's nutritional value, the time it takes to prepare each food, the number of people to be served, and the cost of preparing each food. Each food has its own cooking time and offers different nutrients, so it is important that whoever is preparing the meal chooses to serve foods that satisfy people's nutritional goals without exceeding his or her time constraints for cooking the meal. Since most individuals or organizations will likely have a budgeted amount of money for the meal, they must consider the number of people to be served and how much each food costs to prepare. If the cost is too high, some meals may not be practical to serve to large groups of people. For example, if an individual or organization is interested in serving a good source of protein for a meal, steak might be a good option for a small group of people but would probably be too expensive for a larger group.

Food that might be found in the marketplace

The two primary types of food that an individual can find in the marketplace are animal products and plant products. Animal products include any foods that either are a part of an animal or are produced by an animal, such as meat, milk, assorted dairy products, and honey. Plant products are foods that originate from some sort of vegetation and include foods such as fruits, vegetables, syrup, nuts, oils, and rice. It is important for an individual to understand the difference between these two groups, as animal products often have more foodborne illnesses associated with them than do plant products; because of this, there are different methods of storing and preparing each type of food to minimize these risks. Animal products and plant products provide different nutrients that the body requires to continue functioning normally, so a healthy individual would need to eat both animal and plant products to receive enough of the various nutrients he or she requires without the use of vitamin supplements.

Factors that might influence what foods are available

Some of the major factors that might influence what foods are available to a consumer include the region in which a consumer lives, current weather conditions and seasonal effects, and the demand for a particular type of food. Each geographical region has its own natural resources and different climate, which results in foods unique to the area being readily available. For example, certain crops that react poorly to sudden temperature drops, such as oranges, are easier to grow in areas that have relatively stable and warm climates. Weather and seasonal conditions also play a large role in whether a particular food is available, as certain foods may not be produced during some times of the year in a particular region, while other crops may die as a result of hurricanes, droughts, and other natural disasters. The demand for a particular type of food can also have a significant impact on the availability of that food. Oftentimes, if the demand for a particular type of food increases suddenly, suppliers may have difficulty in meeting that demand.

Unit pricing

Unit pricing is the practice of indicating the price of a product based on the cost per piece or unit included in that product. In other words, unit pricing is a method of determining how much an item costs per unit of measurement. For example, a 12-pack of 12-ounce cans of soda might be $2.99 and have a unit price of $0.70 per liter. Unit pricing is important because it can be extremely useful to a consumer who is attempting to compare two similar products of different sizes to determine which product is less expensive. If, for instance, an individual is trying to decide between a 12-pack of soda that costs $2.99 and has a unit price of $0.70 per liter and a six pack that retails for $1.99 and has a unit price of $0.93 per liter, he or she can easily compare unit prices and see that the 12 pack is the better buy.

Food distributors

Some of the major types of food distributors a consumer might find in the marketplace are chain supermarkets, independent grocery stores, farmers' markets, restaurants, and local farm stands. Each type of food distribution center has its own distinct advantages and disadvantages. Chain supermarkets are large stores that usually offer a large selection of foods at mid-range prices, but foods are often not as fresh and are sometimes of poorer quality than a consumer might find at a farm stand or farmers' market. Independent grocery stores and farmers markets usually have a smaller selection and are slightly more expensive than chain supermarkets, but many consumers prefer to purchase food from these sources because the food is usually locally grown and fresher. Even though restaurants are the most expensive distributors of food because the food is prepared by the restaurant for the consumer, many people appreciate the quality and variety of foods a restaurant can offer. Local farm stands frequently offer the freshest, highest-quality foods for the lowest prices, but they are open for shorter periods of time, often seasonally.

Food consumption patterns

Food consumption patterns are comprised of an analysis of the eating habits of people belonging to a particular region or area. Food consumption patterns indicate that individuals from different regions have very different diets and therefore receive more—or less—of certain nutrients than individuals from other regions. Knowing the kinds of nutrients that are common in the everyday diets of individuals native to a particular area is important, as that information allows health care professionals to understand what types of diseases and deficiencies pose a threat to the people of that region. By understanding which diseases and vitamin deficiencies the individuals of a particular area may be suffering from, resources can be allocated for treating and preventing those diseases. Monitoring food consumption patterns also allows researchers to study these patterns and determine the ingredients in certain foods that may be contributing to illnesses that are prevalent in a particular region.

Eating preferences

Just as every individual is fond of certain foods, her or she dislikes or refuses to eat other types of foods as well. In general, people will find the foods that offer them the most physiological and psychological satisfaction to be the most appealing. Most people who refuse to eat a particular food usually do so for one of three basic reasons: they dislike the taste of the food, the condition of the food or how the food was produced is unappealing to them, or they fear that the food will make them ill. Such preferences are important because they serve as one of the body's safety mechanisms to prevent individuals from eating foods that may be contaminated or foods that the individual may be allergic to. In some circumstances, however, an individual's eating preferences may need to be ignored so that the body can receive all of the nutrients it needs.

Protecting consumers from unsafe foods and keeping food affordable

A number of government regulations in the United States are intended to protect consumers from unsafe foods and help keep food affordable. Some of the most important regulations include food subsidies, price ceilings, tariffs and import quotas, quality-control inspections, and sanitation regulations. Government regulations can manage and even reduce the price of food in several ways: imposing tariffs on imported foods, limiting the amounts of particular foods that can enter the country, offering American farmers and food production facilities financial incentives, and then limiting how much those subsidized producers can charge for their goods. Ideally, these techniques help keep local food sources in business so that the United States does not have to rely too much on outside food sources. Government regulated quality-control inspections and sanitation regulations, such as the Egg Products Inspection Act, the Federal Meat Inspection Act, and the Sanitary Food Transportation Act, all have the purpose of ensuring that foods are produced, stored, and transported following certain guidelines to prevent the food from being contaminated.

Reducing the risk of foodborne illnesses

Some of the methods that can be used to reduce the risk of foodborne illnesses include thawing food appropriately to prevent the growth of bacteria, storing perishable foods in airtight containers and keeping them refrigerated or frozen, and sanitizing all cooking areas and cooking equipment. Individuals should wash their hands before and after handling raw foods, as well as wash fruits and vegetables before eating to remove any bacteria and pesticides. In addition, foods, especially meats, should be cooked at a high enough temperature for a long enough period of time to avoid the growth of bacteria that lead to foodborne illnesses. Perishable foods should be stored in temperatures of 40 degrees Fahrenheit or below to prevent the growth of bacteria, and frozen foods should be thawed in the refrigerator rather than left out to thaw at room temperature because bacteria grows most quickly at temperatures between 41 degrees and 140 degrees Fahrenheit.

Deciding what cooking equipment to purchase

Some of the factors that a consumer should consider when choosing what cooking equipment to purchase include the materials used in the construction of the cooking equipment, the heat conductivity of the materials used, the energy conservation of the cooking equipment, and how easy the equipment is to use and clean. The materials that are used in the construction of a piece of cooking equipment are important because certain materials conduct heat more effectively, retain heat more efficiently, are more durable, and are less expensive than other materials. Certain materials are also rustproof, stick-resistant, and easy to clean, do not flake, and do not react to certain foods. Both the heat conductivity and energy conservation of a piece of cooking equipment are also relevant because the greater the conductivity of the material used in the construction of the equipment and the more efficiently it can retain the heat, the faster the food will cook. Consumers should also know that some types of cooking equipment are easier to use and clean than others, which can make food preparation and clean-up faster.

Food irradiation and shelf life

Food irradiation is the process of using radioactive materials to disinfect and preserve certain types of food. Shelf life refers to how long food will last before it spoils and begins to breed bacteria. Irradiation is important for food manufacturers because it allows a facility to use varying amounts of radiation to kill any bacteria that might be growing on a particular food item, thereby reducing a consumer's risk of foodborne illness. As a result of irradiation techniques that prevent or slow the growth of bacteria, the shelf life of many foods is significantly lengthened. Studies have shown that irradiation methods are completely safe and pose no noticeable risk to individuals who eat foods that have been treated. Foods that are commonly irradiated include apples, bananas, fish, onions, poultry, potatoes, red meats, and strawberries.

Dietary Guidelines for Americans

The Dietary Guidelines for Americans is a combined publication of the United States Department of Health and Human Services and the United States Department of Agriculture that offers advice to consumers about dietary choices that promote good health and reduce the risk of certain diseases, including hypertension, anemia, and osteoporosis. The Dietary Guidelines for Americans offers advice to consumers on a variety of topics such as weight management, appropriate exercise, food safety, and examples of good sources of certain nutrients. This publication is important because it offers a detailed outline of the kinds of foods that an individual should have in their diets, so they do not need to use additional supplements and vitamins. It also informs consumers of the types of exercise that are necessary for an individual to stay healthy as well as the appropriate manner in which to handle and prepare certain foods to minimize the risk of foodborne illness.

The United States Department of Agriculture began issuing nutrition guidelines in 1894, and in 1943 the department began promoting the Basic 7 food groups. In 1956, Basic 7 was replaced with the Basic Four food groups. These were fruits and vegetables, cereals and breads, milk, and meat. Basic Four lasted until 1992, when it was replaced with the Food Pyramid, which divided food into six groups: 1) Bread, cereal, rice, pasta 2) Fruit 3) Vegetables 4) Meat, poultry, fish, dry beans, eggs, nuts 5) Milk, yogurt, cheese 6) Fats, oils, sweets. The Food Pyramid also provided recommendations for the number of daily servings from each group.

The USDA's Food Pyramid was heavily criticized for being vague and confusing, and in 2011 it was replaced with MyPlate. MyPlate is much easier to understand, as it consists of a picture of a dinner plate divided into four sections, visually illustrating how our daily diet should be distributed among the various food groups. Vegetables and grains each take up 30% of the plate, while fruits and proteins each constitute 20% of the plate. There is also a representation of a cup, marked Dairy, alongside the plate. The idea behind MyPlate is that it's much easier for people to grasp the idea that half of a meal should consist of fruits and vegetables than it is for them to understand serving sizes for all the different kinds of foods they eat on a regular basis.

Most experts consider MyPlate to be a great improvement over the Food Pyramid, but it has still come under criticism from some quarters. Many believe too much emphasis is placed on protein, and some say the dairy recommendation should be eliminated altogether. The Harvard School of Public Health created its own Healthy Eating Plate to address what it sees as shortcomings in MyPlate. Harvard's guide adds healthy plant-based oils to the mix, stresses whole grains instead of merely grains, recommends drinking water or unsweetened coffee or tea instead of milk, and adds a reminder that physical activity is important.

Studying moral development

Most laypeople recognize a good person by unconsciously applying the accepted criteria of their culture. Scientists do not disagree about who is a good person but, depending on their field of study, they may define morality differently. The specific age the scientist is researching will also influence his or her definition of morality. Taken together, these scientific viewpoints establish a complex picture of what constitutes a "good person" and how involved the lifelong process of moral development really is.

Psychoanalysts study internalized behavior (conscience or superego) and the way a person reacts to stimuli. Behaviorists study outward behavior such as sharing, helping, and lying. Sociocultural scientists focus on how society's values are passed on, personality traits (moral character), and cognitive behavior. Biologists study neuroanatomy, how genetics influence moral characteristics, and the role hormones play. Cognitive psychologists focus on moral reasoning and the decision-making process.

Attachment bond

Scientists firmly believe that infants must form a secure attachment bond with their primary caregivers in the early years to have a healthy social orientation throughout their entire lives. Studies confirm that establishing a secure attachment bond is an accurate predictor of the ability to form successful relationships later in life. This bond is critical in the child's moral development and in learning to interact appropriately in a social setting. Researchers believe that failure to form a secure attachment bond with the primary caregivers is the most consistent cause of antisocial behavior in childhood because the child did not develop a conscience. Conversely, children who did form a healthy attachment bond are more likely to follow family rules and therefore will also comply with rules imposed by outside authority figures and institutions, including teachers and schools.

Self-control

Some researchers consider self-control, or self-discipline, one of the two most critical building blocks of character. The other is empathy. Between the ages of about five and seven, children should learn to resist temptation, suppress impulses, and delay gratification. The primary caregivers, including parents, babysitters, and teachers, should help children develop self-regulation:
- Providing situational management, which protects children from their impulsive actions.
- Helping children learn to control emotional outbursts by soothing them until they calm down.
- Consistently teaching coping skills when children are confronted with a difficult or unfamiliar situation.
- Explaining the possible consequences if children say or do certain things.
- Showing self-control when dealing with children in challenging situations.

Children are highly influenced by and learn from the behavior of those with whom they interact on a regular basis. For this reason, it is important for children to have good role models to imitate and emulate.

Parenting styles

Most researchers agree there are three parenting styles: authoritarian, permissive, and authoritative.
- Authoritarian parents are controlling, demanding, cold, hostile, and uncommunicative. This style of parenting produces children who have difficulty making decisions, often develop antisocial tendencies, and frequently have trouble making and sustaining relationships.
- Permissive parents tend to be loving but distant, and they usually establish few guidelines about anything. They want to communicate with their children, but frequently do not do so effectively. Their children have difficulty developing self-regulating skills and seem to flounder when confronted with too many choices.
- Authoritative parents are loving, controlling, communicate effectively, and set high expectations. This parenting style produces positive children with higher moral reasoning ability and who are able to form stronger relationships.

Siblings

Studies have shown that siblings influence one another's development in some areas, most notably in developing aggressive behavior and acquiring conflict resolution skills. Scientists believe, but have not conclusively proven, that firstborn children influence the social development and gender identity of later-born children. The overall emotional climate of the family and the different approach parents take with each child has a strong influence on the relationship between the siblings as well as the power one sibling may hold over another.

Researchers are interested in learning why siblings develop differently even though they are exposed to the same environmental dynamics. The theory is that each child experiences the same factors and stimuli differently based on his or her relationship to the parents, siblings, and other family members such as grandparents, aunts, uncles, and cousins. By establishing the nature, extent, and impact of various familial influences, scientists hope to better understand childhood development.

Friends

Between the ages of three and five, a child begins to understand that the other children in the sandbox are different from one another and from him or her. Children realize they like some better than others, even though they do not really know or care to understand why. When children start school, one of their most important social tasks is making friends. They are psychologically ready to develop more complex relationships, and they move their focus from family to friends. School-age children begin spending more time with people outside the family circle. They start confiding in peers and sharing their fears, frustrations, and pleasures with friends. Groups form, and sometimes evolve into cliques, based on many things from appearance and personality to athletics and other extracurricular activities. Peer pressure increases and may include dressing, talking, walking, and acting alike; listening to the same music; and visiting the same Internet sites.

Temperament

The American Heritage College Dictionary defines temperament as "the manner of thinking, behaving, or reacting typical of a specific person." Studies have shown, and casual observation confirms, that a child's temperament will have a direct influence on how he or she behaves in a given situation or reacts to a particular stimuli. For example, if a child has a short attention span, he or she will be challenged in any learning environment that requires him or her to sit still and focus for long periods of time. If a child is shy or easily intimidated by adults, he or she will have a difficult time relating to the teacher, which will have a direct impact on his or her educational experiences. As children age, they will exert more control over their environmental choices, which will affect their interactions. As a result, children usually choose people with whom they are comfortable and situations they perceive to be nonthreatening.

Conflict resolution

A child's ability to resolve conflicts with his or her peers strongly influences his or her acceptance into or rejection from the group. Learning to deal with conflict in a positive manner is critical to developing healthy friendships and has a huge impact on social acceptance. Elementary school children with self-control are better able to find solutions that consider both sides in a dispute, which is the way conflicts should be resolved.

Social acceptance in elementary school is a fairly accurate predictor of how successful a person will be in college and in his or her professional life. Researchers followed two groups of 8-year-olds into their mid-40s. People whose peers rated their social behavior acceptable in elementary school were more successful than those who had social difficulties. A compelling reason to deal with aggressive behavior early in life is that, if left unchecked, it can have serious academic and professional consequences later in life.

Child-centered kindergarten environment

One critical factor to remember is that 5-year-olds learn differently than older children. The physical space and the teacher's approach to instruction should reflect the unique learning requirements of the kindergarten student. Five–year-olds need an environment that grows and changes as they acquire new skills; a curriculum that addresses their physical, social, emotional, and intellectual development; provides lots of different hands-on activities and materials that encourage active participation; and views play as fundamental to their development. Kindergartners' experiences should include opportunities to try new ideas and concepts as well as introduce and celebrate multicultural differences. The physical area should be inviting, colorful, easy to navigate, and encourage interaction. The room should be arranged from the child's viewpoint, with large and small spaces designed for different activities; all areas should be visible to the teacher. Parental involvement should be strongly encouraged, from helping in the classroom to asking about the kindergartner's day.

Child-centered elementary school environment

Elementary school children between the ages of six and nine have progressed beyond learning just through play, although play remains essential to their development. From first grade through fifth grade, children are honing their problem-solving skills and improving their ability to listen, follow instructions and make friends. A child-centered elementary school environment provides students with an active atmosphere and a curriculum that focuses on themes built on topics in which they are interested. When the child feels his or her needs and interests are considered, he or she is more cooperative, happier, less competitive, and involved in fewer conflicts at school and at home. The motivation behind a child-centered learning environment is that children learn by doing as well as by exploring their world in their time and in their way. When the elements that encourage this active learning are present, children's natural curiosity is aroused, and knowledge is acquired.

Practice Test

Literacy and English Language Arts

Multiple choice

1. At what age do children normally demonstrate a speech pattern that is 90% intelligible?
    a. Two years
    b. Three years
    c. Four years
    d. Five years

2. Which of the following genres is most important for children just beginning to become readers in grades K, 1, and 2?
    a. Alphabet books, wordless picture books, and easy-to-read books
    b. Legends and tall tales
    c. Biographies and informational books
    d. Chapter books and fantasy books

3. The statement, "He ran as fast as a startled rabbit," is an example of
    a. Analogy
    b. Metaphor
    c. Symbolism
    d. Repetition

4. Which of the following is NOT a goal of children's literature?
    a. Focus on choices, morals, and values
    b. Instruct students through entertaining stories
    c. Promote an interest in reading itself
    d. Instruct students in the sciences, such as mathematics and biology

5. Young children are more likely to respond to analogies in stories than to metaphors because
    a. They are old enough to understand the abstract thinking and symbolism that analogies express
    b. The ability to understand the kinds of abstraction expressed in metaphors is not developed until later in childhood
    c. They can apply the concepts expressed in analogies to their own daily lives, but metaphors do not compare things that children are familiar with
    d. Metaphors and symbols are usually found only in books that children find boring because of their abstractions

6. In which genre does the literature rely on the reader's suspension of disbelief about magical and mythical creatures?
    a. Science fiction
    b. Fantasy
    c. Action and adventure
    d. Historical fiction

7. Which of the following describes one difference between role-play writing and early writing?
    a. In role-play writing, the child writes in scribbles that are only meaningful to him or her. In early writing, the child uses real letters
    b. In early writing, the child writes in scribbles that are only meaningful to him or her. In role-play writing, the child writes in groups of words with a period at the end
    c. In role-play writing, the child writes in simple forms of language, usually the way the word sounds. In early writing, the child starts to use sight words and familiar text
    d. In early writing, the child has a sense of audience and a purpose for writing. In role-play writing, the child writes from the point of view of an imaginary character

8. A story about a young detective who solves mysteries using mental and physical skills would be classified as
    a. Action and adventure
    b. Historical fiction
    c. Horror and ghost stories
    d. Biography

9. If a child appears delayed in speech development, which of the following is the best course to follow?
    a. Take a wait-and-see approach, as there are wide variations in patterns of speech development
    b. Use in-depth evaluations and early intervention to assist the child with language delays
    c. Help the child with common developmental speech problems, such as saying "w" for "r"
    d. Have the child repeat common words and phrases after an adult pronounces them

10. One of the most important elements in children's literature that captures children's interest is
    a. Character
    b. Accuracy
    c. Information
    d. Vocabulary

11. How should the teacher best deal with an academically talented student who typically finishes work ahead of other students and tends to get into mischief while waiting for others to finish?
    a. Reprimand the student and remind him or her that his talents require setting a good example.
    b. Assign the student an appealing task related to the subject area that requires creativity, research, and/or in-depth study of the subject, such as creating a play or making a collage
    c. Permit the early finisher to have additional play time or extended recess as a reward for rapid completion of assignments
    d. Have the student tutor or help those who are not finished because they are having difficulty with the assignment

12. Which of the following genres takes an opinion and defends it?
    a. Essays
    b. Biographies
    c. Memoirs
    d. Informational texts

13. Which of the following is a developmental skill a child should have before beginning to write?
    a. Large muscle control
    b. Ability to speak coherently
    c. Small muscle control
    d. Ability to hold a pencil correctly

14. The final resolution of a fictional plot is called
    a. Exposition
    b. Rising Action
    c. Falling Action
    d. Denouement

15. When should students be taught to activate their prior knowledge?
    a. Before reading
    b. During reading
    c. After reading
    d. All of the above

16. Activity settings (Tharp and Gallimore, 1988) are aspects of the sociocultural context that affect how students learn and read. Of five activity settings, one is participant identity, or who the students are. Of the other four, which is most related to motivation?
    a. When the activity is done
    b. Why the activity is done
    c. Where the activity is done
    d. How the activity is done

17. In reading instruction, the Three Cueing Systems is one model used. Which of the following represent a valid reading strategy that is NOT a system in the Three Cueing Systems model?
    a. Syntactic cues
    b. Pragmatic cues
    c. Semantic cues
    d. Phonological cues

18. The English word "salary" has a 2,000-year-old etymology to a word meaning...
    a. Salt.
    b. Celery.
    c. Money.
    d. Earnings.

19. Which of the following is NOT a prewriting strategy?
    a. Brainstorming
    b. Visual mapping of ideas
    c. Asking questions
    d. Organizing writing into paragraphs

20. Maria's topic sentence is "My family prepares for holidays in a big way." Which of the following would be the best supporting detail to follow that sentence?
    a. Holidays are just a waste of everyone's time and money
    b. First, we decide who is going to host the holiday dinner
    c. In my family are me, my brother, my sister, and our parents
    d. Afterwards we all help clean up and then relax

21. We are familiar with the modern English meanings of the word "disaster." But in the 16th century, this word meant...
    a. Catastrophe.
    b. Star-crossed.
    c. A misfortune.
    d. Unflowerlike.

22. Students should learn to write for a variety of audiences because
    a. Writing everything just for the teacher is boring
    b. Their classmates are also a potential audience
    c. Students are more involved in their writing if the audience varies
    d. Students can make political statements with letters to the editor

23. Which of the following would you expect children in grades k–2 to learn by being exposed to both fictional and nonfictional literature?
    a. How to tell fiction from nonfiction
    b. How to do research to find information
    c. How to tell if a nonfiction writer is writing from a biased viewpoint
    d. How to understand themes, theories, and settings

24. A patient dies in surgery and the reporting doctor describes the death as a "negative patient outcome." This is *best* identified as an example of...
    a. Jargon.
    b. Ambiguity.
    c. Euphemism.
    d. Connotation.

25. Which of the following should not be capitalized?
    a. State names
    b. Small words like "of" in titles
    c. Proper names
    d. Main words in titles of written work

26. Elena wrote the following paragraph:
I believe that everyone should try to care for our planet. The best ways to do this are through recycling and using natural energy instead of fossil fuels. The supply of fossil fuels such as oil and coal will be used up some day, so we should try now to use less. Solar panels can reduce the use of fossil fuels. Windmills can be used to make electricity. Hybrid cars also use less fuel. If we do not try to be "green," our planet will soon be in trouble from global warming and the absence of fossil fuels. What kind of world would that be?

The purpose of Elena's paragraph was
    a. Narration
    b. Entertainment
    c. Persuasion
    d. Description

27. Which of the following is an example of a portmanteau?
    a. Fax
    b. Brunch
    c. Babysitter
    d. Saxophone

28. Which of the following is not a method of peer editing?
    a. Pairs of students analyze each others' sentences for variety
    b. Groups of students ask questions of the author to make the writing more clear
    c. Students work together to perform a final edit
    d. Students decide whether another student's essay is good writing or poor writing

29. What is the best way for a teacher to make sure that books in the classroom are at an appropriate reading level, neither too easy nor so difficult that beginning readers will become frustrated?
    a. Administer a reading pretest to the class before selecting suitable books
    b. Purchase books that are easy enough for even the most beginning of readers
    c. Make sure that all the books are just slightly above students' reading level, so they will grow
    d. Provide a wide variety of reading materials for children to choose from

30. Assonance means that two or more words
    a. Start with the same sound
    b. End with the same sound
    c. Have the same vowel sound
    d. Sound like an item they portray

31. Of the following sentences, which one appeals to emotion?
    a. It is dangerous to use a cell phone while driving because you steer one-handed.
    b. Statistics of accident risk show that cell-phone use while driving is dangerous.
    c. It is really stupid to use a cell phone when you drive because it is so dangerous.
    d. Many state laws ban cell-phone use when driving due to data on more accidents.

32. The adaptation of language in a piece of writing to meet the author's purpose or audience is called
    a. Theme
    b. Point of view
    c. Style
    d. Voice

33. The English language word "quark" is an example of the result of which linguistic process?
    a. Blending
    b. Conversion
    c. Neologisms
    d. Onomatopoeia

34. The perspective from which a story is told is called
    a. Theme
    b. Point of view
    c. Style
    d. Voice

35. A distinguishing feature of the form known as haiku is…
    a. 5/7/5 syllables per line
    b. An ABA rhyme scheme
    c. Perfectly regular meter
    d. Lengthy epic narratives

36. In Mr. Booker's first grade classroom, students are studying marine animals in science. Mr. Booker wants to select a book to read to the class that will enhance their understanding of this subject while at the same time capturing their interest in a story. Which of the following would be the best choice?
    a. *The Wild Whale Watch*, part of the Magic School bus series, a chapter book about whales
    b. *The Whale Watchers Guide*, a book designed to help plan a whale-watching trip
    c. *Moby Dick*, a famous 19th century novel about a man and a white whale
    d. *The Pacific Ocean*, a book describing the ocean floor, tides, wave formation, and currents

37. When students compare nonfiction literature to fictional literature, what differences will they find?
    a. Nonfiction stories will be told in logical order and will relate only the facts, while fictional stories are never told in logical order
    b. Fictional stories deal with plot, characters, setting, and themes, and nonfiction does not
    c. In addition to plot, character, setting, and theme, a nonfiction work will also introduce interpretations, theory, and research
    d. Students will find few, if any, differences between these two types of literature because they are essentially the same

38. A child using the prewriting strategy called "free writing" will
    a. Make a list of all ideas connected with the chosen topic
    b. Create a visual map on paper to connect ideas
    c. Ask the questions "Who?," "What?," "When?," and "Where?"
    d. Write thoughts and ideas without stopping to edit them

39. In selecting literature for children, the most important first step a teacher should perform is to evaluate
    a. Whether the characters are interesting
    b. Whether the plots are appealing
    c. Class composition and preferences
    d. The reading level of the material

40. The basics of writing to a particular audience do NOT include
    a. Precise vocabulary
    b. Correct facts
    c. Figurative language
    d. Illustrations or examples

Constructed response

400-600 word response
In this constructed response activity, you will be presented with a sample of a student's response to an assignment. You must respond by identifying a student's noteworthy strengths and their weaknesses, presenting evidence of each. Then, you must describe how you would provide an instructional intervention which builds from the student's strength to address the student's needs. Then explain how your intervention will be effective in meeting the student's needs. Your response should be between 400 and 600 words.

Exhibit 1: Lesson goal
Mrs. Harris, a 2nd-grade teacher is assessing Charlie's reading comprehension of a story that he reads fluently and accurately by having Charlie retell the story in his own words. The goal of this activity is to assess and improve on reading comprehension and paraphrasing ability.

Exhibit 2: Reading material
    Bobby is at the park. He plays a new game. A boy tells him how to play the game. First, Bobby has to run as fast as she can. He likes to run. When he runs fast, he feels like he is flying.
    Next, the boy says, "Red light!" Bobby has to stop. He must stand very still. Then the boy says, "Green light!" Now, Bobby can run again. He runs fast. Bobby likes the new game. He wants to play it with his friend Jimmy at school.

Exhibit 3: Conversation transcript
Teacher: Can you tell me what you were reading about?

Charlie: It's a story about some boys. One boy is named Bobby. He doesn't know how to cross the street.

Teacher: How do you know that Bobby needs to learn about crossing the street?

Charlie: Because he doesn't even know about red lights and green lights. How red is for stop and green is for go. I think he's a little kid.

Teacher: What happens to Bobby in this story?

Charlie: This other boy bosses him around. Bobby wants to pretend he is flying. The other boy makes him stop. He yells, "Red light!" and then Bobby stops. I think the other boy tells him about the street when the cars stop. So, he learns about it.

Teacher: What else do you think Bobby will do?

Charlie: Maybe he'll tell the boy to stop bossing him around.

Response
Provide a response between 400 and 600 words on a separate piece of paper.

Mathematics

Multiple Choice

1. What linear equation includes the data in the table below?

X	Y
−3	1
1	−11
3	−17
5	−23
9	−35

    a. $y = -3x - 11$
    b. $y = -6x - 8$
    c. $y = -3x - 8$
    d. $y = -12x - 11$

2. Geometric figures can be classified by
    a. The number of sides
    b. The angles where sides meet
    c. Whether they are polygons or solids
    d. All of the above

3. A dress is marked down by 20% and placed on a clearance rack, on which is posted a sign reading, "Take an extra 25% off already reduced merchandise." What fraction of the original price is the final sales price of the dress?
    a. $\frac{9}{20}$
    b. $\frac{11}{20}$
    c. $\frac{2}{5}$
    d. $\frac{3}{5}$

4. Mrs. Vories, a fifth grade teacher, asks her class to use compatible numbers to help her determine approximately how many chicken nuggets she needs to buy for a school-wide party. The school has 589 students and each student will be served nine nuggets. Which student correctly applied the concept of compatible numbers?
    a. Madison estimates: $500 \times 10 = 5,000$ nuggets
    b. Audrey estimates: $600 \times 5 = 3,000$ nuggets
    c. Ian estimates: $600 \times 10 = 6,000$ nuggets
    d. Andrew estimates: $500 \times 5 = 2,500$ nuggets

5. A number system in which the position of a digit in a number determines its value is called a
    a. Relationship system
    b. Place value system
    c. Regrouping system
    d. Tens and hundreds system

6. For three days, Mr. Hanson had his students keep track of how many times each of them used a pencil during the school day. What is the best kind of graph to use to display these data?
   a. Bar graph
   b. Circle graph
   c. Pictograph
   d. Line graph

7. Paper strips and Cuisenaire rods are manipulatives used to teach
   a. Place value
   b. Fractions
   c. Addition of whole numbers
   d. Percents

8. Which of the following is the correct solution for x in the system of equations $x - 1 = y$ and $y + 3 = 7$?
   a. $x = 6$
   b. $x = 5$
   c. $x = 4$
   d. $x = 8$

9. John drew two triangles on a piece of paper, like this:

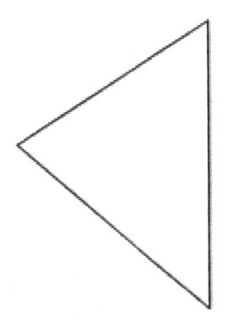

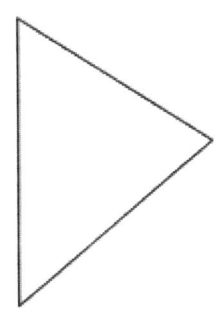

They were facing away from each other, but had the exact same size and shape. This is best described as an example of which geometrical concept?
   a. Rotation
   b. Reflection
   c. Translation
   d. Magnification

10. The table below shows the average amount of rainfall Houston receives during the summer and autumn months.

Month	Amount of Rainfall (in inches)
June	5.35
July	3.18
August	3.83
September	4.33
October	4.5
November	4.19

What percentage of rainfall received during this timeframe, is received during the month of October?
    a. 13.5%
    b. 15.1%
    c. 16.9%
    d. 17.7%

11. Amy saves $450 every 3 months. How much does she save after 3 years?
    a. $4,800
    b. $5,200
    c. $5,400
    d. $5,800

12. A decimal can be converted to a percent by
    a. Moving the decimal point two places to the right
    b. Dividing by 100
    c. Doubling the number
    d. Moving the decimal point one place to the left

13. The 6th grade teachers at Washington Elementary School are doing a collaborative unit on cherry trees. Miss Wilson's math classes are making histograms summarizing the heights of black cherry trees located at a local fruit orchard. How many of the trees at this local orchard are 73 feet tall?

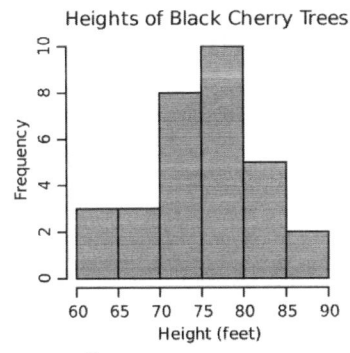

Heights of Black Cherry Trees

   a. 8
   b. That information cannot be obtained from this graph.
   c. 9
   d. 17

14. A third-grade teacher decides to introduce new vocabulary words using a word association game. What is required in order for the students to succeed with word associations?
   a. The definition of the new words.
   b. Prior knowledge.
   c. The spelling of the word.
   d. Synonyms of the new words.

15. Which of the following is an example of an ordinal number?
   a. 13
   b. One-half
   c. Second
   d. Ten

16. Which of the following formulas may be used to represent the sequence 8, 13, 18, 23, 28, …?
   a. $a_n = 5n + 3$
   b. $a_n = n + 5$
   c. $a_n = n + 8$
   d. $a_n = 5n + 8$

17. When deciding to measure the sides of a two-dimensional object, what attributes of that object should be considered?
   a. Volume and liquid measurement
   b. Length and width
   c. Weight and mass
   d. Perimeter and area

18. The ratio of employee wages and benefits to all other operational costs of a business is 2:3. If a business's total operating expenses are $130,000 per month, how much money does the company spend on employee wages and benefits?
   a. $43,333.33
   b. $86,666.67
   c. $52,000.00
   d. $78,000.00

19. Given that x is a prime number and that the greatest common factor of x and y is greater than 1, compare the two quantities.

   Quantity A | Quantity B
   y | the least common multiple of x and y

   a. Quantity A is greater.
   b. Quantity B is greater.
   c. The two quantities are the same.
   d. The relationship cannot be determined from the given information.

20. By rewriting 5 times 9 as 9 + 9 +9 + 9 + 9, students will learn
   a. The commutative property of numbers
   b. The relationship between multiplication and addition
   c. The relationship between addition and division
   d. The associative property of numbers

21. A 6th grade math teacher is introducing the concept of positive and negative numbers to a group of students. Which of the following models would be the most effective when introducing this concept?
   a. Fraction strips
   b. Venn diagrams
   c. Shaded regions
   d. Number lines

22. A missing object problem like the one below is one way of helping students learn what concept?
Truck car bike train truck car bike _____ truck car bike train
   a. Counting
   b. Problem solving
   c. Manipulation of objects
   d. Basic addition

23. What is the slope of the leg marked x in the triangle graphed below?

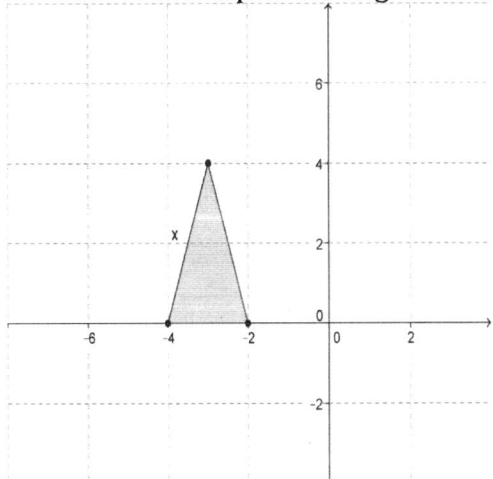

a. 2
b. 3.5
c. 4
d. 4.5

24. What is the educational purpose of having students measure the length of an object, such as their desk or table, with non-standard measuring units smaller than the object, such as crayons?
   a. Measuring with small units is easier for young children
   b. Children cannot read the markings on a standard ruler or yard stick
   c. Students learn to measure something larger than a unit with repetitive use of that unit
   d. Students will later be able to transfer measurements from meters to yards

25. The property of numbers that states that 1 + 3 is the same as 3 + 1 is called
   a. Associative
   b. Distributive
   c. Inverse
   d. Commutative

26. Tom needs to buy ink cartridges and printer paper. Each ink cartridge costs $30. Each ream of paper costs $5. He has $100 to spend. Which of the following inequalities may be used to find the combinations of ink cartridges and printer paper that he may purchase?
   a. $30c + 5p \leq 100$
   b. $30c + 5p < 100$
   c. $30c + 5p > 100$
   d. $30c + 5p \geq 100$

27. Solve $\frac{x-2}{x-1} = \frac{x-1}{x+1} + \frac{2}{x-1}$.
   a. $x = 2$
   b. $x = -5$
   c. $x = 1$
   d. No solution

28. Elementary teachers in one school surveyed their students and discovered that 15% of their students have iPhones. Which of the following correctly states 15% in fraction, decimal, and ratio equivalents?

 a. $\frac{3}{20}$, 0.15, 3:20
 b. $\frac{3}{25}$, 0.15, 3:25
 c. $\frac{15}{10}$, 1.5%, 15:10
 d. $\frac{2}{1}$, 1.5%, 2:1

29. Hannah spends at least $16 on 4 packages of coffee. Which of the following inequalities represents the possible costs?

 a. $16 \geq 4p$
 b. $16 < 4p$
 c. $16 > 4p$
 d. $16 \leq 4p$

30. What is the area of the shaded region in the figure shown below?

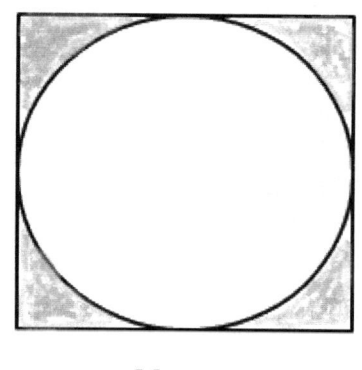

30 cm

30 cm

 a. 177 cm²
 b. 181 cm²
 c. 187 cm²
 d. 193 cm²

31. Given this stem and leaf plot, what are the mean and median?

Stem	Leaf
1	6 8
2	0 1
3	4
4	5 9

 a. Mean = 28 and median = 20
 b. Mean = 29 and median = 20
 c. Mean = 29 and median = 21
 d. Mean = 28 and median = 21

32. Katrina wanted to solve this math problem: "If there are 30 days in a month and today is the 12th, how many days until the end of the month?" What should be her first problem-solving step?
   a. Devise a plan for solving the problem
   b. Carry out the plan she created
   c. Look back to check that her answer is correct
   d. Understand what the problem is asking

33. Which of the following is NOT a model that helps students understand subtraction?
   a. Take away
   b. Missing addend
   c. Number line
   d. Adding zero

34. What is the perimeter of the trapezoid graphed below?

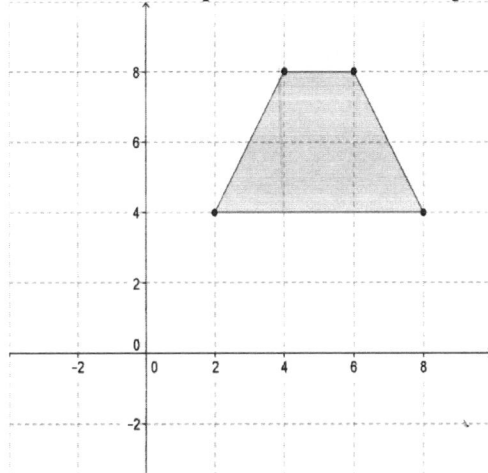

   a. $4 + \sqrt{10}$
   b. $8 + 4\sqrt{5}$
   c. $4 + 2\sqrt{5}$
   d. $8 + 2\sqrt{22}$

35. Sophia is at the market buying fruit for her family of four. Kiwi fruit is only sold in packages of three. If Sophia would like each family member to have the same number of kiwi fruits, which of the following approaches can Sophia use to determine the fewest number of kiwi fruits she should buy?
   a. Sophia needs to determine the greatest common multiple of 3 and 4.
   b. Sophia needs to determine the least common multiple of 3 and 4.
   c. Sophia needs to determine the least common divisor of 3 and 4.
   d. Sophia needs to determine the greatest common divisor of 3 and 4.

36. If a, b, and c are even integers and $3a^2 + 9b^3 = c$, which of these is the largest number which must be factor of c?
   a. 2
   b. 3
   c. 6
   d. 12

37. Elijah pays a $30 park entrance fee, plus $4 for every ticket purchased. Which of the following equations represents the cost?
   a. y = 30x + 4
   b. y = 34x
   c. y = 4x + 30
   d. y = 34x + 30

38. Which of these is **NOT** a net of a cube?

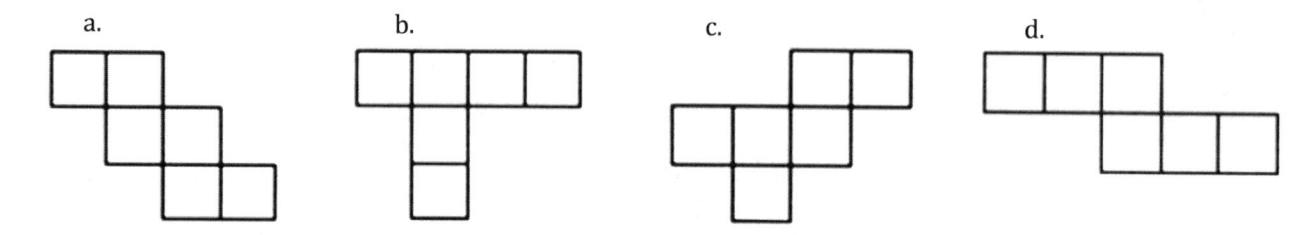

   a.　　　　　　　b.　　　　　　　c.　　　　　　　d.

39. Which of these tables properly displays the measures of central tendency which can be used for nominal, interval, and ordinal data?

   a.

	Mean	Median	Mode
Nominal			x
Interval	x	x	x
Ordinal		x	x

   b.

	Mean	Median	Mode
Nominal			x
Interval	x	x	x
Ordinal	x	x	x

   c.

	Mean	Median	Mode
Nominal	x	x	x
Interval	x	x	x
Ordinal	x	x	x

   d.

	Mean	Median	Mode
Nominal			x
Interval	x	x	
Ordinal	x	x	x

40. Which of the following is NOT a way to teach young children to recognize patterns?
   a. Count by twos beginning with 5
   b. Comparing geometric shapes
   c. Solving for x in an equation
   d. Analyzing the results of a class survey

Constructed response

400-600 word response
In this constructed response activity, you will be presented with a sample of a student's response to an assignment. You must respond by identifying a student's noteworthy strengths and their weaknesses, presenting evidence of each. Then, you must describe how you would provide an instructional intervention which builds from the student's strength to address the student's needs. Then explain how your intervention will be effective in meeting the student's needs. Your response should be between 400 and 600 words.

Exhibit 1: Background information and description of class activity
Mr. Romero recently taught a lesson on simple fractions to his second grade class. This was demonstrated by breaking a chocolate bar into fourths and by drawing the chocolate bar on the board and showing how two halves and one whole are the same. The lesson progressed into demonstrating fractions of halves, thirds, fourths, and fifths. Students were then given small round candies and were required to arrange their candies to correspond with written fractions. The students were also given Popsicle sticks to help separate out their candies into the proper groupings

Exhibit 2: Calvin's work
Key: On this assignment, students are to arrange their candies into groups based on denominator. They then would draw circles and lines representing their candies. The students would then color in those which represent the numerator.

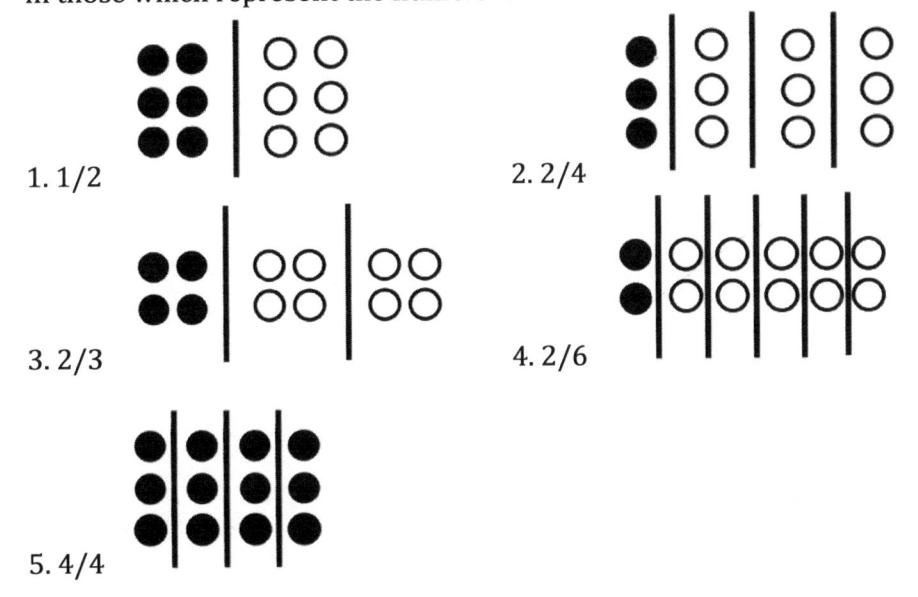

1. 1/2

2. 2/4

3. 2/3

4. 2/6

5. 4/4

Response
Provide a response between 400 and 600 words on a separate piece of paper.

Arts and Sciences

1. What steps should precede drawing a conclusion about a hypothesis?
    a. Testing, observing, and recording data
    b. Communicating the hypothesis to others
    c. Comparing data with data of other groups
    d. Writing the results so they can be replicated

2. The density of a material refers to:
    a. Mass per volume
    b. Mass per mole
    c. Molecular weight per volume
    d. Moles per volume

3. What is the difference between mass and weight?
    a. There is no difference; they are the same
    b. Mass is the amount of matter in an object; weight is the pull of gravity on the object
    c. Mass determines the amount of volume of an object; weight does not
    d. Mass is the amount of cubic space that an object occupies. Cubic space is not related to weight

4. Which of these refers to the oceans and water areas of earth?
    a. Atmosphere
    b. Hydrosphere
    c. Exosphere
    d. Lithosphere

5. What is a practical purpose for the glass walls of skyscrapers?
    a. Decoration
    b. Insulation
    c. Privacy
    d. Support

6. What effect does science have on technology?
    a. Science verifies what technology discovers
    b. Technology often results from scientific discoveries
    c. Science has no effect on technology; each is independent of the other
    d. Scientific progress is dependent on technology

7. Repetition is important to scientific inquiry because
    a. It is the only way to prove that an experiment is valid
    b. It adds to the number of statistics supporting the concept
    c. It assists the scientist in determining which data to consider
    d. It requires many groups of investigators working on a project

8. Which of the following statements is true about the physical properties of liquids and gases?
    I. Liquids and gases are both compressible
    II. Liquids flow, but gases do not
    III. Liquids flow and gases are incompressible
    IV. Liquids flow and gases are compressible
    V. Gases flow and liquids are incompressible
   a. I and III
   b. II and IV
   c. III and V
   d. IV and V

9. Which of the following explains why less force is required to throw a tennis ball a certain distance than a shot put?
   a. The shot put must overcome inertia.
   b. The tennis ball has more potential energy.
   c. The shot put has greater mass.
   d. The tennis ball requires horizontal projection.

10. World weather patterns are very much influenced by
    a. Wind belts
    b. The Earth's orbit
    c. Ocean currents
    d. Atmospheric conditions

11. In the technological design process, after the problem has been identified and a possible solution selected, what is the next step?
    a. Propose designs
    b. Evaluate the solution
    c. Try out the proposed solution
    d. Report results

12. When deciding to measure the sides of a two-dimensional object, what attributes of that object should be considered?
    a. Volume and liquid measurement
    b. Length and width
    c. Weight and mass
    d. Perimeter and area

13. Students are planning to assemble and operate a small gasoline engine. Which safety concern should have the highest priority?
    a. An open fuel tank could release sickening fumes.
    b. Fingers could be injured if caught in the gears.
    c. Spilled liquids may cause a short in the starter.
    d. The exhaust fumes require adequate ventilation.

14. Adding a catalyst to a reaction will do which of the following to that reaction:
    a. Shift the reaction equilibrium towards the products
    b. Increase the temperature of the reaction
    c. Decrease the energy of activation for the reaction
    d. Increase the purity of the reaction products

15. A space station is revolving in a circular orbit around Earth. Consider the following three statements:

   I. The center of mass of the space station is necessarily located at its geometric center.
   II. The center of mass is moving at a constant velocity.
   III. The center of mass of the space station is moving at a constant speed.

Which of the following statements is true?
   a. I is true.
   b. II is true.
   c. III is true.
   d. I, II, and III are not true.

16. Which of the following are required by all organisms in order to survive?
   a. Water, cells, shelter, and space
   b. Food, water, cellular growth, nurturing
   c. Food, water, sunlight, and air
   d. Air, shelter, space, and companionship

17. The results of increased production of crops and a managed approach to agriculture is called
   a. The industrial revolution
   b. The information revolution
   c. The agricultural revolution
   d. The scientific revolution

18. Which map describes the movement of people, trends, or materials across a physical area?
   a. Political Map
   b. Cartogram
   c. Qualitative Map
   d. Flow-line Map

19. It is snack time in your kindergarten class, and you pour two children equal amounts of water; however, one child's cup is bigger. The child with the bigger cup complains that he has less water. In terms of cognitive development, what can you determine by this complaint?
   a. The child has a developmental delay because he does not understand conservation.
   b. The child has not reached the concrete operational stage and does not understand conservation; this is normal for a child of this age.
   c. The child is displaying a delay in intuitive processes commonly acquired during the pre-operational stage of cognitive development.
   d. The child is displaying a preconceptual process that is common among this age group.

20. Ivy loses her job because her skills as a seamstress are no longer required due to a new piece of machinery that does the work of a seamstress more quickly and for less money. Which type of unemployment is this?
   a. Frictional
   b. Structural
   c. Cyclical
   d. Careless

21. Due process means
    a. It's important for every citizen to follow the laws of their state and country
    b Any accused person may confront the accuser and provide a defense
    c. Capital punishment is appropriate if a person is convicted of murder
    d. An accused person is considered guilty until proven to be innocent

22. Which type of chart is best at representing the cycle of demographic transition?
    a. Pie chart
    b. Political map
    c. Line graph
    d. Flow-line map

23. Which of the following was *not* an immediate effect of rapid urban growth in the 1800s?
    a. Poor sanitation conditions in the cities
    b. Epidemics of diseases in the cities
    c. Inadequate police and fire protection
    d. Widespread urban political corruption

24. Which of the following are not included in a geographical definition of Southeast Asia?
    a. Myanmar, Laos, Cambodia, and Thailand
    b. Vietnam, the Malay Peninsula, and Brunei
    c. East Malaysia, Indonesia, and the Philippines
    d. These are all geographical parts of Southeast Asia

25. Social and behavioral theories of learning stress the importance of
    a. Good behavior on the part of students
    b. The social interactions of students that aid or inhibit learning
    c. A reward system for good behavior or growth in skills
    d. The direct connection between thoughts and speech

26. Inflation has what effects?
    a. Harms all members of an economy
    b. Helps all members of an economy
    c. Harms no members of an economy
    d. Harms some members of an economy, helps others

27. In the Constitution of the United States, which of the following powers are reserved for the states?
    a. Taxation
    b. Declaring war
    c. Regulation of intrastate trade
    d. Granting patents and copyrights

28. On a map of Africa, there is a small box around Nairobi. This city is depicted in greater detail in a box at the bottom of the map. What is the name for this box at the bottom of the map?
    a. Inset
    b. Legend
    c. Compass Rose
    d. Key

29. Which of the following choices is/are *not* considered among causes of the French Revolution?
    a. Famines causing malnutrition and starvation
    b. War debt, Court spending, bad monetary system
    c. Resentment against the Catholic Church's rule
    d. Resentment against the Protestant Reformation

30. What is the most common type of volcano on earth?
    a. Lava dome
    b. Composite volcano
    c. Shield volcano
    d. Cinder cone

31. Which of the following is an important aspect of allowing and encouraging children's play?
    a. Children need frequent opportunities to rest and relax
    b. Play teaches children cooperation and sharing
    c. Play encourages competition and opposition
    d. Play time gives the teacher a much needed rest period

32. Which of the following best defines American GDP?
    a. The value, in American dollars, of all goods and services produced within American borders during one calendar year
    b. The value, in American dollars, of all goods and services produced by American companies during one calendar year
    c. The total value, in American dollars, of all American household incomes during one calendar year
    d. The value, in American dollars, of a "market basket" of goods and services in one year divided by the value of the same market basket in a previous year multiplied by 100

33. Which of the following is not one of the primary elements of art?
    a. Dimension
    b. Unity
    c. Texture
    d. Space

34. When encountering a difficult passage, how do musicians most effectively practice that passage?
    a. Playing it as fast as possible
    b. Studying it away from the instrument
    c. Playing it slowly and thoughtfully
    d. Playing the sections before and after

35. To ensure maximum dramatic effect, a director places actors onstage precisely where he wants them. What is this called?
    a. Positioning
    b. Staging
    c. Choreography
    d. Blocking

36. Which of these facts about smoking is LEAST likely to discourage a 14-year-old boy from taking up the habit?
    a. Smokers are ten times more likely to die of lung cancer than nonsmokers.
    b. Smoking is a very expensive habit.
    c. Many girls won't date a boy who smokes.
    d. Smoking can seriously impair athletic performance.

37. Which of the following kinds of activities are BEST suited for developing perceptual-motor skills in adolescents?
    a. one-step physical activities to build foundational skills
    b. fun physical activities that consist of identifiable steps
    c. any physical activities at all, as long as they are fun
    d. any activities that involve hearing, seeing, or touching

38. According to Kohlberg, at which developmental level do children understand that good behavior is expected?
    a. Post-Conventional
    b. Conventional
    c. Pre-Conventional
    d. Adolescent

39. Which of the following represents a discretionary expense?
    a. Textbook
    b. Rent
    c. DVD
    d. Groceries

40. What type of business is the most common employer of high-school students?
    a. Grocery stores
    b. Movie theaters
    c. Clothing stores
    d. Restaurants

Answers and Explanations

Literacy and English Language Arts

1. C: Four years. One hundred percent language development is not achieved until age five.

2. A: Alphabet books, wordless picture books, and easy-to-read books. The other genres are more suitable for older children with well-developed reading skills.

3. A: Analogy. The statement is not a metaphor because it contains the word "like." A metaphor does not. An example of a metaphor would be "He was a frozen statue, motionless beside the door." There is no symbolism in the statement, "He ran as fast as a rabbit," nor is there any repetition.

4. D: Instruct students in sciences, such as mathematics and biology. Textbooks have that goal. Children's literature is designed to enhance moral values, instruct through entertaining stories, and promote a life-long interest in reading.

5. B: The ability to understand the abstract concept expressed in metaphors is not developed until later in childhood. Analogies are easier for children to understand because they compare known items, whereas metaphors require abstract thinking.

6. B: Fantasy. Fantasy stories and books revolve around magical or supernatural creatures. The Harry Potter books are one example of this genre. Science fiction is a similar genre, but relies on the portrayal of a future world, creatures from other planets or galaxies, etc. Action and Adventure involves solving mysteries. Historical fiction stories are set sometime in the past and are usually accurate in their historical information.

7. A: In role playing writing, the child writes in scribbles that are only meaningful to him or her. In early writing, the child begins to use real letters.

8. A: Action and Adventure. One example of this genre is Nancy Drew. Action and Adventure stories do not rely on magical or supernatural events as do Fantasy, Horror, and Ghost stories. They are not biographical unless telling the life of a real person.

9. B: Use in-depth evaluation and early intervention to assist the child with language delays. Research shows that early intervention is highly successful, while a wait-and-see approach just prolongs the delayed language development. Common developmental problems like saying "w" instead of "r" disappear on their own as the child matures and do not need intervention.

10. A: Characters. Children enjoy identifying with a character and experiencing life from that character's point of view. If readers do not bond with a character, they will not enjoy the story.

11. B: Assign the student an appealing task related to the subject area that requires creativity, research, or in-depth study, such as making a collage or creating a play. Assigning the student to tutor classmates does not assist in the intellectual growth of an academically talented student, and the student is apt to resent such an assignment. The teacher needs to be aware that academically

talented students also have special academic needs and continue to challenge them with meaningful assignments.

12. A: Essays. In an essay, the writer defends an opinion, giving reasons for that opinion. Biographies are written to narrate the life of a person. Memoirs detail a person's own life and do not defend opinions. Informational texts are factual.

13. C: Small muscle control. Small muscles are those that enable us to make precise motions, such as gripping a pencil and writing letters with it. Large muscle control involves activities such as running or jumping. The ability to speak is not a developmental skill leading to the ability to write.

14. D: Denouement. The denouement is the end of the story. The other choices are intermediate steps in writing a story.

15. D: Reading instructors should teach students to activate their prior knowledge because it will improve their reading comprehension. Before reading (A), teachers should discuss and model connections with existing knowledge to prepare students by helping them consider what they already know about the subject of the text. While they read (B), students can make better sense of the text by considering how it fits with what they already know. After reading (C), teachers can lead discussions helping students focus on how the connections they made between the text and their previous knowledge informed their understanding of the text, and on how the text helped them build on their foundations of existing knowledge.

16. B: Why the students participate in a reading/learning activity refers to the motivation for the activity. Option A refers to the timing of the reading/learning activity. Option C refers to the place or physical setting of the learning activity. Option D refers to the way(s) in which the learning activity is defined and executed. All of these activity settings are factors that influence learning differently according to the different cultural, social, and economic factors involved in each specific situation.

17. B: Pragmatics is the study of how language is used socially for communication. In reading instruction, pragmatic cues relate to the reader's purposes for reading and the reader's understanding of the workings of textual structures. Although pragmatic cues are valid and important, the Three Cueing Systems model does not include a pragmatic "system." The three cueing systems named in this theory are the phonological system of sound cues (D), the Semantic system of meaning cues (C), and the Syntactic system of sentence-structure cues (A).

18. A: The Latin word *sal* meant "salt." According to the famous ancient historian Pliny the Elder, "in Rome, a soldier was paid in salt," as it was a means of preserving food in the days before refrigeration and was thus a very valuable commodity. The Latin term *salarium*, from the root *sal*, originally meant the salt paid to soldiers but eventually became generalized to mean any kind of payment. (The expression "worth your salt" also derives from this origin.) "Salary" may sound similar to "celery" (B), but their roots and meanings are not the same. While salt eventually referred to any kind of payment including money or other kinds, it never originally meant *money* (C). "Earnings" (D) is a Modern English synonym for "salary" rather than the original meaning of its root word.

19. D: Organizing writing into paragraphs is done either during the writing process or afterwards in the revision stage. It is not a prewriting strategy.

20. B: "First we decide who is going to host the holiday dinner." A clue is found in the word "first." A list of actions or ideas often follows a topic sentence.

21. B: In Old Italian, the word *disastro* meant unfavorable in one's stars. It was commonplace to attribute bad fortune to the influences of the stars in the Medieval and Renaissance eras. The Old Italian word came into English in the late 1500s as "disaster" and was used by Shakespeare (cf. *King Lear*). The word's Latin root is *astrum*, meaning "star," and the Latin prefix *dis-*, meaning "apart" and signifying negation. *Catastrophe* (A) and *misfortune* (C) are both Modern English meanings of the word "disaster," whereas the "ill-starred" meaning used in Elizabethan times has now become archaic or obsolete. The root means "star," not the aster flower (D).

22. C: Students are more involved in their writing if the audience varies. Examples of varied audiences include letters to the editor, letters to a friend, an essay written for a community group, and a story written for younger children or beginning readers.

23. A: How to tell fiction from nonfiction. This is a skill that children learn by following clues within the literature that point out whether the story is true or not. Young children are not yet ready to distinguish bias in an author's writing or understand themes and theories.

24. C: A euphemism is an expression used instead of more literal words to make a harsh expression sound softer, to make an impolite description sound more polite, or to make a description less polite (such as saying "bit the dust" instead of "died" in a formal setting). Jargon (A) is the specialized terminology of a specific field or group. This example, however, is NOT medical jargon; a better example might be "expired" or "deceased." Ambiguity (B) means unclear and/or open to multiple interpretations. A better example of ambiguity in this scenario might be, "The surgery did not obtain all of the desired outcomes." This can mean a greater number of things than that the patient died. A connotation (D) is a suggested meaning associated with the literal meaning of a word. For example, "The surgery was abortive" does not state that the patient died, but if the surgery was meant to save the patient's life, the adjective "abortive," meaning unsuccessful or failing to obtain the desired result, could connote that the patient died.

25. B: Small words in titles like "the" and "of." State names, proper names, and main words in titles should all be capitalized.

26. C: Persuasion. Elena's paragraph was written to persuade. Clues to her purpose can be found in the first and last sentences, which clearly try to influence the reader.

27. B: The word "brunch" is a blend of "breakfast" and "lunch". Blends of two or more words are known as portmanteau words. (*Portmanteau* is a French word meaning a suitcase.) "Fax" (A) is an example of clipping, or shortening a word, from its original "facsimile." "Babysitter" (C) is an example of compounding, or combining two or more words into one. "Saxophone" (D) is an example of proper noun transfer: A Belgian family that built musical instruments had the last name of Sax, and this wind instrument was named after them. These represent some of the ways that new words have entered—and still do enter—the English language.

28. D: Students decide whether another student's essay is good writing or poor writing. Peer editing should consist of suggestions for improvement and never involve judgmental decisions about quality.

29. D: Provide a wide variety of reading materials for children to choose from. Each classroom will have students who are just beginning to read and some that are reading fluently above grade level. Providing reading materials with an appealing variety of subject matter and broad distribution of reading levels will ensure that every child in the class can select an appropriate book to read.

30. C: Have the same vowel sound. Words with assonance have the same vowel sound. An example would be cow and loud.

31. C: This sentence appeals to the reader's emotions by stating simply that it is dangerous and "really stupid" to use a cell phone while driving; it does not provide any evidence or logic to support the statement. Choice A offers a logical, common-sense argument in that steering one-handed makes driving more dangerous. Choice B refers to statistics of greater accident risk to support the statement that cell phone use while driving is dangerous. Such supporting evidence is an appeal to logic. Choice D cites the fact that many state laws ban cell phone use while driving to support the idea that it is dangerous, and also refers to data on more accidents from doing so. These pieces of supporting evidence also appeal to logic rather than emotion.

32. C: Style. An author writing a humorous book will use a different style than an author writing a biography.

33. C: Neologisms (from *neo-* meaning "new"), also known as "creative coinages," are new words sometimes invented by people which then become parts of our vocabulary. The word "quark" was first coined by the great Irish author James Joyce; he used it in his last novel, *Finnegans Wake*. The physicist Murray Gell-Mann then chose this word from Joyce's work to name the model of elementary particles he proposed (also proposed concurrently and independently by physicist George Zweig) in 1964. Blending (A) is another way new words come into our language; for example, "moped" is a blend of the respective first syllables of "motor" and "pedal." Conversion (B), also called functional shift, changes a word's part of speech. For example, the common nouns "network," "microwave," and "fax," along with the proper noun "Google" have all been converted to verbs in modern usage. Onomatopoeia (D) means words that imitate associated sounds, such as "meow" and "click."

34. B: Point of view. The point of view is generally first or third person. Stories in the second person exist, but these are rare.

35. A: The haiku, originating in Japanese poetry and since adopted in English-language poetry, is a short poem of only three lines, often with 17 syllables, with the first and third lines having five syllables and the second line having seven syllables. (In Japanese there are many other rules, which become very complicated.) Haiku are typically unrhymed, so they do not have a rhyme scheme (B). Similarly, they do not employ any regular meter (C). Because haiku are typically 17 syllables or fewer, they do not involve long narratives (D).

36. A: The *Wild Whale Watch*, part of the Magic School bus series, a chapter book about whales. First graders love to listen to chapter books, but most first graders are not quite able to read chapter books on their own. The undersea fictional adventures in this book will impart a great deal of marine information while simultaneously capturing students' attention with the story. The *Whale Watchers Guide* is not a good choice since the class is not planning a whale watching trip. *Moby Dick* is a well-known adult book, which first graders would not understand. *The Pacific Ocean* will probably offer a lot of marine information, but may not capture first graders' interests.

37. C: In addition to plot, character, setting, and theme, a nonfictional work will also introduce interpretations, theories, and research. For example, a biography is a type of nonfiction that may have plot, character, setting, and theme, and in addition it will introduce interpretations and theories (of the person's life and actions) as well as evidence of the author's research.

38. D: Write thoughts and ideas without stopping to edit them. Freewriting is a prewriting strategy that asks the writer to simply write without any internal editing or concern about formalities, such as spelling or punctuation. The purpose of freewriting is to get the flow of ideas going.

39. C: Class composition and preferences. Before selecting literature for the classroom, the teacher needs to assess the class, considering where they are with their reading skills and what their current interests are. After determining these things, the teacher would next evaluate books that seem appropriate for this particular group of children in terms of plot, character, and reading level.

40. B: Correct and accurate facts are not part of the basics of writing to a particular audience. Some writing for some audiences will not be factual at all, for example, a fairy tale written for young children. The basics of writing to a particular audience include precise vocabulary, figurative language, and illustrations or examples.

Sample constructed response

Charlie's response demonstrates that he is able to recognize key words and pull from his personal experiences to make some sense of the material he is reading. Charlie clearly employs a strategy of identifying and remembering specific content words and phrases, such as "red-light" and "run." These are likely sight words, which he has frequently come into contact with before. Making a meaningful connection with the words which he does know, he extrapolates that a young boy is learning about crossing a street safely. This is a great strategy which will help Charlie out when encountering new words later on.

Charlie is straightforward about having missed details. He indicates this by using the phrase "I think" in the fourth and sixth lines of the transcript. He probably does not have the reading recognition skills to easily notice words and phrases he probably knows well, but has not encountered in a written format. The phrase, "plays a new game," would have been a very good phrase for Charlie to notice to have a more full understanding of what the story was about. Charlie is good at recognizing some words and phrases but relies more on his context clues than trying to work through unknown words. In response, it would be effective to re-read the story with Charlie phrase by phrase and have him work his way through the words which he does not know. Making use of his verbal response, I would try to have Charlie point out the details for why he thinks the boys are talking about crossing the street. This helps Charlie learn to independently look for details which can help him understand. When he comes across words which he does not recognize, I would have him try to sound out and write them down for himself to improve vocabulary recognition and reading retention.

This strategy would be effective for addressing Charlie's reading comprehension weaknesses by helping him learn to identify the words he knows and the words which he does not know. Charlie is likely in a rush to finish this activity as he did not seem to put much effort into working through more difficult words. One of his biggest needs is to slow down and go through each word so that he does not miss important details later on. One way of helping him keep track would be to ask him step by step the five W questions to identify key facts before trying to come up with a solution. This strategy needs to be accompanied by praise when Charlie recognizes missed words and when he realizes where he missed the key points of the passage.

Mathematics

1. C: Using the points (−3, 1) and (1, −11), the slope may be written as $m = \frac{-11-1}{1-(-3)}$ or $m = -3$. Substituting the slope of −3 and the x- and y-values from the point (−3, 1), into the slope-intercept form of an equation gives $1 = -3(-3) + b$, which simplifies to $1 = 9 + b$. Subtracting 9 from both sides of the equation gives $b = -8$. Thus, the linear equation that includes the data in the table is $y = -3x - 8$.

2. D: All of the above. Geometric figures can be classified in a number of ways, including the number of sides, the angles where sides meet, and as polygons or solids.

3. D: When the dress is marked down by 20%, the cost of the dress is 80% of its original price; thus, the reduced price of the dress can be written as $\frac{80}{100}x$, or $\frac{4}{5}x$, where x is the original price. When discounted an extra 25%, the dress costs 75% of the reduced price, or $\frac{75}{100}\left(\frac{4}{5}x\right)$, or $\frac{3}{4}\left(\frac{4}{5}x\right)$, which simplifies to $\frac{3}{5}x$. So the final price of the dress is three-fifths of the original price.

4. C. The number 589 can be estimated to be 600. The number 9 can be estimated to be 10. The number of chicken nuggets is approximately 600 × 10, which is 6,000 nuggets. Therefore, the correct choice is C.

5. B: A place value system. That is the system that requires the position of a digit in a number to determine the digit's value. For example, in the number 123, the digit two is in ten's place, and its value is 20.

6. A: Bar graph. A bar graph is used to compare quantities. A circle is used to compare parts of a whole. A pictograph shows comparison of quantities using symbols. A line graph shows trends over a period of time.

7. B: Fractions. Students can manipulate the different lengths of materials like paper strips and Cuisenaire rods, in order to determine that one rod is one half the length of the other, for example.

8. B: The equation $y + 3 = 7$ is solved by subtracting 3 from both sides to yield $y = 4$. Substituting $y = 4$ into $x - 1 = y$ yields $x - 1 = 4$. Adding 1 to both sides of this equation yields $x = 5$. Therefore, the correct choice is B.

9. B: Reflection. One triangle faces the other. They are alike in all other ways. In a rotation, two like figures are rotated about a central point. A translation is a change in the position of a geometric figure. Magnification refers to a change in size of the figure.

10. D: The total rainfall is 25.38 inches. Thus, the ratio $\frac{4.5}{25.38}$, represents the percentage of rainfall received during October. $\frac{4.5}{25.38} \approx 0.177$ or 17.7%.

11. C: There are 36 months in 3 years. The following proportion may be written: $\frac{450}{3} = \frac{x}{36}$. The equation $3x = 16200$, may be solved for x. Dividing both sides of the equation by 3 gives $x = 5,400$.

12. A: Moving the decimal point two places to the right. For example, the decimal 3.42 stands for 342.0 percent of something.

13. B: The histogram only shows that there are eight trees between 70 and 75 feet tall. It does not show the individual heights of the trees. That information cannot be obtained from this graph. Therefore, the correct choice is B.

14. B: Word associations require a student to pull from previous knowledge or experience. For example, if the student is presented with the word "aardvark" but has never seen or heard of an The settlers had not brought enough aardvark, he or she will not be able to make associations. While word association may be a good activity for students after they have reviewed the vocabulary words, it may be counterproductive if the students are unfamiliar with the words. Teachers should also be mindful of cultural differences that may account for a variation in previous knowledge.

15. C: Second. Ordinal numbers are first, second, third, fourth, etc.

16. A: The sum of 3 and the product of each term number and 5 equals the term value. For example, for term number 4, the value of 23 is equal to $5(4) + 3$, or 23.

17. B: Length and width. Since the object is not a solid, no other dimensions are needed.

18. C: Since the ratio of wages and benefits to other costs is 2:3, the amount of money spent on wages and benefits is $\frac{2}{5}$ of the business's total expenditure. $\frac{2}{5} \cdot \$130,000 = \$52,000$.

19. C: If x is a prime number and that the greatest common factor of x and y is greater than 1, the greatest common factor of x and y must be x. The least common multiple of two numbers is equal to the product of those numbers divided by their greatest common factor. So, the least common multiple of x and y is $\frac{xy}{x} = y$. Therefore, the values in the two columns are the same.

20. B: The relationship between multiplication and addition. By performing these activities, students will see that multiplication is just the repetitive addition of a number a certain number of times.

21. D: Number lines can help students understand the concepts of positive and negative numbers. Fraction strips are most commonly used with fractions. Venn diagrams are commonly used when comparing groups. Shaded regions are commonly used with fractions or percentages. Therefore, the correct choice is D.

22. B: Problem solving. Because an item is missing in the middle of the pattern, the process asked for cannot be counting or addition. Solving this puzzle does not involve manipulation of objects.

23. C: The slope of a line can be found from any two points by the formula $slope = \frac{y_2 - y_1}{x_2 - x_1}$. A quick sketch of the point in choice C reveals a line with a negative slope. Substituting the last two points into the formula yields $slope = \frac{-3 - 1}{0 - (-6)}$ which reduces to $\frac{-4}{6}$ or $\frac{-2}{3}$. The points in choice A form a line

with a positive slope. The points in choice B form a line with a negative slope of $\frac{-3}{2}$. The points in choice D form a horizontal line. Therefore, the correct choice is C.

24. C: Students learn to measure something larger than a unit by repetitive use of that unit.

25. D: Commutative. The property that states that the order in which numbers are added does not change the answer is called the commutative property.

26. A: The inequality will be less than or equal to, since he may spend $100 or less on his purchase.

27. B: Notice that choice C cannot be correct since $x \neq 1$. ($x = 1$ results in a zero in the denominator.)

$$\frac{x-2}{x-1} = \frac{x-1}{x+1} + \frac{2}{x-1}$$
$$(x-1)(x+1)\left(\frac{x-2}{x-1} = \frac{x-1}{x+1} + \frac{2}{x-1}\right)$$
$$(x+1)(x-2) = (x-1)^2 + 2(x+1)$$
$$x^2 - x - 2 = x^2 - 2x + 1 + 2x + 2$$
$$x^2 - x - 2 = x^2 + 3$$
$$-x = 5$$
$$x = -5$$

28. A: To a convert a percent to a fraction, remove the percent sign and place the number over 100. That means 15% can be written as $\frac{15}{100}$, which reduces to $\frac{3}{20}$. To covert a percent to a decimal, remove the percent sign and move the decimal two places to the left. To convert a percent to a ratio, first write the ratio as a fraction, and then rewrite the fraction as a ratio. Therefore, the correct choice is A.

29. D: Since she spends at least $16, the relation of the number of packages of coffee to the minimum cost may be written as $4p \geq 16$. Alternatively, the inequality may be written as $16 \leq 4p$.

30. D: The area of the square is equal to $(30)^2$, or 900 square centimeters. The area of the circle is equal to $\pi (15)^2$, or approximately 707 square centimeters. The area of the shaded region is equal to the difference of the area of the square and the area of the circle, or 900 cm² - 707 cm², which equals 193 cm². So the area of the shaded region is about 193 cm².

31. C: The mean is the average of the data and can be found by dividing the sum of the data by the number of data: $\frac{16 + 18 + 20 + 21 + 34 + 45 + 49}{7} = 29$. The median is the middle data point when the data are ranked numerically. The median is 21. Therefore, the correct choice is C.

32. D: Understand what the problem is asking. Before you can solve a problem, you must decide what it is about.

33. D: Adding zero. Adding zero does not assist students in understanding subtraction. Physically taking some objects away from an array of objects, working a problem with a missing addend like 7 + __ = 13 helps students learn that 13-7 = 6. Moving to the left on a number line is another way of helping students understand subtraction.

34. B: The perimeter is equal to the sum of the lengths of the two bases, 2 and 6 units, and the diagonal distances of the other two sides. Using the distance formula, each side length may be represented as $d = \sqrt{20} = 2\sqrt{5}$. Thus, the sum of the two sides is equal to $2\sqrt{20}$, or $4\sqrt{5}$. The whole perimeter is equal to $8 + 4\sqrt{5}$.

35. B: Sophia needs to find multiples of 3 (3, 6, 9, 12, 15...) and multiples of 4 (4, 8, 12, 16,...) and find the least common multiple between them, which is 12. The greatest common divisor of 3 and 4 is 1. The least common divisor between two numbers is always 1. The greatest common multiple can never be determined. Therefore, the correct choice is B.

36. D: Since a and b are even integers, each can be expressed as the product of 2 and an integer. So, if we write $a = 2x$ and $b = 2y$, $3(2x)^2 + 9(2y)^3 = c$.
$$3(4x^2) + 9(8y^3) = c$$
$$12x^2 + 72y^3 = c$$
$$12(x^2 + 6y^3) = c$$
Since c is the product of 12 and some other integer, 12 must be a factor of c. Incidentally, the numbers 2, 3, and 6 must also be factors of c since each is also a factor of 12.

37. C: The slope is equal to 4 since each ticket costs $4. The y-intercept is represented by the constant fee of $30. Substituting 4 for m and 30 for b into the equation $y = mx + b$ gives $y = 4x + 30$.

38. B: A cube has six square faces. The arrangement of these faces in a two-dimensional figure is a net of a cube if the figure can be folded to form a cube. Figures A, C, and D represent three of the eleven possible nets of a cube. If choice B is folded, however, the bottom square in the second column will overlap the fourth square in the top row, so the figure does not represent a net of a cube.

39. A: Nominal data are data that are collected which have no intrinsic quantity or order. For instance, a survey might ask the respondent to identify his or her gender. While it is possible to compare the relative frequency of each response (for example, "most of the respondents are women"), it is not possible to calculate the mean, which requires data to be numeric, or median, which requires data to be ordered. Interval data are both numeric and ordered, so mean and median can be determined, as can the mode, the interval within which there are the most data. Ordinal data has an inherent order, but there is not a set interval between two points. For example, a survey might ask whether the respondent whether he or she was very dissatisfied, dissatisfied, neutral, satisfied, or very satisfied with the customer service received. Since the data are not numeric, the mean cannot be calculated, but since ordering the data is possible, the median has context.

40. C: Solving for x in an equation. Young children are not ready for algebraic equations, but they can learn to recognize patterns by counting by twos, comparing geometric shapes, and analyzing data they have collected.

Sample constructed response

In the skill of visually assembling fractions with counters, a student must understand multiple steps of a process. This process involves first dividing the pieces into appropriate groups based on the denominator. Then the student must draw his groupings and finally select and color in the proper number representing the numerator. In this exercise, Calvin was given twelve small candies, which he grouped appropriately in each of the five problems given to him. Calvin did very well to split the candies equally and into the proper number, which shows a strong understanding of grouping by denominator. This is shown in his splitting twelve into two groups in question 1, four groups in questions two and five, three groups in question three, and finally six groups in question four. Calvin also demonstrates that he knows that the numerator can change, as is demonstrated in question five. He does not seem to grasp this rule fully, however, as demonstrated by his always coloring only one group in questions two, three, and four. Calvin is in specific need of having numerators demonstrated thoroughly.

> At this point in Calvin's understanding, he cannot proceed in further instruction in fractions without having a more clear understanding of variance possible in numerators. Instructional intervention should build from his understanding of denominators to isolate his need. This would best be approached by starting with a fraction he can recognize, such as one fourth. I would ask Calvin to identify the fraction and then show him two fourths. At this point, Calvin should independently come to the conclusion that one fourth and two fourths are differentiated by the change in colored in markers rather than by the number of groups. This form of instruction is best suited to one on one intervention, rather than as a class. Once Calvin has been capable of showing the differences between each of the fourth fractions, I would then change the denominator and have him work through similar exercises with thirds, fifths, and sixths with an increasing degree of independence.

Following the independent instruction, Calvin should be given the opportunity to make corrections to his worksheet and asked to explain what he did wrong before. This would be an adequate way of assessing Calvin's level of understanding following the instructional intervention. After proceeding through corrections, Calvin should also be given plenty of opportunity to practice over the following week. Calvin's strong skills in denominators are likely to have strong foundation, but in areas that are new or weaker, retention of new instruction may be an issue. Additional practice is supportive in building retention of new skills.

Arts and Sciences

1. A: Testing, observing, and recording data. Before drawing a conclusion about a hypothesis, one should test and observe it and record data about the test results.

2. A: Density is mass per volume, typically expressed in units such as g/cm³, or kg/m³.

3. B: Mass. Mass is the amount of matter in an object. Weight is the measure of the pull of gravity on an object.

4. B: Hydrosphere. The earth's environment consists of the atmosphere, (the air we breathe), the hydrosphere (water), and the lithosphere (the land).

5. B: Large buildings with visible exteriors made almost entirely of glass are often considered to be designed as such for aesthetic architectural purposes, although there are practical advantages. One of these is the insulating property of glass, a particularly useful aspect on very tall buildings, where the ambient outside temperatures and wind patterns are irregular and undesirable. Little support is provided by glass walls, so these buildings usually have a core of steel girders. Decoration is by definition not a practical purpose, nor does glass help issues of tenant privacy.

6. B: Technology often results from scientific discoveries. The relationship between science and technology is evident when scientific discoveries prompt technologic advances.

7. A: It is the only way to prove that an experiment is valid. If an experiment can't be successfully repeated with the same outcome, one cannot determine that the experimental results are valid. Repetition is the key to scientific progress.

8. D: Both liquids and gases are fluids and therefore flow, but only gases are compressible. The molecules that make up a gas are very far apart, allowing the gas to be compressed into a smaller volume.

9. C: The greater the mass of an object, the greater the force necessary to move it. A shot put has greater mass than a tennis ball; therefore, more force is required to throw it a certain distance than is required to a throw a tennis ball the same distance (conversely, less force is required to throw the tennis ball that distance than the shot put). Option A does not explain the difference (both the tennis ball and the shot put are governed by the principle of inertia, meaning that force must be applied to both to set them in motion). Potential energy does not explain the difference in necessary force; neither is it clear that the tennis ball has more potential energy – this eliminates option B. Typically to throw both the tennis ball and the shot put, one would throw them horizontally; this doesn't explain the difference in necessary force (this eliminates option D).

10. Ocean currents. Wind belts, the Earth's orbit, and atmospheric conditions have some effect on weather, but ocean currents have the greatest influence.

11. C: Try out the proposed solution. The first step is to identify a problem and propose a solution. Trying the solution comes next, followed by evaluation and reporting the results.

12. B: Length and width. Since the object is not a solid, no other dimensions are needed.

13. D: Exhaust fumes are an ever-present concern, while the others are incidents that might or might not occur. A combustion engine of any kind produces fumes which can rapidly cause health damage, brain damage or death if allowed to fill an inadequately ventilated space. Therefore activities of this kind are usually conducted near an open garage door or loading dock if not out-of-doors. A situation guaranteed to happen--the production of fumes--is of higher priority than incidental dangers.

14. C: Catalysts lower the energy barrier between products and reactants and thus increase the reaction rate.

15. C: In a uniform gravitational field, such as occurs near Earth's surface, an object will move like a point mass located at the center of mass. However, this does not necessarily mean that the geometrical center of an object is the same as its center of mass, depending on its shape, design and mass distribution. The center of mass of a sphere or cube is at its geometric center because you can imagine the sphere as consisting of a large number of point masses located at certain points in space. Multiplying the point masses by their location and dividing by the total mass gives the center of mass. I is not true because the space station may not be completely symmetrical. III is true because the space station is undergoing uniform circular motion around Earth. If the orbit had been elliptical, this would not be true because the speed would have changed depending on the station's position. However, even though the speed is constant in a circular orbit, the velocity is not. Since velocity has a direction associated with it, and the space station is moving in a circular path, its velocity is constantly changing.

16. C: Food, water, sunlight, and air. All living organisms need food, water, sunlight and air. Shelter, space, and nurturing are nice to have but not crucial to sustaining life.

17. C: The agricultural revolution. A dependable food supply is essential to all populations. The agricultural revolution, an organized, almost scientific approach to agriculture, increased the food supply necessary for a growing world population.

18. D: A flow-line map describes the movement of people, trends, or materials across a physical area. The movements depicted on a flow-line map are typically represented by arrows. In more advanced flow-line maps, the width of the arrow corresponds to the quantity of the motion. Flow-line maps usually declare the span of time that is being represented. A political map depicts the man-made aspects of geography, such as borders and cities. A cartogram adjusts the size of the areas represented according to some variable. For instance, a cartogram of wheat production would depict Iowa as being much larger than Alaska. A qualitative map uses lines, dots, and other symbols to illustrate a particular point. For example, a qualitative map might be used to demonstrate the greatest expansion of the Persian Empire.

19. B: The child is developing normally; typical of his age group, he is in the preoperational stage of development and has not yet mastered conservation. Conservation is the ability to use logical reasoning to determine quantity. In this case, the child thinks one glass has more water simply because the glass is bigger. As this child enters into the concrete operational stage of development, he will understand that two amounts can be equal despite the size or shape of the container they are in. However, since this skill is not yet developed, the child will continue to believe one has more. If the teacher pours the water from the bigger glass into a glass that equals the size of his classmate's, the child will have a different reaction and possibly think the two are now equal.

20. B: Structural unemployment is unemployment that results from a mismatch of job skills or location. In this case, Ivy's job skill—her ability to work as a seamstress—is no longer desired by employers. Frictional and cyclical are other forms of unemployment; economists do not use the term careless unemployment.

21. B: The right of a defendant to confront accusers and to provide a defense.

22. C: The cycle of demographic transition is best illustrated by a line graph. Demographic transition is a phenomenon in which a region's growth rate increases rapidly, peaks, and then decreases slowly over a long time. In the early phase of a region's development, both the birth and death rates are high, which can cause the population to fluctuate. As the people of the region become settled, the growth rate calms down, and the region enters a period of rapid increase. Political maps are better at depicting borders and the locations of cities, while pie charts are better at representing proportions. Flow-line maps are good for illustrating the movement of people, goods, or trends across a physical area.

23. D: Political corruption was not an immediate effect of the rapid urban growth during this time. The accelerated growth of cities in America did soon result in services being unable to keep up with that growth. The results of this included deficiencies in clean water delivery and garbage collection, causing poor sanitation (a). That poor sanitation led to outbreaks of cholera and typhus, as well as typhoid fever epidemics (b). Police and fire fighting services could not keep up with the population increases, and were often inadequate (c). With people moving to the cities at such a fast rate, there were also deficits in housing and public transportation.

24. D: These are all geographically parts of Southeast Asia. The countries of Myanmar (Burma), Laos, Cambodia, and Thailand (a) are considered Mainland Southeast Asia, as are Vietnam and the Malay Peninsula (b). Brunei (b), East Malaysia, Indonesia, and the Philippines (c) are considered Maritime Southeast Asia, as are Singapore and Timor-Leste. The Seven Sister States of India are also considered to be part of Southeast Asia, geographically and culturally. (The Seven Sister States of India are Arunachal Pradesh, Assam, Nagaland, Meghalaya, Manipur, Tripura, and Mizoram, which all have contiguous borders in northeastern India.)

25. B: The social interaction of students that aid or inhibit learning. According to these theories, students do not just learn in isolation or in a one-on-one relationship with a teacher. They also learn attitudes toward education from their peers, sometimes positive and sometimes negative.

26. D: While rising prices may hurt many members of an economy, those same rising prices may benefit other members of the same economy. For example, rising prices may help those who sell goods and services and are able to keep their costs of production low, increasing their profit margin. Meanwhile, rising prices can hurt consumers because their income is now able to purchase fewer goods and services than before.

27. C: Regulate intrastate trade. Intrastate trade is solely within a state, so the state has jurisdiction over it. Taxation is a right granted to both federal and state authorities. Declaring war is a national decision. Patents and copyrights apply to goods made and/or sold throughout the country; therefore, they are a federal responsibility.

28. A: A smaller box in which some part of the larger map is depicted in greater detail is known as an inset. Insets provide a closer look at parts of the map that the cartographer deems to be more important (for instance, cities, national parks, or historical sites). Often, traffic maps will include

several insets depicting the roads in the most congested area of the city. Legends, also known as keys, are the boxes in which the symbols used in the map are explained. A legend, or key, might indicate how railroads and boundaries are depicted, for example. A compass rose indicates how the map is oriented along the north-south axis. It is common for cartographers to tilt a map for ease of display, such that up may not be due north.

29. D: Resentment against the Protestant Reformation was not a cause given for the French Revolution. Choices (a), (b), and (c) are just a few among many causes cited for the war. Famines caused malnutrition and even starvation among the poorest people (a). Escalating bread prices contributed greatly to the hunger. Louis XV had amassed a great amount of debt from spending money on many wars in addition to the American Revolution. Military failures as well as a lack of social services for veterans exacerbated these debts. In addition, the Court of Louis XVI and Marie Antoinette spent excessively and obviously on luxuries even while people in the country were starving, and France's monetary system was outdated, inefficient, and thus unable to manage the national debt (b). Much of the populace greatly resented the Catholic Church's control of the country (c). However, there was not great resentment against the Protestant Reformation (d); there were large minorities of Protestants in France, who not only exerted their influence on government institutions, but undoubtedly also contributed to the resentment of the Catholic Church. Because (d) is not a cause of the French Revolution as the other choices are, answer, all of these, is incorrect.

30. B: The composite volcano, sometimes called the stratovolcano, is the most common type of volcano on earth. A composite volcano has steep sides, so the explosions of ash, pumice, and silica are often accompanied by treacherous mudslides. Indeed, it is these mudslides that cause most of the damage associated with composite volcano eruptions. Krakatoa and Mount Saint Helens are examples of composite volcanoes. A lava dome is a round volcano that emits thick lava very slowly. A shield volcano, one example of which is Mt. Kilauea in Hawaii, emits a small amount of lava over an extended period of time. Shield volcanoes are not known for violent eruptions. A cinder cone has steep sides made of fallen cinders, which themselves are made of the lava that intermittently shoots into the air.

31. B: Play teaches children cooperation and sharing. Play is one way a child learns to relate to other children in a positive way.

32. A: Answer B is a definition of gross national product, and answers C and D define other economic measures.

33. B: Dimension, texture, and space are all *elements* of art, while unity is one of the *principles* of art. Unity in artwork is achieved when an artist's use of the elements produces a sense of wholeness or completeness in the finished product.

34. C: When encountering a difficult passage, musicians most effectively practice that passage slowly and thoughtfully. Playing through a challenging passage quickly can be detrimental to the learning process. Studying away from the instrument and practicing the sections before and after can be helpful, but will not address the difficult passage in the most effective manner.

35. D: Director placement of an actor onstage could be considered *positioning,* but the technical theatre term is *blocking,* so answer choice A is incorrect. Staging is related to set design and prop placement, and has nothing to do with the placement of actors. Therefore, answer choice B can be eliminated. Choreography is related to actor placement onstage, but only when specific dance movements are involved, making answer choice C incorrect.

36. A: Young people generally feel themselves to be invincible and show little regard for the future consequences of their behavior. More immediate concerns are shortages of cash, romantic rejection, and athletic inadequacy.

37. B: To develop perceptual-motor skills, it is best to engage students in physical activities that they find fun or enjoyable and that can be described and taught in terms of particular steps. These activities should involve uses of the senses such as sight, hearing, and touch. For example, shooting hoops can be described in particular steps, it involves holding and throwing a basketball, and seeing the basketball hoop. If shooting hoops is an activity students enjoy, this is a good activity to help students develop perceptual-motor skills. Answer A and C can be rejected because it is best to use activities that involve sequential steps; answer D can be rejected because it does not involve steps, nor necessarily significant motor skills (for example, watching a movie involves hearing and seeing, but it is not a way to build perceptual-motor skills in adolescents).

38. B: Conventional. There is actually a hint to this answer in its name. According to Kohlberg, the stage of development during which children learn conventional behavior—e.g., good behavior—is the Conventional Stage.

39. C: Purchasing a DVD is a discretionary expense because it is based on personal desire rather than need. In other words, it is an expense made at the discretion of the consumer. Discretionary expenses are those over which a consumer has the most control. A comprehensive budget must include discretionary expenses as well as fixed and variable expenses. Fixed expenses, such as rent, are the same every month. Variable expenses, including groceries and school supplies, vary in amount over the course of a year.

40. D: Restaurants are the most common employer of high-school students, based on data from the United States Bureau of Labor Statistics. These students will have direct experience with the cost of food, as well as with the nutritional choices available in a restaurant.

Secret Key #1 - Time is Your Greatest Enemy

Pace Yourself

Wear a watch. At the beginning of the test, check the time (or start a chronometer on your watch to count the minutes), and check the time after every few questions to make sure you are "on schedule."

If you are forced to speed up, do it efficiently. Usually one or more answer choices can be eliminated without too much difficulty. Above all, don't panic. Don't speed up and just begin guessing at random choices. By pacing yourself, and continually monitoring your progress against your watch, you will always know exactly how far ahead or behind you are with your available time. If you find that you are one minute behind on the test, don't skip one question without spending any time on it, just to catch back up. Take 15 fewer seconds on the next four questions, and after four questions you'll have caught back up. Once you catch back up, you can continue working each problem at your normal pace.

Furthermore, don't dwell on the problems that you were rushed on. If a problem was taking up too much time and you made a hurried guess, it must be difficult. The difficult questions are the ones you are most likely to miss anyway, so it isn't a big loss. It is better to end with more time than you need than to run out of time.

Lastly, sometimes it is beneficial to slow down if you are constantly getting ahead of time. You are always more likely to catch a careless mistake by working more slowly than quickly, and among very high-scoring test takers (those who are likely to have lots of time left over), careless errors affect the score more than mastery of material.

Secret Key #2 - Guessing is not Guesswork

You probably know that guessing is a good idea. Unlike other standardized tests, there is no penalty for getting a wrong answer. Even if you have no idea about a question, you still have a 20-25% chance of getting it right.

Most test takers do not understand the impact that proper guessing can have on their score. Unless you score extremely high, guessing will significantly contribute to your final score.

Monkeys Take the Test

What most test takers don't realize is that to insure that 20-25% chance, you have to guess randomly. If you put 20 monkeys in a room to take this test, assuming they answered once per question and behaved themselves, on average they would get 20-25% of the questions correct. Put 20 test takers in the room, and the average will be much lower among guessed questions. Why?
1. The test writers intentionally write deceptive answer choices that "look" right. A test taker has no idea about a question, so he picks the "best looking" answer, which is often wrong. The monkey has no idea what looks good and what doesn't, so it will consistently be right about 20-25% of the time.
2. Test takers will eliminate answer choices from the guessing pool based on a hunch or intuition. Simple but correct answers often get excluded, leaving a 0% chance of being correct. The monkey has no clue, and often gets lucky with the best choice.

This is why the process of elimination endorsed by most test courses is flawed and detrimental to your performance. Test takers don't guess; they make an ignorant stab in the dark that is usually worse than random.

$5 Challenge

Let me introduce one of the most valuable ideas of this course—the $5 challenge:
- *You only mark your "best guess" if you are willing to bet $5 on it.*
- *You only eliminate choices from guessing if you are willing to bet $5 on it.*

Why $5? Five dollars is an amount of money that is small yet not insignificant, and can really add up fast (20 questions could cost you $100). Likewise, each answer choice on one question of the test will have a small impact on your overall score, but it can really add up to a lot of points in the end.

The process of elimination IS valuable. The following shows your chance of guessing it right:

If you eliminate wrong answer choices until only this many remain:	Chance of getting it correct:
1	100%
2	50%
3	33%

However, if you accidentally eliminate the right answer or go on a hunch for an incorrect answer, your chances drop dramatically—to 0%. By guessing among all the answer choices, you are GUARANTEED to have a shot at the right answer.

That's why the $5 test is so valuable. If you give up the advantage and safety of a pure guess, it had better be worth the risk.

What we still haven't covered is how to be sure that whatever guess you make is truly random. Here's the easiest way:
- *Always pick the first answer choice among those remaining.*

Such a technique means that you have decided, **before you see a single test question**, exactly how you are going to guess, and since the order of choices tells you nothing about which one is correct, this guessing technique is perfectly random.

This section is not meant to scare you away from making educated guesses or eliminating choices; you just need to define when a choice is worth eliminating. The $5 test, along with a pre-defined random guessing strategy, is the best way to make sure you reap all of the benefits of guessing.

Secret Key #3 - Practice Smarter, Not Harder

Many test takers delay the test preparation process because they dread the awful amounts of practice time they think necessary to succeed on the test. We have refined an effective method that will take you only a fraction of the time.

There are a number of "obstacles" in the path to success. Among these are answering questions, finishing in time, and mastering test-taking strategies. All must be executed on the day of the test at peak performance, or your score will suffer. The test is a mental marathon that has a large impact on your future.

Just like a marathon runner, it is important to work your way up to the full challenge. So first you just worry about questions, and then time, and finally strategy:

Success Strategy

1. Find a good source for practice tests.
2. If you are willing to make a larger time investment, consider using more than one study guide. Often the different approaches of multiple authors will help you "get" difficult concepts.
3. Take a practice test with no time constraints, with all study helps, "open book." Take your time with questions and focus on applying strategies.
4. Take a practice test with time constraints, with all guides, "open book."
5. Take a final practice test without open material and with time limits.

If you have time to take more practice tests, just repeat step 5. By gradually exposing yourself to the full rigors of the test environment, you will condition your mind to the stress of test day and maximize your success.

Secret Key #4 - Prepare, Don't Procrastinate

Let me state an obvious fact: if you take the test three times, you will probably get three different scores. This is due to the way you feel on test day, the level of preparedness you have, and the version of the test you see. Despite the test writers' claims to the contrary, some versions of the test WILL be easier for you than others.

Since your future depends so much on your score, you should maximize your chances of success. In order to maximize the likelihood of success, you've got to prepare in advance. This means taking practice tests and spending time learning the information and test taking strategies you will need to succeed.

Never go take the actual test as a "practice" test, expecting that you can just take it again if you need to. Take all the practice tests you can on your own, but when you go to take the official test, be prepared, be focused, and do your best the first time!

Secret Key #5 - Test Yourself

Everyone knows that time is money. There is no need to spend too much of your time or too little of your time preparing for the test. You should only spend as much of your precious time preparing as is necessary for you to get the score you need.

Once you have taken a practice test under real conditions of time constraints, then you will know if you are ready for the test or not.

If you have scored extremely high the first time that you take the practice test, then there is not much point in spending countless hours studying. You are already there.

> Benchmark your abilities by retaking practice tests and seeing how much you have improved. Once you consistently score high enough to guarantee success, then you are ready.

If you have scored well below where you need, then knuckle down and begin studying in earnest. Check your improvement regularly through the use of practice tests under real conditions. Above all, don't worry, panic, or give up. The key is perseverance!

Then, when you go to take the test, remain confident and remember how well you did on the practice tests. If you can score high enough on a practice test, then you can do the same on the real thing.

General Strategies

The most important thing you can do is to ignore your fears and jump into the test immediately. Do not be overwhelmed by any strange-sounding terms. You have to jump into the test like jumping into a pool—all at once is the easiest way.

Make Predictions

As you read and understand the question, try to guess what the answer will be. Remember that several of the answer choices are wrong, and once you begin reading them, your mind will immediately become cluttered with answer choices designed to throw you off. Your mind is typically the most focused immediately after you have read the question and digested its contents. If you can, try to predict what the correct answer will be. You may be surprised at what you can predict.

Quickly scan the choices and see if your prediction is in the listed answer choices. If it is, then you can be quite confident that you have the right answer. It still won't hurt to check the other answer choices, but most of the time, you've got it!

Answer the Question

It may seem obvious to only pick answer choices that answer the question, but the test writers can create some excellent answer choices that are wrong. Don't pick an answer just because it sounds right, or you believe it to be true. It MUST answer the question. Once you've made your selection, always go back and check it against the question and make sure that you didn't misread the question and that the answer choice does answer the question posed.

Benchmark

After you read the first answer choice, decide if you think it sounds correct or not. If it doesn't, move on to the next answer choice. If it does, mentally mark that answer choice. This doesn't mean that you've definitely selected it as your answer choice, it just means that it's the best you've seen thus far. Go ahead and read the next choice. If the next choice is worse than the one you've already selected, keep going to the next answer choice. If the next choice is better than the choice you've already selected, mentally mark the new answer choice as your best guess.

The first answer choice that you select becomes your standard. Every other answer choice must be benchmarked against that standard. That choice is correct until proven otherwise by another answer choice beating it out. Once you've decided that no other answer choice seems as good, do one final check to ensure that your answer choice answers the question posed.

Valid Information

Don't discount any of the information provided in the question. Every piece of information may be necessary to determine the correct answer. None of the information in the question is there to throw you off (while the answer choices will certainly have information to throw you off). If two seemingly unrelated topics are discussed, don't ignore either. You can be confident there is a relationship, or it wouldn't be included in the question, and you are probably going to have to determine what is that relationship to find the answer.

Avoid "Fact Traps"

Don't get distracted by a choice that is factually true. Your search is for the answer that answers the question. Stay focused and don't fall for an answer that is true but irrelevant. Always go back to the question and make sure you're choosing an answer that actually answers the question and is not just a true statement. An answer can be factually correct, but it MUST answer the question asked. Additionally, two answers can both be seemingly correct, so be sure to read all of the answer choices, and make sure that you get the one that BEST answers the question.

Milk the Question

Some of the questions may throw you completely off. They might deal with a subject you have not been exposed to, or one that you haven't reviewed in years. While your lack of knowledge about the subject will be a hindrance, the question itself can give you many clues that will help you find the correct answer. Read the question carefully and look for clues. Watch particularly for adjectives and nouns describing difficult terms or words that you don't recognize. Regardless of whether you completely understand a word or not, replacing it with a synonym, either provided or one you more familiar with, may help you to understand what the questions are asking. Rather than wracking your mind about specific detailed information concerning a difficult term or word, try to use mental substitutes that are easier to understand.

The Trap of Familiarity

Don't just choose a word because you recognize it. On difficult questions, you may not recognize a number of words in the answer choices. The test writers don't put "make-believe" words on the test, so don't think that just because you only recognize all the words in one answer choice that that answer choice must be correct. If you only recognize words in one answer choice, then focus on that one. Is it correct? Try your best to determine if it is correct. If it is, that's great. If not, eliminate it. Each word and answer choice you eliminate increases your chances of getting the question correct, even if you then have to guess among the unfamiliar choices.

Eliminate Answers

Eliminate choices as soon as you realize they are wrong. But be careful! Make sure you consider all of the possible answer choices. Just because one appears right, doesn't mean that the next one won't be even better! The test writers will usually put more than one good answer choice for every question, so read all of them. Don't worry if you are stuck between two that seem right. By getting down to just two remaining possible choices, your odds are now 50/50. Rather than wasting too much time, play the odds. You are guessing, but guessing wisely because you've been able to knock out some of the answer choices that you know are wrong. If you are eliminating choices and realize that the last answer choice you are left with is also obviously wrong, don't panic. Start over and consider each choice again. There may easily be something that you missed the first time and will realize on the second pass.

Tough Questions

If you are stumped on a problem or it appears too hard or too difficult, don't waste time. Move on! Remember though, if you can quickly check for obviously incorrect answer choices, your chances of guessing correctly are greatly improved. Before you completely give up, at least try to knock out a couple of possible answers. Eliminate what you can and then guess at the remaining answer choices before moving on.

Brainstorm

If you get stuck on a difficult question, spend a few seconds quickly brainstorming. Run through the complete list of possible answer choices. Look at each choice and ask yourself, "Could this answer the question satisfactorily?" Go through each answer choice and consider it independently of the others. By systematically going through all possibilities, you may find something that you would otherwise overlook. Remember though that when you get stuck, it's important to try to keep moving.

Read Carefully

Understand the problem. Read the question and answer choices carefully. Don't miss the question because you misread the terms. You have plenty of time to read each question thoroughly and make sure you understand what is being asked. Yet a happy medium must be attained, so don't waste too much time. You must read carefully, but efficiently.

Face Value

When in doubt, use common sense. Always accept the situation in the problem at face value. Don't read too much into it. These problems will not require you to make huge leaps of logic. The test writers aren't trying to throw you off with a cheap trick. If you have to go beyond creativity and make a leap of logic in order to have an answer choice answer the question, then you should look at the other answer choices. Don't overcomplicate the problem by creating theoretical relationships or explanations that will warp time or space. These are normal problems rooted in reality. It's just that the applicable relationship or explanation may not be readily apparent and you have to figure things out. Use your common sense to interpret anything that isn't clear.

Prefixes

If you're having trouble with a word in the question or answer choices, try dissecting it. Take advantage of every clue that the word might include. Prefixes and suffixes can be a huge help. Usually they allow you to determine a basic meaning. Pre- means before, post- means after, pro - is positive, de- is negative. From these prefixes and suffixes, you can get an idea of the general meaning of the word and try to put it into context. Beware though of any traps. Just because con- is the opposite of pro-, doesn't necessarily mean congress is the opposite of progress!

Hedge Phrases

Watch out for critical hedge phrases, led off with words such as "likely," "may," "can," "sometimes," "often," "almost," "mostly," "usually," "generally," "rarely," and "sometimes." Question writers insert these hedge phrases to cover every possibility. Often an answer choice will be wrong simply because it leaves no room for exception. Unless the situation calls for them, avoid answer choices that have definitive words like "exactly," and "always."

Switchback Words

Stay alert for "switchbacks." These are the words and phrases frequently used to alert you to shifts in thought. The most common switchback word is "but." Others include "although," "however," "nevertheless," "on the other hand," "even though," "while," "in spite of," "despite," and "regardless of."

New Information

Correct answer choices will rarely have completely new information included. Answer choices typically are straightforward reflections of the material asked about and will directly relate to the question. If a new piece of information is included in an answer choice that doesn't even seem to relate to the topic being asked about, then that answer choice is likely incorrect. All of the information needed to answer the question is usually provided for you in the question. You should not have to make guesses that are unsupported or choose answer choices that require unknown information that cannot be reasoned from what is given.

Time Management

On technical questions, don't get lost on the technical terms. Don't spend too much time on any one question. If you don't know what a term means, then odds are you aren't going to get much further since you don't have a dictionary. You should be able to immediately recognize whether or not you know a term. If you don't, work with the other clues that you have—the other answer choices and terms provided—but don't waste too much time trying to figure out a difficult term that you don't know.

Contextual Clues

Look for contextual clues. An answer can be right but not the correct answer. The contextual clues will help you find the answer that is most right and is correct. Understand the context in which a phrase or statement is made. This will help you make important distinctions.

Don't Panic

Panicking will not answer any questions for you; therefore, it isn't helpful. When you first see the question, if your mind goes blank, take a deep breath. Force yourself to mechanically go through the steps of solving the problem using the strategies you've learned.

Pace Yourself

Don't get clock fever. It's easy to be overwhelmed when you're looking at a page full of questions, your mind is full of random thoughts and feeling confused, and the clock is ticking down faster than you would like. Calm down and maintain the pace that you have set for yourself. As long as you are on track by monitoring your pace, you are guaranteed to have enough time for yourself. When you get to the last few minutes of the test, it may seem like you won't have enough time left, but if you only have as many questions as you should have left at that point, then you're right on track!

Answer Selection

The best way to pick an answer choice is to eliminate all of those that are wrong, until only one is left and confirm that is the correct answer. Sometimes though, an answer choice may immediately look right. Be careful! Take a second to make sure that the other choices are not equally obvious. Don't make a hasty mistake. There are only two times that you should stop before checking other answers. First is when you are positive that the answer choice you have selected is correct. Second is when time is almost out and you have to make a quick guess!

Check Your Work

Since you will probably not know every term listed and the answer to every question, it is important that you get credit for the ones that you do know. Don't miss any questions through careless mistakes. If at all possible, try to take a second to look back over your answer selection and make sure you've selected the correct answer choice and haven't made a costly careless mistake (such as marking an answer choice that you didn't mean to mark). The time it takes for this quick double check should more than pay for itself in caught mistakes.

Beware of Directly Quoted Answers

Sometimes an answer choice will repeat word for word a portion of the question or reference section. However, beware of such exact duplication. It may be a trap! More than likely, the correct choice will paraphrase or summarize a point, rather than being exactly the same wording.

Slang

Scientific sounding answers are better than slang ones. An answer choice that begins "To compare the outcomes..." is much more likely to be correct than one that begins "Because some people insisted..."

Extreme Statements

Avoid wild answers that throw out highly controversial ideas that are proclaimed as established fact. An answer choice that states the "process should used in certain situations, if..." is much more likely to be correct than one that states the "process should be discontinued completely." The first is a calm rational statement and doesn't even make a definitive, uncompromising stance, using a hedge word "if" to provide wiggle room, whereas the second choice is a radical idea and far more extreme.

Answer Choice Families

When you have two or more answer choices that are direct opposites or parallels, one of them is usually the correct answer. For instance, if one answer choice states "x increases" and another answer choice states "x decreases" or "y increases," then those two or three answer choices are very similar in construction and fall into the same family of answer choices. A family of answer choices consists of two or three answer choices, very similar in construction, but often with directly opposite meanings. Usually the correct answer choice will be in that family of answer choices. The "odd man out" or answer choice that doesn't seem to fit the parallel construction of the other answer choices is more likely to be incorrect.

Special Report: How to Overcome Test Anxiety

The very nature of tests caters to some level of anxiety, nervousness, or tension, just as we feel for any important event that occurs in our lives. A little bit of anxiety or nervousness can be a good thing. It helps us with motivation, and makes achievement just that much sweeter. However, too much anxiety can be a problem, especially if it hinders our ability to function and perform.

"Test anxiety," is the term that refers to the emotional reactions that some test-takers experience when faced with a test or exam. Having a fear of testing and exams is based upon a rational fear, since the test-taker's performance can shape the course of an academic career. Nevertheless, experiencing excessive fear of examinations will only interfere with the test-taker's ability to perform and chance to be successful.

There are a large variety of causes that can contribute to the development and sensation of test anxiety. These include, but are not limited to, lack of preparation and worrying about issues surrounding the test.

Lack of Preparation

Lack of preparation can be identified by the following behaviors or situations:
- Not scheduling enough time to study, and therefore cramming the night before the test or exam
- Managing time poorly, to create the sensation that there is not enough time to do everything
- Failing to organize the text information in advance, so that the study material consists of the entire text and not simply the pertinent information
- Poor overall studying habits

Worrying, on the other hand, can be related to both the test taker, or many other factors around him/her that will be affected by the results of the test. These include worrying about:
- Previous performances on similar exams, or exams in general
- How friends and other students are achieving
- The negative consequences that will result from a poor grade or failure

There are three primary elements to test anxiety. Physical components, which involve the same typical bodily reactions as those to acute anxiety (to be discussed below). Emotional factors have to do with fear or panic. Mental or cognitive issues concerning attention spans and memory abilities.

Physical Signals

There are many different symptoms of test anxiety, and these are not limited to mental and emotional strain. Frequently there are a range of physical signals that will let a test taker know that he/she is suffering from test anxiety. These bodily changes can include the following:
- Perspiring
- Sweaty palms
- Wet, trembling hands
- Nausea
- Dry mouth
- A knot in the stomach
- Headache
- Faintness
- Muscle tension
- Aching shoulders, back and neck
- Rapid heart beat
- Feeling too hot/cold

To recognize the sensation of test anxiety, a test-taker should monitor him/herself for the following sensations:
- The physical distress symptoms as listed above
- Emotional sensitivity, expressing emotional feelings such as the need to cry or laugh too much, or a sensation of anger or helplessness
- A decreased ability to think, causing the test-taker to blank out or have racing thoughts that are hard to organize or control.

Though most students will feel some level of anxiety when faced with a test or exam, the majority can cope with that anxiety and maintain it at a manageable level. However, those who cannot are faced with a very real and very serious condition, which can and should be controlled for the immeasurable benefit of this sufferer.

Naturally, these sensations lead to negative results for the testing experience. The most common effects of test anxiety have to do with nervousness and mental blocking.

Nervousness

Nervousness can appear in several different levels:
- The test-taker's difficulty, or even inability to read and understand the questions on the test
- The difficulty or inability to organize thoughts to a coherent form
- The difficulty or inability to recall key words and concepts relating to the testing questions (especially essays)
- The receipt of poor grades on a test, though the test material was well known by the test taker

Conversely, a person may also experience mental blocking, which involves:
- Blanking out on test questions
- Only remembering the correct answers to the questions when the test has already finished.

Fortunately for test anxiety sufferers, beating these feelings, to a large degree, has to do with proper preparation. When a test taker has a feeling of preparedness, then anxiety will be dramatically lessened.

The first step to resolving anxiety issues is to distinguish which of the two types of anxiety are being suffered. If the anxiety is a direct result of a lack of preparation, this should be considered a normal reaction, and the anxiety level (as opposed to the test results) shouldn't be anything to worry about. However, if, when adequately prepared, the test-taker still panics, blanks out, or seems to overreact, this is not a fully rational reaction. While this can be considered normal too, there are many ways to combat and overcome these effects.

Remember that anxiety cannot be entirely eliminated, however, there are ways to minimize it, to make the anxiety easier to manage. Preparation is one of the best ways to minimize test anxiety. Therefore the following techniques are wise in order to best fight off any anxiety that may want to build.

To begin with, try to avoid cramming before a test, whenever it is possible. By trying to memorize an entire term's worth of information in one day, you'll be shocking your system, and not giving yourself a very good chance to absorb the information. This is an easy path to anxiety, so for those who suffer from test anxiety, cramming should not even be considered an option.

Instead of cramming, work throughout the semester to combine all of the material which is presented throughout the semester, and work on it gradually as the course goes by, making sure to master the main concepts first, leaving minor details for a week or so before the test.

To study for the upcoming exam, be sure to pose questions that may be on the examination, to gauge the ability to answer them by integrating the ideas from your texts, notes and lectures, as well as any supplementary readings.

If it is truly impossible to cover all of the information that was covered in that particular term, concentrate on the most important portions, that can be covered very well. Learn these concepts as best as possible, so that when the test comes, a goal can be made to use these concepts as presentations of your knowledge.

In addition to study habits, changes in attitude are critical to beating a struggle with test anxiety. In fact, an improvement of the perspective over the entire test-taking experience can actually help a test taker to enjoy studying and therefore improve the overall experience. Be certain not to overemphasize the significance of the grade - know that the result of the test is neither a reflection of self worth, nor is it a measure of intelligence; one grade will not predict a person's future success.

To improve an overall testing outlook, the following steps should be tried:
- Keeping in mind that the most reasonable expectation for taking a test is to expect to try to demonstrate as much of what you know as you possibly can.

- Reminding ourselves that a test is only one test; this is not the only one, and there will be others.
- The thought of thinking of oneself in an irrational, all-or-nothing term should be avoided at all costs.
- A reward should be designated for after the test, so there's something to look forward to. Whether it be going to a movie, going out to eat, or simply visiting friends, schedule it in advance, and do it no matter what result is expected on the exam.

Test-takers should also keep in mind that the basics are some of the most important things, even beyond anti-anxiety techniques and studying. Never neglect the basic social, emotional and biological needs, in order to try to absorb information. In order to best achieve, these three factors must be held as just as important as the studying itself.

Study Steps

Remember the following important steps for studying:
- Maintain healthy nutrition and exercise habits. Continue both your recreational activities and social pass times. These both contribute to your physical and emotional well being.
- Be certain to get a good amount of sleep, especially the night before the test, because when you're overtired you are not able to perform to the best of your best ability.
- Keep the studying pace to a moderate level by taking breaks when they are needed, and varying the work whenever possible, to keep the mind fresh instead of getting bored.
- When enough studying has been done that all the material that can be learned has been learned, and the test taker is prepared for the test, stop studying and do something relaxing such as listening to music, watching a movie, or taking a warm bubble bath.

There are also many other techniques to minimize the uneasiness or apprehension that is experienced along with test anxiety before, during, or even after the examination. In fact, there are a great deal of things that can be done to stop anxiety from interfering with lifestyle and performance. Again, remember that anxiety will not be eliminated entirely, and it shouldn't be. Otherwise that "up" feeling for exams would not exist, and most of us depend on that sensation to perform better than usual. However, this anxiety has to be at a level that is manageable.

Of course, as we have just discussed, being prepared for the exam is half the battle right away. Attending all classes, finding out what knowledge will be expected on the exam, and knowing the exam schedules are easy steps to lowering anxiety. Keeping up with work will remove the need to cram, and efficient study habits will eliminate wasted time. Studying should be done in an ideal location for concentration, so that it is simple to become interested in the material and give it complete attention. A method such as SQ3R (Survey, Question, Read, Recite, Review) is a wonderful key to follow to make sure that the study habits are as effective as possible, especially in the case of learning from a textbook. Flashcards are great techniques for memorization. Learning to take good notes will mean that notes will be full of useful information, so that less sifting will need to be done to seek out what is pertinent for studying. Reviewing notes after class and then again on occasion will keep the information fresh in the mind. From notes that have been taken summary sheets and outlines can be made for simpler reviewing.

A study group can also be a very motivational and helpful place to study, as there will be a sharing of ideas, all of the minds can work together, to make sure that everyone understands, and the studying will be made more interesting because it will be a social occasion.

Basically, though, as long as the test-taker remains organized and self confident, with efficient study habits, less time will need to be spent studying, and higher grades will be achieved.

To become self confident, there are many useful steps. The first of these is "self talk." It has been shown through extensive research, that self-talk for students who suffer from test anxiety, should be well monitored, in order to make sure that it contributes to self confidence as opposed to sinking the student. Frequently the self talk of test-anxious students is negative or self-defeating, thinking that everyone else is smarter and faster, that they always mess up, and that if they don't do well, they'll fail the entire course. It is important to decreasing anxiety that awareness is made of self talk. Try writing any negative self thoughts and then disputing them with a positive statement instead. Begin self-encouragement as though it was a friend speaking. Repeat positive statements to help reprogram the mind to believing in successes instead of failures.

Helpful Techniques

Other extremely helpful techniques include:
- Self-visualization of doing well and reaching goals
- While aiming for an "A" level of understanding, don't try to "overprotect" by setting your expectations lower. This will only convince the mind to stop studying in order to meet the lower expectations.
- Don't make comparisons with the results or habits of other students. These are individual factors, and different things work for different people, causing different results.
- Strive to become an expert in learning what works well, and what can be done in order to improve. Consider collecting this data in a journal.
- Create rewards for after studying instead of doing things before studying that will only turn into avoidance behaviors.
- Make a practice of relaxing - by using methods such as progressive relaxation, self-hypnosis, guided imagery, etc - in order to make relaxation an automatic sensation.
- Work on creating a state of relaxed concentration so that concentrating will take on the focus of the mind, so that none will be wasted on worrying.
- Take good care of the physical self by eating well and getting enough sleep.
- Plan in time for exercise and stick to this plan.

Beyond these techniques, there are other methods to be used before, during and after the test that will help the test-taker perform well in addition to overcoming anxiety.

Before the exam comes the academic preparation. This involves establishing a study schedule and beginning at least one week before the actual date of the test. By doing this, the anxiety of not having enough time to study for the test will be automatically eliminated. Moreover, this will make the studying a much more effective experience, ensuring that the learning will be an easier process. This relieves much undue pressure on the test-taker.

Summary sheets, note cards, and flash cards with the main concepts and examples of these main concepts should be prepared in advance of the actual studying time. A topic should never be eliminated from this process. By omitting a topic because it isn't expected to be on the test is only setting up the test-taker for anxiety should it actually appear on the exam. Utilize the course syllabus for laying out the topics that should be studied. Carefully go over the notes that were made in class, paying special attention to any of the issues that the professor took special care to emphasize while lecturing in class. In the textbooks, use the chapter review, or if possible, the chapter tests, to begin your review.

It may even be possible to ask the instructor what information will be covered on the exam, or what the format of the exam will be (for example, multiple choice, essay, free form, true-false). Additionally, see if it is possible to find out how many questions will be on the test. If a review sheet or sample test has been offered by the professor, make good use of it, above anything else, for the preparation for the test. Another great resource for getting to know the examination is reviewing tests from previous semesters. Use these tests to review, and aim to achieve a 100% score on each of the possible topics. With a few exceptions, the goal that you set for yourself is the highest one that you will reach.

Take all of the questions that were assigned as homework, and rework them to any other possible course material. The more problems reworked, the more skill and confidence will form as a result. When forming the solution to a problem, write out each of the steps. Don't simply do head work. By doing as many steps on paper as possible, much clarification and therefore confidence will be formed. Do this with as many homework problems as possible, before checking the answers. By checking the answer after each problem, a reinforcement will exist, that will not be on the exam. Study situations should be as exam-like as possible, to prime the test-taker's system for the experience. By waiting to check the answers at the end, a psychological advantage will be formed, to decrease the stress factor.

Another fantastic reason for not cramming is the avoidance of confusion in concepts, especially when it comes to mathematics. 8-10 hours of study will become one hundred percent more effective if it is spread out over a week or at least several days, instead of doing it all in one sitting. Recognize that the human brain requires time in order to assimilate new material, so frequent breaks and a span of study time over several days will be much more beneficial.

Additionally, don't study right up until the point of the exam. Studying should stop a minimum of one hour before the exam begins. This allows the brain to rest and put things in their proper order. This will also provide the time to become as relaxed as possible when going into the examination room. The test-taker will also have time to eat well and eat sensibly. Know that the brain needs food as much as the rest of the body. With enough food and enough sleep, as well as a relaxed attitude, the body and the mind are primed for success.

Avoid any anxious classmates who are talking about the exam. These students only spread anxiety, and are not worth sharing the anxious sentimentalities.

Before the test also involves creating a positive attitude, so mental preparation should also be a point of concentration. There are many keys to creating a positive attitude. Should fears become rushing in, make a visualization of taking the exam, doing well, and seeing an A written on the paper. Write out a list of affirmations that will bring a feeling of confidence, such as "I am doing well in my English class," "I studied well and know my material," "I enjoy this class." Even if the affirmations aren't believed at first, it sends a positive message to the subconscious which will result in an alteration of the overall belief system, which is the system that creates reality.

If a sensation of panic begins, work with the fear and imagine the very worst! Work through the entire scenario of not passing the test, failing the entire course, and dropping out of school, followed by not getting a job, and pushing a shopping cart through the dark alley where you'll live. This will place things into perspective! Then, practice deep breathing and create a visualization of the opposite situation - achieving an "A" on the exam, passing the entire course, receiving the degree at a graduation ceremony.

On the day of the test, there are many things to be done to ensure the best results, as well as the most calm outlook. The following stages are suggested in order to maximize test-taking potential:

- Begin the examination day with a moderate breakfast, and avoid any coffee or beverages with caffeine if the test taker is prone to jitters. Even people who are used to managing caffeine can feel jittery or light-headed when it is taken on a test day.
- Attempt to do something that is relaxing before the examination begins. As last minute cramming clouds the mastering of overall concepts, it is better to use this time to create a calming outlook.
- Be certain to arrive at the test location well in advance, in order to provide time to select a location that is away from doors, windows and other distractions, as well as giving enough time to relax before the test begins.
- Keep away from anxiety generating classmates who will upset the sensation of stability and relaxation that is being attempted before the exam.
- Should the waiting period before the exam begins cause anxiety, create a self-distraction by reading a light magazine or something else that is relaxing and simple.

During the exam itself, read the entire exam from beginning to end, and find out how much time should be allotted to each individual problem. Once writing the exam, should more time be taken for a problem, it should be abandoned, in order to begin another problem. If there is time at the end, the unfinished problem can always be returned to and completed.

Read the instructions very carefully - twice - so that unpleasant surprises won't follow during or after the exam has ended.

When writing the exam, pretend that the situation is actually simply the completion of homework within a library, or at home. This will assist in forming a relaxed atmosphere, and will allow the brain extra focus for the complex thinking function.

Begin the exam with all of the questions with which the most confidence is felt. This will build the confidence level regarding the entire exam and will begin a quality momentum. This will also create encouragement for trying the problems where uncertainty resides.

Going with the "gut instinct" is always the way to go when solving a problem. Second guessing should be avoided at all costs. Have confidence in the ability to do well.

For essay questions, create an outline in advance that will keep the mind organized and make certain that all of the points are remembered. For multiple choice, read every answer, even if the correct one has been spotted - a better one may exist.

Continue at a pace that is reasonable and not rushed, in order to be able to work carefully. Provide enough time to go over the answers at the end, to check for small errors that can be corrected.

Should a feeling of panic begin, breathe deeply, and think of the feeling of the body releasing sand through its pores. Visualize a calm, peaceful place, and include all of the sights, sounds and sensations of this image. Continue the deep breathing, and take a few minutes to continue this with closed eyes. When all is well again, return to the test.

If a "blanking" occurs for a certain question, skip it and move on to the next question. There will be time to return to the other question later. Get everything done that can be done, first, to guarantee all the grades that can be compiled, and to build all of the confidence possible. Then return to the weaker questions to build the marks from there.

Remember, one's own reality can be created, so as long as the belief is there, success will follow. And remember: anxiety can happen later, right now, there's an exam to be written!

After the examination is complete, whether there is a feeling for a good grade or a bad grade, don't dwell on the exam, and be certain to follow through on the reward that was promised...and enjoy it! Don't dwell on any mistakes that have been made, as there is nothing that can be done at this point anyway.

Additionally, don't begin to study for the next test right away. Do something relaxing for a while, and let the mind relax and prepare itself to begin absorbing information again.

From the results of the exam - both the grade and the entire experience, be certain to learn from what has gone on. Perfect studying habits and work some more on confidence in order to make the next examination experience even better than the last one.

Learn to avoid places where openings occurred for laziness, procrastination and day dreaming.

Use the time between this exam and the next one to better learn to relax, even learning to relax on cue, so that any anxiety can be controlled during the next exam. Learn how to relax the body. Slouch in your chair if that helps. Tighten and then relax all of the different muscle groups, one group at a time, beginning with the feet and then working all the way up to the neck and face. This will ultimately relax the muscles more than they were to begin with. Learn how to breathe deeply and comfortably, and focus on this breathing going in and out as a relaxing thought. With every exhale, repeat the word "relax."

As common as test anxiety is, it is very possible to overcome it. Make yourself one of the test-takers who overcome this frustrating hindrance.

Additional Bonus Material

Due to our efforts to try to keep this book to a manageable length, we've created a link that will give you access to all of your additional bonus material.

Please visit http://www.mometrix.com/bonus948/nystcemsb-2 to access the information.